D1608898

Allan "Rocky" Lane,
Republic's Action Ace

by
Chuck Thornton
and
David Rothel

Published by
EMPIRE PUBLISHING, INC.
(The *BIG REEL* Folks)
Route 3, Madison, NC 27025
(919) 427-5850

Allan "Rocky" Lane, Republic's Action Ace, by Chuck Thornton and David Rothel

Portions of *Allan "Rocky" Lane, Republic's Action Ace* were published in a limited edition in 1985 under the title *The Western Adventures of Allan Lane.*

Published and printed in the United States of America

Library of Congress Catalog Number 90-081549

ISBN Number 0-944019-09-9

First Printing 1990

CONTENTS

ACKNOWLEDGMENTS

The authors acknowledge with appreciation the help the following organizations and individuals in the preparation of this book: Bob Carman, Ron Honthaner, Jim Rutland, Charles Sharpe, Harold Smith, Phil Smoot, Ken Taylor, Tommy Williamson, Eddie Brandt's Saturday Matinee, Film Favorites, The Shannon Press LTD.

The authors are indebted to Rick Freudenthal of Nashville, Tennessee, for sharing his outstanding collection of Allan "Rocky" Lane photographs for chapter seven of this book.

Great appreciattion goes to Rhonda Lemons and the staff of Empire Publishing Company, Inc. for overseeing the production of this book.

CHAPTER 1

ALLAN "ROCKY" LANE, THE FIGHTIN'EST COWBOY ON THE RANGE

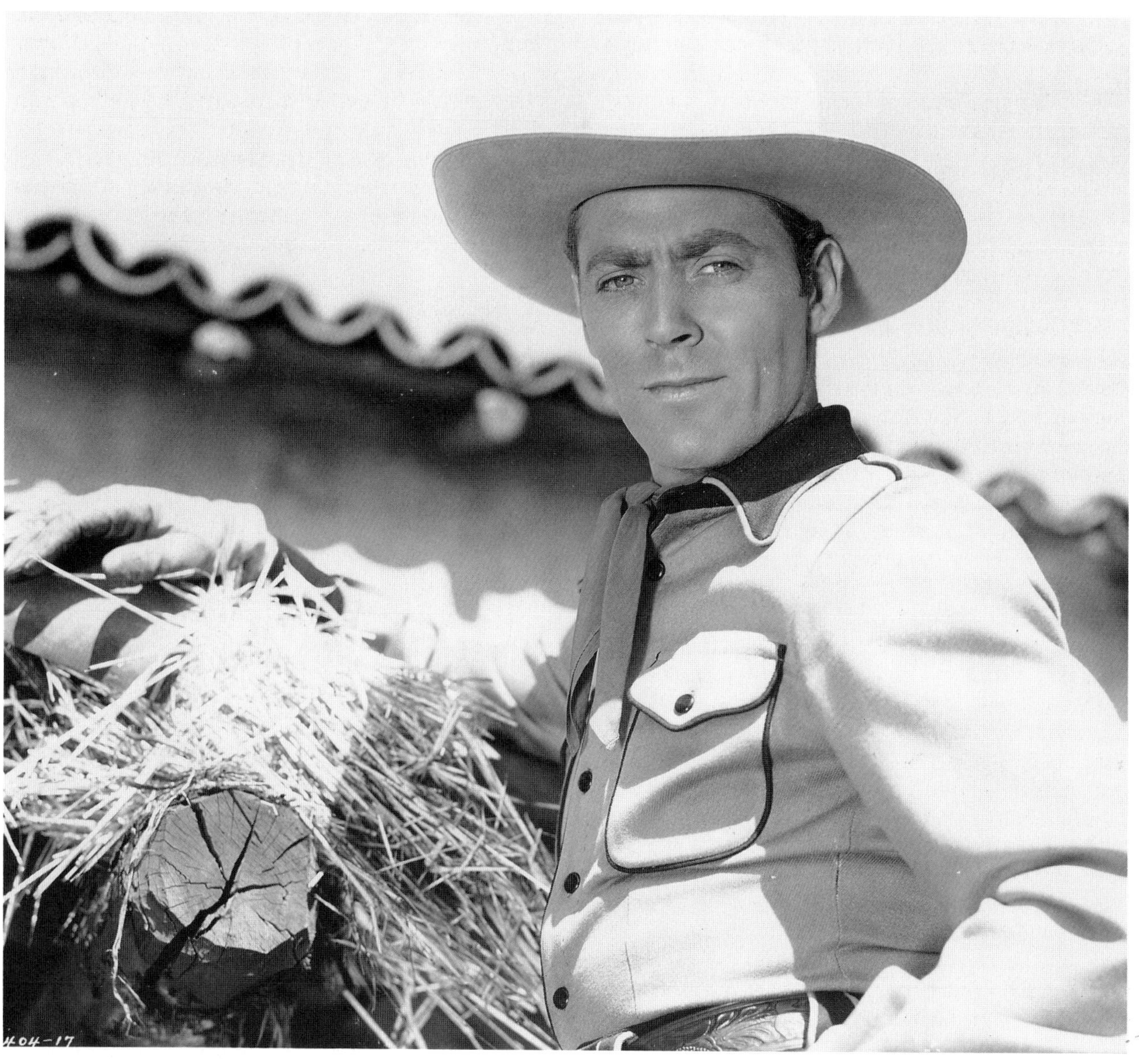

Allan Lane was already forty years old when he began his Western film career for Republic Pictures in 1944. This publicity photo was shot at the time he replaced Don "Red" Barry as a Republic cowboy hero.

The biography most generally accepted lists the birthdate of Allan Lane as September 22, 1904, and relates the fact that he was born at Mishawaka, Indiana, under the name Harry Albershart. From all other indications it appears that the young Hoosier lad's early years were spent enduring typical farm life experiences. And overall this early training probably took place minus a great deal of excitement, but more than likely produced a great deal of hard-nosed teaching that influenced him to a large degree in later life. Symbolic chores such as breaking beans, feeding hogs and weeding peppermint were the order of the day in the life of the Albershart family and it seems that this early training helped Lane develop a fondness for the outdoors that was to remain with him. This part of Lane's life lasted until about the time he finished grammar school. Then, the family vacated Indiana and moved onward to Grand Rapids, Michigan, where Lane finished out his required schooling. Supposedly, sometime between the ages of seven and nine, Lane began to spend his summers on his uncle's ranch located near Clovis, New Mexico. (Attempts to locate relatives in or near the city of Clovis produced no evidence whatsoever, and no records exist of any group of Albersharts in this area. Of course the possibility of the Clovis' uncle still remains due to the fact that I have no means at my disposal to determine the nature of the uncle's true name.) According to Hollywood movie pressbook quotes from Allan Lane (and pressbook quotes most generally are taken with a grain of salt), the thrill of the west was to remain with him after his Clovis ventures. These same quotes also maintain that Allan Lane became a fan of cowboy greats Tom Mix and Ken Maynard along about this time. This much is more than likely true and is no earth-shattering amount of knowledge because, after all, what red-blooded American boy didn't worship such stars during their heyday? Of course, we also must realize that movie publicists many times tend to overdo the build-up portion of an actor's life for reasons related to selling their product.

One biography states that Lane became a good rider while at his uncle's ranch and not only became a top hand but also began to enter Sunday rodeos. He became good enough at this that some of the old hands encouraged him to tour the country, and he did so, picking up small amount of prize money here and there until he finally made his way to California and the Saugus Roundup. There he was discovered by director Avery Edwards and asked to show up in Hollywood to interview for the part of a cowboy in a forthcoming picture. Lane agreed to the interview, got himself a haircut, borrowed some clothes, and arrived for the interview all decked out as a city dude. He then is supposed to have landed the dude part in the picture and some real-life dude is supposed to have landed the

This portrait shot of Allan Lane was taken prior to his years as a Western film star. His classic good looks and mellow voice quality made him an ideal candidate for leading-man roles.

cowboy part. There is little doubt that this story is some publicity agent's idea of a major build-up campaign for Allan Lane. There is no basis whatsoever for authenticity herein. But it has to be admitted that this story sounds good and this was its purpose all along.

Allan Lane finished high school in Grand Rapids and is reported to have done so with honors. Also, his athletic progress was reported to have been above average while completing this part of his education. Most accounts indicate that upon graduation from high school Lane headed back to Indiana and enrolled at the University of Notre Dame. While attending Notre Dame for three years, Lane was reported to have starred in three sports: football, baseball, and basketball. This certainly would have been no small accomplishment if it were true. However, no proof of Lane's Notre Dame tenure can be found. in corresponding with Mr. Edward Krause, Director of Athletics at Notre Dame University, and in receiving replys from both Mr. Krause and from the university's Sports Information Department, again a lack of information. Not only was there no record of Lane (Harry Albershart) appearing as a Notre Dame athlete, but also nothing could be found that would confirm that Lane had ever even enrolled at Notre Dame. It does seem to be true, however, that Lane became interested in commercial photography during this phase of his career. He founded his own company and had among his customers, Lucky Strike cigarettes, Ford Motor Company, and other famous names of the day. This was also the time when Lane became interested in acting and toured New York with a Cincinnati road show company. Most sources indicate that at this time the name Allan Lane was created. Lane landed the leading part in the production of HIT THE DECK. For a period of at least two years Lane alternated between acting in such productions and in operating his photography business.

Sports heroes becoming movie stars became a not uncommon combination in the late twenties and early thirties, and Allan Lane fit into this category nicely. For regardless of whether or not Lane actually starred at Notre Dame, he certainly possessed the physical characteristics necessary for athletic achievements. During his prime Lane stood in at 6'2" tall and tipped the scales at 190 pounds. He was also endowed with a fine speaking voice and was exceedingly handsome. All in all, it could be said of Lane that he issued forth a hard-he-man type of appearance. In 1929 (this account seems to be more accurate) Lane came to the attention of Fox Film Corporation President Windfred Sheehan and was placed in a film entitled: NOT QUITE DECENT. THE FORWARD PASS was also released in 1929 and offered Lane another small part. *Wild West Stars* Publications (in an article by Lewis Bagwell-issue #28) confronts us with the idea that THE FORWARD PASS may have been released before NOT QUITE DECENT. Whatever the case, Allan Lane appeared in 16 full length features (he was cut from the final release of Warner Brothers SMART MONEY in 1931), and in a number of short subjects such as the Fox three reeler, DETECTIVES WANTED, released in 1929 and starring a comedy team known as Clark and McCullough. (The team of Bobby Clark and Paul McCullough starred in fourteen three reelers for Fox before the series was moved over to the RKO lot late in 1929.) Lane was featured in short subject number eleven in the series, KNIGHTS OUT, and in the fourteenth and last Fox Release, DETECTIVES WANTED. He also was featured in Hal Roach's MGM two-reeler, WAR MAMAS, in 1931. The MGMer was part of a short series starring Zasu Pitts and Thelma Todd for producer Hal Roach. A note of further interest is that another future Red Ryder also made one of his first screen appearances for Roach. This was Bill Elliott, who was among the cast for the very first of these two-reelers called LETS DO THINGS. Another top Western name appearing with Lane in WAR MAMAS, the fourth in order of release, was Guinn "Big Boy" Williams.

In 1932 Allan Lane decided to drop his motion picture career interest and return to New York and stage work. He also planned to re-establish his photography business. Some indication has been made that Lane also supplemented his income at this time by trying his hand at both pro football and pro baseball, but again I have not been able to find any evidence that this is so. If it could be proven that Lane tried all the various occupations credited to him, it could truly be said that he was a very dynamic and energetic man. Anyway, beginning in 1932, Allan Lane began what was to be a long and often up-hill climb to success.

Lane's motion picture career remained dormant between the years 1932 and 1936. He did return to Hollywood in 1936 and began to appear regularly in featured roles from out of all the major studios. He supported Shirley Temple in STOWAWAY in 1936 and landed a big part in 20th Century Fox's 1937 release of CHARLIE CHAN AT THE OLYMPICS. It was in 1937 that Lane performed in his first role for the then newly formed Republic Pictures Corporation. The film was entitled THE DUKE COMES BACK, and Lane was so impressive in his role as a boxer that he was signed on by RKO. His elation was short-lived however as his RKO contract did not earn him the success he sought. Lane was cast in twelve drawing room dramas for RKO during the 1938-39 season and found himself stalemated in the same type of pictures that his previous ten years had produced. He did manage to rate a sixth-billed supporting job in the Harry Carey Western of

1938, THE LAW WEST OF TOMBSTONE. This picture was noteworthy as also being the one in which young Tim Holt made his initial adult Western appearance.

Allan Lane was still seeking greater screen recognition following his RKO contract days and reached the verge of almost forgetting stardom. Then along came Republic. And then the part of the Allan Lane story that remains with us that put a permanent impression on our minds came into being. In 1940 Lane had supported Roy Acuff in GRAND OLE OPRY and renewed the attention of Republic's golden-age serial producer, Hiram S. Brown. It seems Brown remembered Lane from THE DUKE COMES BACK and became interested in Lane testing for the role of Sergeant King of the Royal Mounted (a forthcoming Republic chapter-play based on the famous Zane Grey mountie), Lane received the part, acted in three other serials for Republic, and at long last had answered his calling. Now he was to become a big name to the Saturday matinee set and his name was to become synonymous with the word action. For the next thirteen years Allan Lane was to remain predominantly at the top of his industry and in a role that he, at least most of the time, enjoyed. Besides the 1940 production of KING OF THE ROYAL MOUNTED, Lane also starred in the 1942 sequel, KING OF THE MOUNTIES, DAREDEVILS OF THE WEST in 1943, and in THE TIGER WOMAN, with serial queen Linda Stirling, in 1944.

Along about this time Republic decided to promote Don "Red" Barry to leading man roles (either because of a shortage of leading-man material due to the war or because Barry had ambitions of becoming another James Cagney). Whatever the reason for this change, Barry's successful Western series left an opening for a replacement. Allan Lane fit in nicely. He even seemed

Just prior to starting his first Western series for Republic, Allan Lane starred with Janet Martin in CALL OF THE SOUTH SEAS (1944). In those years, it was not common for the main character to have a thin-line mustache such as Lane possesses on his upper lip in the photo above.

It was Republic's custom to call new contract players onto a sound stage and shoot a series of stills for publicity purposes. It was Allan Lane's turn to pose for the camera on this day in 1944. Here he looks sternly heroic.

to don Barry's wearing apparel, at least almost. There the similarity ended, because even though Lane's acting abilities approached those of Barry, Lane produced more personal action in his films. He seemed to handle the action in better fashion, to be more of the man of few words type whose words carried more weight when he spoke. Barry's last sidekick, Wally Vernon, supported Lane in the first two films of this new series and certainly did nothing to help the cause. However, the films were very acceptable and were not lacking for action. SILVER CITY KID, the first of the six films, was loaded with several tough fistfights between Lane and adversaries Harry Woods, Tom Steele and Bud Geary. The third film was more than likely the best of the group, thanks to the comic talents of Max Terhune and the able support of Duncan Renaldo. After the fifth of the series was released in 1945, Lane guest-starred (he had a small speaking part) along with Don Barry, Bob Livingston, Sunset Carson and Wild Bill Elliott in Roy Roger's BELLS OF ROSARITA. The last film of the series, TRAIL OF KIT CARSON, was then completed. Overall, this was a very respectable beginning for the new Western star and should have put him well on his way in this line of endeavor. But for some reason or another Lane was now thrust back to the drawing room. Who knows why! Maybe it was a promotion and maybe it was a leading-man shortage necessity. Anyway, after three films of this variety, Lane climbed back into the saddle again for another guest appearance. This time he supported Monte Hale (another slow starter who after several supporting roles was being built up in a new Magnacolor-Trucolor series) in OUT CALIFORNIA WAY along with Roy Rogers, Dale Evans and Don Barry. And while all this was going on, Allan Lane was preparing himself for what was to become the second finest series of his career, Wild Bill Elliott's now discontinued Red Ryder offerings.

Republic wasn't about to leave the now vacant (Elliott dropped the "Wild Bill" moniker and became the more sophisticated-sounding William Elliott in a group of grade A productions for Republic that have been compared to John Wayne films of that time. Personally, I like them.) Red Ryder role inactive as all the Elliott jobs had been highly popular and had ignited that all-important principle: profit at the box office. Herbert J. Yates, President of Republic Productions, is said to have first considered Marshall Reed for the role but leaned toward Lane after viewing footage from Lane's earlier series for his studio. Lane got the role. He

In this shot Lane displays his don't-fool-with-me smiling-eyes pose.

Allan Lane took over the Red Ryder series from Wild Bill Elliott in 1946. Here he is seen in the Red Ryder garb with the horse named Thunder. The picture was taken on the back lot of Republic, beside the ranch house and barn of the Duchess.

played the Red Ryder character during the 1946-47 season, which resulted in seven fine, action-packed sagebrushers. Bobby Blake retained the role of Little Beaver from the Elliott series. Martha Wentworth was the duchess. And, of course, villains such as Roy Barcroft and Gene Roth didn't harm the proceedings by hanging around from picture to picture and doing evil things. Lane seemed to be gaining more poise and stature as the series rolled along and looked very impressive in the Red Ryder garb. One reason given for the demise of the Ryders after the seventh offering, MARSHAL OF CRIPPLE CREEK, has been that Blake was outgrowing the Little Beaver character and that searching world-wide for a replacement was out of the question. Perhaps this was true and perhaps it just happened that the regulars grew restless in their roles. It does appear that the Lane-Blake tandem never achieved the same rapport as the Elliott-Blake combination. Blake's part in the series is said to have diminished as the series neared it's end, but in my comparisons of the Ryder films that I have been privileged to view, I can spot no major differences in Blake's length of film footage per picture. I do feel that the Lane-Ryders and the Elliott-Ryders compare favorably in every respect. Both series were, I believe, some of Republic's best and hurt neither man's career.

Allan Lane next entered into the final phase of his B Western career. This phase covered the years 1947-1953 and made Lane one of the last stars to discontinue the programmer Western. What was to become the mark of immortality for Allan Lane (now called Allan "Rocky" Lane), was a group of what I believe to be among the finest series Westerns available. Several things were happening to help force the B oaters to make an exodus toward an eternal sunset. Things such as rising production costs, television, a supposed lack of concern among producers, and, I think, a more sophisticated audience, as well as groups of more color productions on the market, helped to ring the final death knell. But before this came into being Allan Lane truly left his mark for the public to critique. He starred in thirty-eight films, beginning with THE WILD FRONTIER in 1947 and ending with EL PASO STAMPEDE in 1953, and each offering issued forth an almost continuous piece of action and was constantly fast moving. True, stock footage may have entered more and more into the later entries of the series as budgets were slashed, but, if so, this footage was hidden fairly well. And in praise to Lane's dead serious professionalism, his restrained personality seemed to mold his work together (much like Tim Holt at RKO). The original twenty-eight Lanes ran from fifty-nine to sixty minutes in length and the last ten features in this series saw running times cut to fifty-four minutes. This was more than likely done for two reasons: cutting costs and for possible television sales in the future.

Allan Lane's Westerns were in contrast to most other Western series of his time due to a larger emphasis on plot realism. Direction was generally good and the overall quality of acting was above average, especially for this type of programmer, Lane played the part of a forceful hero who could work his way out of tight spots in a logical way, usually in no small part due to good scripts. Eddy Waller played Lane's sidekick in thirty-two of the thirty-eight films (Chubby Johnson aided Lane in three films, Walter Baldwin, Irving Bacon and Clem Bevens each in one film). Waller supplied above-average comedy relief as grizzled old Nugget Clark, a character not overly blessed with smarts, but who, on the other hand, wasn't a completely helpless and bungling idiot. Production values and technical details usually reached high standards in this series. After watching several offerings from the Rocky Lane series of films, this conclusion has been reached: Lane's films illuminated a dark, somber-type quality that gave them a trademark all their own. This was in direct contrast to the usual brightness prevalent in other Republic Westerns.

The supporting cast was effective by and large in almost all of these films, and each film, when viewed even today, still moves fairly smoothly and always swiftly. The observer could usually expect a fast pace from the opening reel to the fadeout. I suppose the most commonly used adjectives from Lane's movie ads most ably describe the man's films: Allan "Rocky" Lane sinks flying fists and hot lead into bandit gangs. Very few critics, whether Lane fans or not, could dispute this statement. Allan Lane had come close before, but now he captured the character that best suited his particular abilities.

After the completion of EL PASO STAMPEDE, which was released on September 8, 1953, Allan "Rocky" Lane faded into B Western obscurity. He, like the business to which he had devoted himself, became a thing of the past. This man whose perfectionist demands of himself and others while on the sets, now discovered that fame was a fleeting thing. He had made enemies and perhaps this hurt him. Perhaps he couldn't see things as others saw them and only performed in the way that he saw fit, the way that he believed. Whatever the case, Allan Lane now found himself with only an occasional featured role in the GUNSMOKE television series. To support himself he became a Los Angeles car salesman and was probably greatly enlightened when in 1955 he was offered the chance to once again play the Red Ryder character in a TV pilot that was to launch the series into action. Unfortunately, Lane was outfitted in a sort of outlandish garb that immediately turned viewers off. Why this was done, nobody knows. Perhaps it was an attempt to meet the needs of the time. Anyway, it failed, and with its failure Allan Lane's last chance at stardom ended. The show is high on collectors' lists today if that is any consolation.

After the TV try at a new Red Ryder series failed, Allan Lane was to make three more theatrical appearances. In 1958 he obtained a featured part in a Rory Calhoun Western for Universal called THE SAGA OF HEMP BROWN and for the same Studio he also played two very minor roles in Audie Murphy starrers. These films were HELL BENT FOR LEATHER (1960) and POSSE FROM HELL (1961). He was reportedly bitter because the movie industry seemed to have

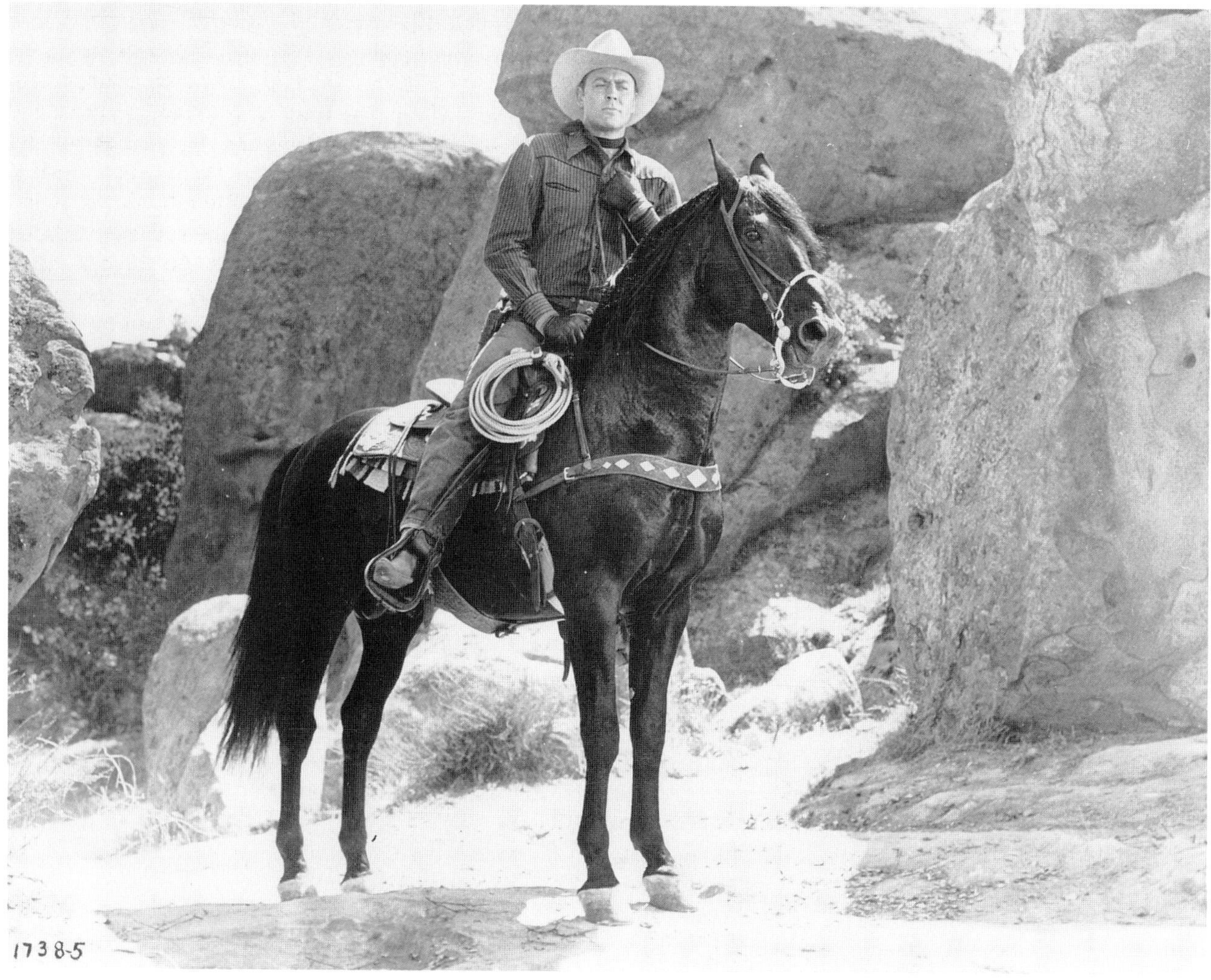

In 1947 the Red Ryder films were discontinued, and Allan Lane was given his own starring series. During the next seven years he made thirty-eight films in which he played a character called "Rocky" Lane. He wore a dark-striped shirt (shown above) and Levi jeans. His horse was a stallion (Yes, really!) named Blackjack.

turned its back on him. Personal feelings aside, it is difficult to understand why this fine actor didn't at least land some sort of TV series. He still retained his athletic build and good looks when viewed in POSSE FROM HELL in 1961.

Actually, Allan Lane did not disappear entirely from the scene. Quite by accident he became the off-camera voice for MR ED, the talking horse of TV fame and performed this act from 1961-1966. According to star Alan Young (from an interview taped with Les Adams in 1975), Young and producer, Leonard Goldstein overheard Lane talking while visiting a Hollywood stable in their search for the proper horse to portray Mr. Ed. Goldstein liked the sound of Lane's voice, and after a bit of inquiring, offered him the unusual job of supplying the sound for the talking horse. Lane needed the work but his pride entered into the picture, and he agreed to accept the offer only if a contract would be drawn up and signed that provided an outlet to prevent embarrassment to Lane. So, Allan Lane became a part of the MR. ED show but saw to it that his name was not listed in the credits. Later, after the show became a success, it was indicated that Lane tried to get the terms of the contract changed so that he might receive credit for his part. His earnings in this venture supplied Allan Lane with enough income to retire and live comfortably until his death from bone cancer on October 27, 1973. He resided in Los Angeles at this time.

According to Lewis Bagwell's article on Allan Lane, which was written for Jim Ward's fine publication, *Wild West Stars* (Issue #28), Lane was twice married: first to the former Gladys Leslie and later to actress Sheila Ryan. Both marriages ended in divorce. Lane's obituary listed his mother as sole survivor.

Allan Lane was said to be a ready conversationalist with close friends, a man who studied Western history, knew much about saddle and Indian lore, and could discuss and analyze fine horses with the best. He also was a man who, once during a fit of anger, tried to force a co-star over a cliff during a filming sequence. On another occasion he had a featured player thrown off the studio lot for arriving in Levis. It seems his contract stated that only Lane would be allowed to wear such apparel in the picture, and he intended to see to it that the terms of the contract were upheld.

At the end there didn't appear to be an overabundance of friends available. True, many of Rocky's saddle pals had already passed on and others were either scattered or were unable to attend, and perhaps there were other reasons; but only four persons showed up for his funeral. Besides his mother and the ministers, Lane's funeral was attended by two friends, whose names will be withheld for personal reasons.

Allan Lane twice made the list of top-ten Western stars as reported by *Motion Picture Herald and Fan Magazines*, 1951-#8, and 1953-#5. *Who's Who in Western Stars Magazine* #2, 1952, relates that Lane planned to become a paniolo, Hawaiian cowboy. He planned on starring in a series of Westerns produced on the islands. Of course, this never came about and perhaps was exaggerated to begin with. In conclusion, it could be said that Allan Lane lived through a period of movie history that will never be repeated and produced thrills that can never be recaptured. And regardless of how complex his personality really was, few could argue that his contributions to the field of endeavor that he engaged in, the B Western, were immense. Allan Lane rewarded his many fans' dimes and quarters many times over. And, somehow, it is hard to realize that this great action star is gone from the scene, because, as long as film historians and enthusiasts remain, Allan "Rocky" Lane will continue to ride the range.

CHAPTER 2

EARNING HIS SPURS; THE FIRST ALLAN LANE WESTERN SERIES

Allan Lane gets a leg up on the action for his first Western film series

In 1940 Allan Lane was put under non-exclusive contract to Republic Pictures and cast in several forgettable features and four memorable serials. The features were low-budget time-fillers, for the most part, that were aimed at the lower half of double-bills. For Republic he made GRAND OLD OPRY (1940), and CALL OF THE SOUTH SEAS (1944).

United Artists starred him in a piece of fluff called ALL-AMERICAN CO-ED (1940), and Twentieth Century-Fox cast him in a totally negligible opus entitled THE DANCING MASTERS (1943). In-between these features, Lane had the opportunity to establish himself as an action performer in four fine serials—KING OF THE ROYAL MOUNTED (1940), KING OF THE MOUNTIES (1942), DAREDEVILS OF THE WEST (1943), and THE TIGER WOMAN (1944).

KING OF THE ROYAL MOUNTED and KING OF THE MOUNTIES, according to writer Alan Barbour in his book entitled *Cliffhanger,* "firmly established the actor as a leading Republic hero and are among the most thrilling productions (with beautifully staged fight sequences and wonderful miniature work) ever made for Saturday matinee fans." Of DAREDEVILS OF THE WEST Barbour writes, it is "one of the most action-packed serials ever made" and "one of Republic's all-time best action serials." Jim Harmon and Donald F. Glut, in their book *The Great Movie Serials,* praise THE TIGER WOMAN as "a slick Republic serial, with the fast action scenes that were a mixture of Western, jungle, and detective elements, and (containing) perfect special effects that became a trademark of the studio."

In each of the serials Allan Lane displayed the action skills that would later make him a top Western star for Republic. The two Mountie serials and DAREDEVILS OF THE WEST were the best of the four for Lane. His part in THE TIGER WOMAN was somewhat dissipated by the casting of Linda Sterling as title character and Duncan Renaldo as his cohort in the action scenes.

During the time Lane was completing CALL OF THE SOUTH SEAS, he learned that Don "Red" Barry was moving on to "bigger" features at Republic and that the studio planned to cast him in the remaining films that were originally scheduled for Barry. Unfortunately, he was also saddled with Barry's sidekick, Wally Vernon (a misplaced Damon Runyon-type character who fumbled through Lane's first two entries), and a precocious little blond tot named Twinkle Watts. It was rumored at the time that Republic had thoughts of turning Twinkle into the next Shirley Temple, but, ultimately, that was not to be—probably because of the ire expressed by Western fans who found the cutsy kid a trial in the Barry Westerns and even more of a pain in the six features that comprised Allan Lane's first Western series for Republic.

SILVER CITY KID (1944) got the series off to a fast-moving start by director John English. Strong support was offered by heroine Peggy Stewart and old standbys Harry Woods, Glenn Strange, Tom London, and Tom Steele. John English, who had directed Allan

Allan Lane could dish it out.

And he could take it!

Lane in three of his serials for Republic, had a passionate dislike for the actor and never again directed him in a picture.

Less than two months later STAGECOACH TO MONTEREY (1944) was released. Lesley Selander helmed this one, a less rousing entry in the fledgling series, which signaled the demise of Wally Vernon from the Lane pictures but again featured the talents of leading lady Peggy Stewart.

Next came SHERIFF OF SUNDOWN (1944), again directed by Selander and providing Lane a reunion with Linda Stirling and Duncan Renaldo, who had been featured with him in THE TIGER WOMAN earlier the same year. Max Terhune was a welcome sidekick addition, providing some comic relief with his dummy Elmer. With Terhune and Renaldo on board, it seemed like shades of the Three Mesquiteers series to many Western fans.

The second half of Lane's six-pack series began in early 1945 with the release of THE TOPEKA TERROR, an action-packed episode with the usual Republic stock company of performers. Look for young Monte Hale in a small part. The studio had put the future singing cowboy under contract just a few months before and within a year he would be starring in his own series.

The next entry, CORPUS CHRISTI BANDITS (1945), was an oddball film by B Western standards and was a bit on the ambitious side. The first part of the picture reveals Lane as a returned bomber pilot from World War II. We then flashback to the old West as he tells his kid sister (Twinkle Watts) the story of their grandfather, Corpus Christi Jim. More than one B Western theatre patron wondered why Republic went to all the trouble, but Lane did turn in a fine performance in both the modern and flashback sequences, and the plot did contain interesting parallels to soldiers returning from World War II and the Civil War.

The final film in Lane's first series was TRAIL OF KIT CARSON (1945), which, not surprisingly, had nothing to do with Kit Carson. Directed by Leslie Selander, it was only a fair conclusion to an above average but still rather uninspired series for Allan Lane.

Peggy Stewart was Allan Lane's leading lady in both SILVER CITY KID and STAGECOACH TO MONTEREY.

There were better things just ahead for the cowboy star.

SILVER CITY KID

55 Mins .... July 20, 1944

ALLAN LANE .... Jack Adams
PEGGY STEWART .... Ruth Clayton
WALLY VERNON .... Wildcat Higgins
TWINKLE WATTS .... Twinkle Clayton
HARRY WOODS .... Sam Ballard
FRANK JAQUET .... William Stoner
LANE CHANDLER .... .Steve Clayton
GLENN STRANGE .... Garvey
BUD GEARY .... Yager
TOM STEELE .... Utah
TOM LONDON .... Sheriff Gibson
JACK KIRK .... Tom
SAM FLINT .... Mr. Andrews

ASSOC. PRODUCER .... Stephen Auer
DIRECTED BY .... .John English
ORIGINAL STORY .... Bennett Cohen
SCREENPLAY BY .... Taylor Caven
PHOTOGRAPHED BY .... Reggie Lanning
MUSICAL SCORE .... Joseph Dubin

In 1885 the only deposit of molybdenum in the United States is found in Redwood County. William Stoner, local banker and owner of the Redwood Mine, has received an offer from The National Steel Company to buy the output of the mine. Stoner and his Attorney Sam Ballard, who is also acting judge, have discovered that the vein runs under the ranch of Steve Clayton.

Stoner and Ballard are thought to be respectable men, but Steve Clayton learns otherwise and discovers that they are tampering with the vein under his property. Clayton is shot by Garvey, one of Ballard's henchmen. Jack Adams and his pal Wildcat Higgins ride up with guns blazing to help their friend and succeed in running the gunmen off. Taking their wounded friend back to his ranch, Clayton begins to make an incriminating statement to his sister Ruth about Garvey before succumbing to his wounds. Jack vows to avenge the death of his friend.

Jack goes to town to seek permission from Stoner to take a look at the mine for clues. Stoner gives his approval but after Jack leaves, he and Ballard continue their talk on how to get control of the Clayton property before others discover their chicanery. The first step in their plan is to dispatch Garvey and his ruffians to intercept Jack and prevent him from reaching the mine. An over anxious Garvey misses Jack with his rifle, so he and his men beat a hasty retreat so they won't be recognized. Jack finds a spur part at the scene and holds onto it as a clue.

Back in town Ruth loudly accuses Stoner of knowing something of her brother's death, since Steve was near Stoner's mine when he was shot. Stoner tries to calm her but to no avail. Jack and Wildcat arrive in town and head for the saloon to gain information. Jack sees that Yager is missing the spur part he found and accuses him of taking a shot at him. Garvey and Yager engage Jack and Wildcat in a brawl that decimates the saloon. Sheriff Gibson arrives and jails Yager, Jack, and Wildcat. Fearing that Yager will talk, Garvey later shoots him from the rear of the jail. Ballard sends a letter to Ruth by Utah to which he has signed Stoner's name. The letter asks that she be in Stoner's office at eight that night. Meanwhile Ballard forces Stoner to sign over the mine to him. Moments before Ruth arrives, Ballard kills Stoner so that Ruth will be blamed. She picks up the gun with which Ballard shot Stoner and is found with it in her hand when Ballard and the others arrive. Ruth is, in fact, accused of the murder but escapes from her captors.

At the jail Jack has been released by the Sheriff and is deputized to find Yager's killer. Ballard arrives at the jail to swear out a warrant for the arrest of Ruth Clayton. Jack's first job is to bring Ruth in. He reluctantly accepts the job and does so only after being told by Acting Judge Ballard that he will release her on bond if she is brought in. Jack finds Ruth and after convincing her that Stoner's murder was a deliberate attempt to get her out the way, she agrees to turn herself in. After Jack brings Ruth in, Ballard reneges on his agreement to free her on bail. An incensed Jack beats two of Ballards heavies in the fight which follows and then turns in his badge, vowing to find Clayton's killer.

Jack returns to the Clayton ranch and finds an eviction notice ordering the ranch vacated within twenty-four hours. Jack and Wildcat later learn that Ballard has had Ruth released in his custody. Jack and Wildcat return to the Clayton Ranch and are met by gunfire from the six-guns of Ballard and Garvey and his men. After Ruth escapes, Ballard and Garvey seek refuge in the barn only to have Jack force them out by torching it. Garvey is gunned down by Jack who then chases the hard-riding Ballard and knocks him from his horse. Ballard falls to his death from a cliff during a fight with Jack.

Ruth is made head of the Redwood mine with Jack and Wildcat staying on to help out.

STAGECOACH TO MONTEREY

55 Mins .... Sept. 15, 1944

ALLAN LANE .... Chick Weaver
PEGGY STEWART .... Jessie Wade
WALLY VERNON .... Throckmorton Snodgrass
TWINKLE WATTS .... Inky Wade
TOM LONDON .... Chester Wade
LEROY MASON .... Black Jack Barstow
ROY BARCROFT .... J. Rodney Stevens
KENNE DUNCAN .... Joe
BUD GEARY .... Dan
CARL SEPULVEDA .... Roy
JACK KIRK .... Bartender
FRED GRAHAM .... Mac

ASSOC. PRODUCER .... Stephen Auer
DIRECTED BY .... Lesley Selander
ORIGINAL SCREENPLAY .... NormanS. Hall
PHOTOGRAPHED BY .... William Bradford
MUSICAL SCORE .... Joseph Dubin

Bruce Redmond, Special Agent for the U.S. Treasury Department, using the name Chick Weaver, stops a Monterey bound stage and seeks a ride under the pretense that his horse has broken a leg. After obtaining a ride, Weaver converses with fellow passengers, J. Rodney Stevens of the U.S. Silver Foundation and Throckmorton Snodgrass, the self-proclaimed best stamp printer west of the Mississippi. Their conversation is ended by gunfire. The stage is stopped by a group of outlaws headed by Dan who claims that they are looking for Bruce Redmond. After all passengers identify themselves, the stage is allowed to continue on its journey.

Once arriving in Monterey, Snodgrass manages to get a job at the *Monterey Clarion*, run by Chester Wade and his daughter Jessie. As Jessie gets a story from Chick about the stage and its passengers, Stevens, the third passenger, goes to the Four Aces Saloon. He learns that saloon owner Black Jack Barstow is the man responsible for dispatching outlaws to stop the stage in the search for Redmond. Stevens confides to Barstow that his U.S. Silver Foundation is a bogus operation devised to sell phony mint certificates to unwary victims in order to capitalize on legitimate silver strikes in the area. Barstow gets in on the action since

Look out, Allan. You're dealing with two shady characters (Roy Barcroft and LeRoy Mason) in fancy suits. You can bet they're up to no good.

Twinkle Watts demonstrates some of her endearing qualities to Wally Vernon, Allan Lane, Tom London, and Peggy Stewart in this scene from STAGECOACH TO MONTEREY.

Chester Wade is in debt to him with no way to pay off. He has the reluctant Wade help by printing the phony certificates.

Snodgrass in reality is also a treasury agent and shares his room at the *Clarion* with Chick, the man with whom he is secretly working. The treasury agents leave their room in search of information on the bogus operation. Their search takes them to Barstow's saloon where they are confronted by the hoodlums who stopped the stage and are drawn into a fight. After toppling the ruffians, Chick informs Barstow that he needs a job. The not-so-subtle Barstow offers him a job for $100 per month and tells him that he is to do away with Bruce Redmond when he shows up.

While playing cards at the Four Aces that night, Chick sees Barstow leave and decides that he and Snodgrass will follow him. As Barstow threatens Wade inside the hideout for wanting to quit, Chick and Snodgrass spot a deserted shack and prepare to search it before being shot at by two gunmen. The gunmen flee after failing to kill the intruders but are chased by Chick who shoots one of them. Chick and Snodgrass recognize the dead man as being a frequent patron of the Four Aces.

Chick and his partner return to the deserted ranch the next day and discover a ladder inside the well while drawing water for their horses. They examine the well and find a printing press, some phony mint certificates, and an article of Wade's printing attire. Arriving in town to question Jessie, they still remain incognito but tell the woman to have her father be careful. Realizing that Chick is really a treasury agent from an accidental discovery of his badge, Jessie informs her father and questions him about his activities.

Meanwhile, Stevens receives a letter from a fellow crook which includes a photo of Bruce Redmond. After learning from Joe that Weaver chased him the previous night and seeing the photo that Stevens received, Barstow orders henchmen Joe, Dan, and Roy to eliminate Chick and Snodgrass. All but Roy are killed in the gun battle with the agents.

Chick and Snodgrass confront Wade and identify themselves to him. After revealing that Barstow intimidated him and forced him to print the certificates, Wade is deputized by Chick and joins him and Snodgrass as they head for a confrontation with Barstow and Stevens.

The trio is met by gunfire from Barstow and Stevens who have gone to dispose of the printing press. The crooks flee in a buckboard after wounding Wade. Chick chases them and shoots Barstow. Stevens, the mastermind of the scheme, dies when he loses control of the buckboard, which overturns.

After the funds of Barstow and Stevens are attached and distributed to those swindled, Chick informs Wade that he has been cleared of any wrongdoing and has been offered a job with the Treasury as a printing expert.

It's a tense moment in STAGECOACH TO MONTEREY as Allan Lane and Wally Vernon come to the rescue of the wounded Tom London.

Peggy Stewart, Tom London, Wally Vernon, and Allan Lane enjoy a chuckle in this relaxed scene from STAGECOACH TO MONTEREY.

SHERIFF OF SUNDOWN

55 Mins .... Nov. 7, 1944

ALLAN LANE .... Tex Jordan
LINDA STIRLING .... Lois Carpenter
MAX TERHUNE .... Third Grade Simms
TWINKLE WATTS .... .Little Jo Craig
ROY BARCROFT .... Jack Hatfield
DUNCAN RENALDO .... Chihuahua Ramirez
BUD GEARY .... Ward
JACK KIRK .... Andy Craig
HERBERT RAWLINSON. .... Governor Brainerd
TOM LONDON .... Sheriff Tom Carpenter
KENNE DUNCAN .... Albert Wilkes
BOB WILKE .... .Bradley

ASSOC. PRDODUCER. .... Stephen Auer
DIRECTED BY .... Lesley Selander
ORIGINAL SCREENPLAY .... Norman S. Hall
PHOTOGRAPHED BY .... Bud Thackery
MUSICAL SCORE .... Joseph Dubin

Cattleman Tex Jordan is headed for the town of Sundown to sell a herd of cattle, his last before calling it quits and heading East to see the country.

Tex and his friends Third Grade Simms and Chihuahua Ramirez arrive in Sundown to sell the cattle

Duncan Renaldo and Max Terhune look on as Allan Lane stops Roy Barcroft from harming Jack Kirk in SHERIFF OF SUNDOWN.

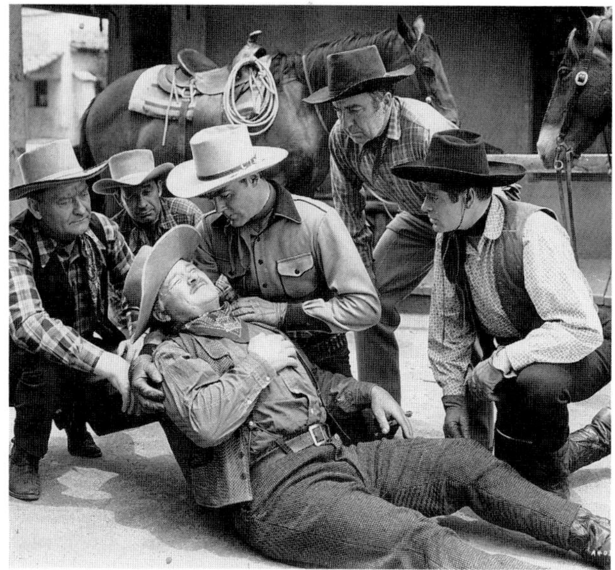

Allan Lane comes to the aid of Jack Kirk as Max Terhune (left), Duncan Renaldo (right), and a couple of townspeople look on.

to Jack Hatfield of the Hatfield Land and Cattle Company. Hatfield virtually runs the town since he also owns the Cattlemen's Exchange Bank as well as the saloon and other businesses. Hatfield rules with an iron hand as he forces the small cattlemen to sell below market value but pays fair prices to the big cattlemen like Tex who can afford to go elsewhere. Hatfield pulls a gun and prepares to shoot complaining cattleman Andy Craig in the back but is stopped by Tex and his pals, precipitating a wild free-for-all.

Outside the saloon, Tex consoles his friend Craig and buys his cattle at a fair price, planning to later sell them to Hatfield. Tex, who threatens to tell other Texas cattlemen about Hatfield's unfair business practices, is talking with Hatfield when a gunshot rings out. Tex's friend Craig has been shot by Ward, a Hatfield henchman. Tex is asked by his dying friend to take care of his daughter, Little Jo. Tex and his pals ride out to the Craig Ranch to break the news to her but can't and join her for dinner.

Allan Lane and Duncan Renaldo pretend to have a falling out so that Duncan can go underground to trap bad guy Roy Barcroft. That's Jack O'Shea on the left fooling with his chips.

The next morning Tex returns to town and discusses his dilemma with Sheriff Carpenter and his daughter Lois. Tex accuses Hatfield of being behind Craig's killing but is dejected to learn that Hatfield can't be arrested without evidence. Tex vows to get Hatfield legally and leaves the Sheriff's office, but he, Third Grade and Chihuahua are fired upon by Hatfield's men. An exchange of gunfire follows. Sheriff Carpenter stops the shoot-out and prepares to make arrests but is stopped by Hatfield who requests that Tex and friends not be arrested.

Tex and cohorts head for Capital City to talk with Governor Brainerd about the problems in Sundown. The Governor agrees to help Tex, especially since he knows that Hatfield is plotting to replace him as governor. Governor Brainerd makes Tex a special investigator and gives him the power to deputize men to help him. Before Tex can leave, Albert Wilkes, a worker in the governor's office and secret spy for Hatfield, delivers a letter revealing that Sheriff Carpenter, the man that Tex had spoken so highly of to the Governor, has been shot and killed.

Tex returns to Sundown and opens the Cattlemen's Cooperative Exchange, an organizatlion established to see that all cattlemen get a fair price for their herds. This organization is not to Hatfield's liking since it cuts into his profits. After learning from Wilkes that the governor is behind Tex, Hatfield orders Ward to attack the cattlemen coming into Sundown to encourage them to deal with him and not Tex Jordan.

With no end to the raids and killings in sight and upon learning from the governor that Wilkes has been supplying info to Hatfield, Tex devises a plan to get proof that Hatfield is behind the chicanery, Tex and his friend Chihuahua pretend to have a falling out so that Chihuahua can gain inside information on Hatfield. To convince the villains that they are on the outs, Tex confronts Chihuahua in the saloon and trades punches with him. After the fight Tex pays Chihuahua his back wages and fires him. Chihuahua gains the confidence of Hatfield and friends and joins their side.

The plan works for a while, but Hatfield is alerted to the ruse when Wilkes writes him that Tex is out to get him. Hatfield has Chihuahua write Tex a letter asking that they meet at Rock Creek Canyon alone. Fearing a trap of some sort, Chihuahua includes a code word in the letter to alert his partner to the possible danger. Tex arrives at Rock Creek Canyon and eludes the sentry before joining his Mexican friend in battling Hatfield and Ward. Tex shoots Ward, who has wounded Chihuahua, and mounts his sturdy steed to chase Hatfield. Hatfield is roped from his horse by Tex but pulls a knife on his surprised adversary. Fists fly as the badman is subdued.

With Hatfield sentenced to hang, Tex makes Little Jo the owner of the Cattlemen's Cooperative Exchange and Lois Carpenter the trustee, Tex departs with a promise to return and organize territorial rangers at a later date.

THE TOPEKA TERROR

55 Mins .... Jan. 26, 1945

ALLAN LANE .... Chad Stevens
LINDA STERLING .... June Hardy
EARLE HODGINS .... Don Quixote Martingale
TWINKLE WATTS .... Midge Hardy
ROY BARCROFT .... Ben Jode
BUD GEARY .... Clyde Flint
TOM LONDON .... William Hardy
FRANK JAQUET .... Trent Parker
JACK KIRK .... Joe Green
EVE NOVAK .... Mrs. Green
BOB WILKE .... Townsman
HANK BELL .... Stage Driver

ASSOC. PRODUCER .... Stephen Auer
DIRECTED BY .... Howard Bretherton
SCREENPLAY .... Patricia Harper & Norman S. Hall
ORIGINAL STORY. .... Patricia Harper
PHOTOGRAPHED BY .... Bud Thackery
MUSICAL DIRECTOR .... Richard Cherwin

The granting of two million acres of land by the U.S. Government to homesteaders proved a godsend to many a settler. However, the landrush which followed brought forth many a crook to capitalize on the homesteaders' good fortune.

Ben Jode, crooked representative of the Great Eastern Finance Company, arrives in the town of Red Dust to see Clyde Flint, owner of the lucky Chance Saloon. Jode and Flint have plans to acquire the lands granted the homesteaders and are aided by Trent Parker, the local land agent, who because he owes a great deal of money to Flint, is easy prey for his swindling pals.

William Hardy and his youngest daughter Midge are enroute to town to meet June, his eldest daughter who has preceded them into town to file their claim, when Midge accidentally discharges a shotgun and causes their wagon to run away. Chad Stevens, a secret investigatior for the U.S. Territorial Land Department is close by and stops the wagon. Chad and the Hardys happen upon an unclaimed parcel of land at which Chad instructs them to stay while he rides ahead to tell June.

Chad arrives in town and is greeted by gunfire from Flint, Jode, and their men who have taken exception to the homesteaders attempt to get the land record book when told that their claims belong to others. Chad joins the melee before insisting that the homesteaders leave town and regroup. After informing Hardy of the trouble, Chad suggests that the homesteaders join forces and fight for their rights. He instructs Hardy to go into town and file a claim on the parcel that they happened upon when he stopped the runaway wagon.

Hardy is accompanied into town by Don Quixote Martingale, one of the more outspoken of the settlers. Martingale, a lawyer by profession, advocates taking their claim to the Supreme Court—or higher, if necessary, to get justice. The duo spots a poster in the land office proclaiming Flint to be the best man running for the job of sheriff. Realizing that Jode was one of the men who shot at them, Hardy and Martingale join Chad at the saloon to show their displeasure at having been shot at. Jode recognizes Chad as the straight shooter who helped the homesteaders and a fight breaks out. The villains go down to defeat at the hands of the brawling Chad.

They return to the land office where they are told that they can't vote in the election because they aren't legal residents, Chad advocates that they build their own town on Hardy's six-hundred acres, but Parker claims this to be illegal. The secret investigator recites a law which makes it legal, causing Parker to go into his back office to check on its legality. Jode is in the back room, and, upon learning that Chad is right, he reenters the land office from the front and offers to buy Hardy's land. Hardy refuses to sell out his friends, so he turns down Jode's most generous offer.

The homesteaders manage to get financing for their town and supplies from a neighboring town. Flint and his henchmen attack the supply wagons but are turned back by Chad, who suspects that they will have trouble, and others who are hidden inside the wagons. Upset by their failure, Jode orders Parker to entice Hardy and Martinghale into town. Once at the land office, Jode knocks Martingale out after forcing Hardy to sign his land over. Hardy is then shot with Martingale's gun in an attempt to frame the lawyer.

Chad arrives to find Martingale accused of killing Hardy. However, Chad finds that Hardy is only wounded and takes him to the doctor for treatment. After Hardy dies from his wounds, Chad returns to question Parker and finds him cleaning out his desk. The crooked land agent is tricked into revealing the truth about Hardy's shooting and the land swindle. Jode arrives in the office, causing a fight to break out. Jode gets the short end of the stick from Chad who then rescues Martingale from being lynched for murdering Hardy.

His job having been done, Chad reveals his identity to all before returning to headquarters.

CORPUS CHRISTI BANDITS

55 Mins .... April 20, 1945

ALLAN LANE .... Capt. James Christie
Corpus Christi Jim
HELEN TALBOT .... Dorothy Adams
JACK KIRK .... Alonzo Adams
TWINKLE WATTS .... Nancy Adams
FRANCIS MCDONALD .... Dad Christie
ROY BARCROFT .... Wade Larkin
TOM LONDON .... Rocky
KENNE DUNCAN .... Spade
BOB WILKE .... Steve
RUTH LEE .... Mom Christie
ED CASSIDY .... Marshal Dan Adams
EMMETT VOGAN .... The Governor
DICKIE DILLON .... Brush
FREDDIE CHAPMAN .... Stinky
SHELBY BACON .... Moonlight

ASSOC. PRODUCER .... Stephen Auer
DIRECTED BY .... Wallace A. Grissell
ORIGINAL SCREEN PLAY .... Norman S. Hall
PHOTOGRAPHED BY .... Bud Thackery
MUSICAL DIRECTOR .... Richard Cherwin

Captain James Christie, after having flown many combat missions over Europe and returning home to Texas, prepares to head for Austin, Texas, to see the Governor. Before leaving, Captain Christie asks his dad to tell his sister Nancy the story of her grandfather, the legendary Corpus Christi Jim. Dad Christie agrees to tell the story.

In 1865 after the end of the Civil War, Corpus Christi Jim, who fought for the Texas Cavalry, returns home to Corpus Christi to a rather dim future. Not only does he find his parents dead and no jobs in sight, but he is forced to shoot a commissioner in self-defense, only to be imprisoned falsely for murder. Jim and three friends break jail and leave Corpus Christi for greener pastures.

Jim and his partners Rocky, Spade, and Steve arrive beyond the Pecos where little law exists. After not eating for some time, Spade advocates that they rustle a herd of cattle. Jim takes exception to Spade's suggestion because all had agreed that he would run

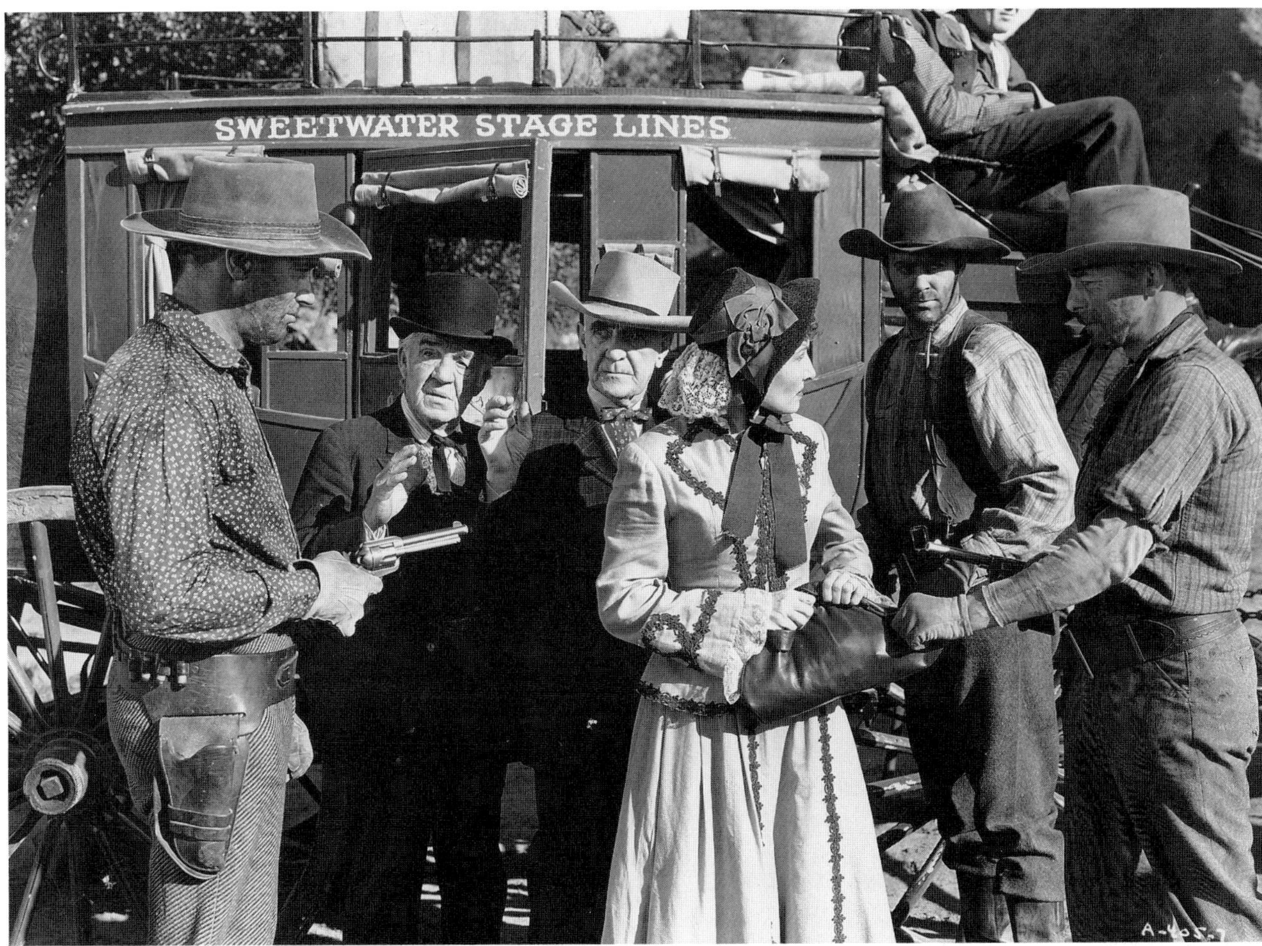

Robert Wilke (left), Kenne Duncan (right), and Allan Lane (next to Duncan) are holding up a stage early in CORPUS CHRISTI BANDITS. Lane doesn't look too happy with Kenne Duncan in this scene.

the outfit. After losing to Jim in a fight, Spade agrees to follow Jim's orders, the first of which is to rob a stage. The stage is robbed out of necessity, so when Spade accosts a female passenger and tries to take her jewelry, he and Jim have words again. After splitting the money to get a fresh start, Jim vows to never resort to robbery again. His new start is to be made in nearby Pecos Wells where he will change his name to Jim Christie.

Jim and his partners arrive in Pecos Wells to find Alonzo Adams, editor of the Pecos Wells Beacon, attempting to get the citizens to sign a petition for a marshal to come to town to eliminate its lawless element. Wade Larkin heads the criminal faction in town and even had the last marshal killed. Larkin, who owns the Lone Star Saloon, has his men shoot up the newspaper office. When they fire shots at Adams' daughter Dorothy, Jim intervenes and runs the men off. Jim learns from a grateful Adams and daughter that Larkin likes to gamble, so he devises a plan to get the ruffian.

Jim tells his partners that he plans to engage Larkin in a card game and advises that they stay out of the game. While Jim and Larkin play cards, Dorothy reads of the stage hold-up and suspects Jim and his partners of the deed. Jim wins over $35,000 from Larkin in the card game and even wins money from Spade, who didn't take Jim's advice to stay out of the game. When Jim bets his stack against the Lone Star, Larkin goes to get a fresh deck from his bartender, telling him to shoot Jim if he stands up after the game. Larkin loses the saloon, after which he loses a fight to Jim, which almost levels the Lone Star.

Jim goes to Adams and informs him that he has won the saloon from Larkin, and he confesses to having robbed the stage. Adams is being given money by Jim to return to the passengers of the stage when the Cherokee Kid, a Larkin cronie, tries to shoot Jim. The kid is quickly dispatched to Boot Hill by Jim's blazing six-shooter. Jim returns to his saloon and offers to make Rocky and Steve his partners if they donate their share of the hold-up money to him. They agree, but a disgrunted Spade is left out since he lost his money in the card game.

Spade learns that the money Jim won will be on the Sweetwater stage, so he tells Larkin and joins him in his plan to reacquire the money. During a newspaper interview with Dorothy, Jim learns that Spade and Larkin have recently been seen together. Smelling trouble, Jim rides off to meet the stage but is too late since Spade and Larkin have killed the drivers and gotten away with the stage. Jim arrives with guns blazing and shoots Larkin. He then chases the stage being driven by Spade. After jumping from his mount to the stage, Jim battles Spade on top and knocks him off.

The *Pecos Wells Beacon* publishes the story of Jim's heroic deed, but the troubles are not over as U.S. Marshal Dan Adams, Alonzo Adams' brother, arrives to serve a murder warrant on Jim. Despite Dorothy's suggestion that he leave town, Jim decides to stay and face the music. Steve pulls a gun to shoot the marshal, but Jim pulls his firearm to protect the marshal, only to be wounded by him. Jim recovers and all learn that he has been exonerated for the killing because of new evidence.

With the story of Corpus Christi Jim over, his grandson Captain James Christie is decorated and is made an honorary Captain of the Texas Rangers by the Governor of the State of Texas.

Lane returns editor Jack Kirk's gun to him as daughter Helen Talbot looks on. The scene is from CORPUS CHRISTI BANDITS.

TRAIL OF KIT CARSON

57 Mins. .... July 11, 1945

ALLAN LANE .... Bill Harmon
HELEN TALBOT .... Joan Benton
TOM LONDON .... John Benton
TWINKLE WATTS .... Peggy Bailey
ROY BARCROFT .... Dr. Charles B. Ryan
KENNE DUNCAN .... Trigger Chandler
JACK KIRK .... Sheriff Buffalo Bailey
BUD GEARY .... Red Snyder
TOM DUGAN .... Bart Hammond
GEORGE CHESEBRO .... Kirby

ASSOC. PRODUCER .... Stephen Auer
DIRECTED BY .... Lesley Selander
SCREENPLAY BY .... Jack Natteford
& Albert DeMond
ORIGINAL STORY BY .... Jack Natteford
PHOTOGRAPHED BY .... Bud Thackery
MUSICAL DIRECTOR .... Richard Cherwin

Bill Harmon departs from Texas and heads for California after receiving a letter from his friend and partner Dave MacRoy informing him that their mine has recently yielded a rich gold strike. Bill arrives to find that his partner has died, supposedly by accident, while cleaning his gun. Bill learns of his friend's death from miner John Benton but suspects that Dave was actually murdered, especially when he learns that Dr. Charles B. Ryan bought the property very cheaply the evening before Dave was found dead.

After finding samples of high grade ore in Dave's cabin, Bill goes to town to have it assayed. While in town he informs Sheriff Buffalo Bailey that he believes that his partner was killed, and he also questions local gunsmith Trigger Chandler, who helped to classify the death as suicide based on his having compared the bullet removed from the body and those remaining in Dave's gun. Refusing to believe Chandler, Bill informs him that he will be around until his friend's killer is apprehended.

Bill, Sheriff Bailey, and Benton then go to see Dr. Ryan and question him about the mine sale. Dr. Ryan shows Bill and the others a receipt that he was given by Dave, which was witnessed by Hammond, the bartender at the Nugget Saloon. Still not convinced, even though the sheriff believes that the respectable Dr. Ryan is telling the truth, Bill questions Hammond and learns that Dave won the money from Ryan in a card game and was given a check by him that he cashed in the saloon. Searching the doctor's office that night, Bill finds the check book entry indicating that money was given to Dave for the purchase of his mine.

The next morning as Bill talks to Benton's daughter Joan. Red Snyder, who has been hired by Ryan to kill Bill, tries to goad him into a fight. Refusing to fight in Joan's presence, Bill heads for the saloon to get an apology. A gunfight takes place with a henchman being shot before Sheriff Bailey arrives and threatens to jail Bill and Red if further problems arise. Red is ordered out of town but is shot and killed by Trigger Chandler, the crooked ally of Dr. Ryan, knowing that Bill will be blamed. Dr. Ryan removes the bullet, and gunsmith Chandler tells the sheriff that the bullet came from Bill's gun. Bill is jailed even though Benton, who was near Snyder at the time of the shooting, swears that Bill could not have shot the ruffian.

While in jail, Bill learns from Peggy Bailey, the sheriff's daughter, that Benton was shot in a card game. Though not known to Bill, Chandler got Benton involved in the game in which Kirby, a hired gun, shot him. Bill escapes jail and eludes the pursuing posse before reaching the Benton ranch. With Dr. Ryan doing the operating, Bill oversees his procedure with shooting arm ready. After Benton is saved, Bill rides back to town to confront Chandler but is fired upon by the posse. Dodging bullets left and right, Bill finds Chandler preparing to leave. Ryan arrives thus causing a three-way slugfest. When the sheriff arrives, Trigger decides to talk but is shot by Ryan, who then escapes.

Bill chases the fleeing villain and ropes him from his horse. Dr. Ryan is tied up and taken back to town where justice awaits him.

Allan Lane strikes a pose for a publicity photo during the filming of his first Western series for Republic Pictures.

CHAPTER 3

THE THIRD RED RYDER; THE SECOND ALLAN LANE WESTERN SERIES

Republic cast Allan Lane in three non-Westerns after he finished his first series. Here he is seen with Jane Frazee in a publicity pose for A GUY COULD CHANGE (1946).

As Allan Lane's first Western series was winding down and before the Red Ryder films began, Republic had him guest star in one of Roy Rogers' musical productions, BELLS OF ROSARITA (1945) —a very popular film of the time. Then the studio cast him in three non-Westerns: THE GAY BLADES (1946); A GUY COULD CHANGE (1946), in which he co-starred with the popular Jane Frazee; and NIGHT TRAIN TO MEMPHIS (1946), a more hillbilly than Western production which starred Roy Acuff and His Smoky Mountain Boys. Lane and Republic leading lady Adele Mara supported the popular Grand Ole Opry star. Then before starting the Red Ryder series, Allan Lane was again a guest star; this time it was in the new Monte Hale series the studio was touting to the Saturday matinee crowd. The picture was titled OUT CALIFORNIA WAY (1946) and also had Roy Rogers, Dale Evans, Trigger, and Donald Barry as guests.

There are a lot of Western fans who feel the Red Ryder serial (starring Don "Red" Barry) and the two Republic Red Ryder series (starring Wild Bill Elliott and

Allan Lane was called into NIGHT TRAIN TO MEMPHIS (1946) to lend strong support to the inexperienced Roy Acuff, seen here with Lane in a still from the picture.

Adele Mara, seen here with Lane in NIGHT TRAIN TO MEMPHIS, was a Republic leading lady who always seemed a little too glamorous for playing Western heroines and a little too sexy for the good girl in Republic's melodramas.

Allan Lane) were some of the best B Western movies ever put on film. The story is told that Don Barry didn't want the role in the serial, THE ADVENTURES OF RED RYDER (1940), but was coerced into it by Herbert Yates, the head of the studio, who promised Barry that he would get better assignments later at the studio. Regardless of the backlot intrigue regarding this first Ryder casting, Barry was a big hit in the serial and was forevermore stuck with the nickname of Red—even though his hair was never of that hue.

Bill Elliott started the film series four years later and made a total of sixteen excellent Red Ryder pictures with Bobby Blake as Little Beaver. The series was well-received by the fans even though Elliott made no attempt to change his stock Wild Bill Elliott character into the famous Fred Harman redheaded cowboy. There was action aplenty, fine stunt work, and strong supporting casts from the Republic stock company of Western players. Elliott, however, longed to climb out of the B Western mold and felt that he might be able to do the John Wayne/STAGECOACH bit and become a star of big-budget A Westerns. Republic, too, thought the strategy might work and agreed to the career change. While his metamorphose from Wild Bill to the

Yes, Roy Barcroft is at his evil ways again! Allan Lane is about to offer Roy a chair in hopes of distracting him from pinching Roy Acuff's head off. The scene is from NIGHT TRAIN TO MEMPHIS.

more sophisticated William Elliott was somewhat successful at first, his career in films started a long, slow slide that found him working in low-budget detective films at Allied Artists (earlier Monogram) at the end of his career a few years later.

Allan Lane would rather have starred in a series of his own, but still he was happy to take over the popular Red Ryder series at the studio. He made seven very successful Red Ryder films during 1946 and 1947 with Bobby Blake, who was retained as Little Beaver. Republic contract director R. G. Springsteen helmed all seven Allan Lane Ryder films.

Fans are mixed regarding their preference in Red Ryders. Don "Red" Barry was well-liked in the role, but most fans consider him out of the running because his performance was a one-time casting in the serial. The relative youthfulness of Allan Lane (compared to Elliott) appealed to many, and there was a feeling that his older brother relationship with Little Beaver played better than the fatherly demeanor exuded by Bill Elliott when he played the role. Others liked the more forceful characterization that Elliott brought to the role. In reality there was little more than the personalities of the actors which made the difference. They played the role in their stock manner with little attempt to develop the character as his originator drew him in the comic pages, but that didn't seem to bother anyone at the time. (Two years later Jim Bannon looked and played the role in a manner closer to the Harmon original in a four-episode color series for Eagle-Lion Pictures, but the low-budget production values and weak scripts left most audiences restless.)

Republic gave Allan Lane the same production quality and strong supporting casts that had been available to Elliott. The first entry in the series, SANTA FE UPRISING (1946), was a strong starter with Barton MacLane as the main heavy and Jack LaRue as his smarmy cohort. One change which hurt the Lane Ryder series a little was the recasting of the Duchess role. Alice Fleming had made such a strong impression in the role during the sixteen Elliott Ryder films that Martha Wentworth—fine actress though she was—could never quite claim the role for her own.

STAGECOACH TO DENVER (1946) proved to be a lesser entry in the series even though it had Roy Barcroft in as the head villain and Peggy Stewart as the

It's time for a shoot out between Red Ryder and the bad guys in this scene from STAGECOACH TO DENVER.

misguided heroine with the intriguing name of Beautiful. A portion of the script dealt with a child who was paralyzed after a stagecoach accident and in need of a delicate operation. Some of the situations were considerably more somber than B Western action fans were accustomed to and the story was, therefore, viewed as something of a downer.

Many fans feel that the third episode, VIGILANTES OF BOOMTOWN (1947), was the best in the Allan Lane series. The script had a boxing plot regarding the bout between "Gentleman" Jim Corbett and Bob Fitzsimmons. Roy Barcroft was again the chief heavy. This time he plotted to steal the box office receipts from the fight. Peggy Stewart was also around again to complicate the situation for Red Ryder. She finds fisticuffs disgusting and wants the fight between Corbett and Fitzsimmons cancelled. Roscoe Karns, a fine character actor who rarely wandered into Westerns, was on hand as the delightfully kooky manager of "Gentleman" Jim Corbett.

HOMESTEADERS OF PARADISE VALLEY (1947) and OREGON TRAIL SCOUTS (1947) were released little more than a month apart in the spring of the year and were followed two months later by RUSTLERS OF DEVIL'S CANYON (1947). They were well-crafted Ryder films but are generally not the ones fans get most excited about in the series. In the view of this writer, Villian Gene Stutenroth in HOMESTEADERS OF PARADISE VALLEY (and later MARSHAL OF CRIPPLE CREEK) always had trouble with serious heavy roles because of his frequent association with The Three Stooges. It was hard to take Stutenroth seriously as a chief heavy after seeing him perform as a comic foil for Larry, Curly and Moe. The offbeat casting of excellent character actor Arthur Space (brother of Barry Fitzgerald) as the slick villain in RUSTLERS OF DEVIL'S CANYON helped to raise the quality of the picture.

The last episode in the series, MARSHAL OF CRIPPLE CREEK, got mixed reviews from authors who write about Western films. Alan Barbour (in his book *The Thrill of it all*) called MARSHAL OF CRIPPLE CREEK "one of the best B-Westerns Republic ever turned out." But writer/B Western fan Michael Pitts (in his book *Western Movies*) writes "it is hardly one of the best" (in the Red Ryder series). Don Miller (in his excellent book entitled *Hollywood Corral*) states that the scriptwriter was "running dry," the producer "wasn't opening the purse strings," and the performers were "restless in their roles."

Differences of opinion are part of what makes film viewing fun. We all appreciate films to different degrees and for different reasons. Regardless of whether MARSHAL OF CRIPPLE CREEK was one of the best in the series or not, I think it can be safely said that the cast was strong (Trevor Bardette, Tom London, Roy Barcroft, to mention only a few) and the action intense. It wasn't too bad a film with which to bid the Red Ryder character adieu at Republic Pictures.

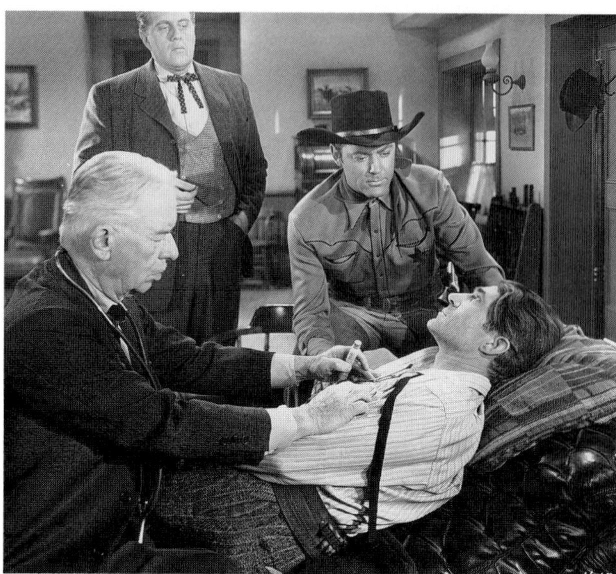

The doctor checks out Trevor Bardette as Gene Stutenroth and Allan Lane look on. The scene is from MARSHAL OF CRIPPLE CREEK.

SANTA FE UPRISING

55 Mins .... Nov. 15, 1946

ALLAN LANE .... Red Ryder
BOBBY BLAKE .... Little Beaver
MARTHA WENTWORTH .... The Duchess
BARTON MACLANE .... Crawford
JACK LARUE .... Bruce Jackson
TOM LONDON .... Lafe Dibble
DICK CURTIS .... Luke Case
FORREST TAYLOR .... Moore
EMMETT LYNN .... Hank
HANK PATTERSON .... Jake
PAT MICHAELS .... Sonny Dibble
EDMUND COBB .... Madison Pike
KENNE DUNCAN .... Henchman
EDYTHE ELLIOTT .... Mrs. Dibble

ASSOC. PRODUCER .... Sidney Picker
DIRECTED BY .... R. G. Springsteen
ORIGINAL SCREENPLAY .... Earle Snell
PHOTOGRAPHED BY .... Bud Thackery
MUSICAL DIRECTOR .... Mort Glickman

The town of Bitter Springs loses its sheriff, the fourth in the last year, to the bullets of outlaws. Although the citizens are very discouraged at the outlawry, Lafe Dibble, one of the more outspoken citizens, tells Mr. Crawford, editor of the *Territorial Gazette*, that his plan to go to the governor for help will do no good. Most of the town's trouble takes place when cattlemen drive their herds across the government road rather than the thirty mile toll road owned by Madison Pike who takes orders from Crawford, the secret leader of the outlaws.

The outspoken Lafe Dibble makes the mistake of letting it be known that he is about to drive his herd across the government road. Camped down for the night, Dibble and his men are attacked by gun wielding bandits. Lafe Dibble is killed in the attack, which sees casualties on both sides. Madison Pike, who owns the toll road, is badly wounded in the exchange of gunfire while riding with the bandits. Bruce Jackson and Luke Case take the wounded man to Crawford's office, where the newspaper editor tries to get him to sign over the toll road. He fails as Pike dies.

The *Territorial Gazette* informs of Pike's death and announces that the toll road as well as Pike's other properties are to be sold by court order since no will exists. Red Ryder and his aunt, the Duchess, a distant cousin of Madison Pike, read the news. Red insists that the Duchess go to claim what is hers and sends a telegram to the editor announcing her arrival. Red and his sidekick Little Beaver plan to leave later.

Determined to get control of the road for himself, Crawford has Luke take over the stage ten miles outside of town in a move designed to get rid of Pike's heir. Luke drives the stage fast and jumps off, hoping that it will wreck. Unknown to him at the time, Red Ryder, who is not far behind, transfers to the stage and saves his aunt from certain death.

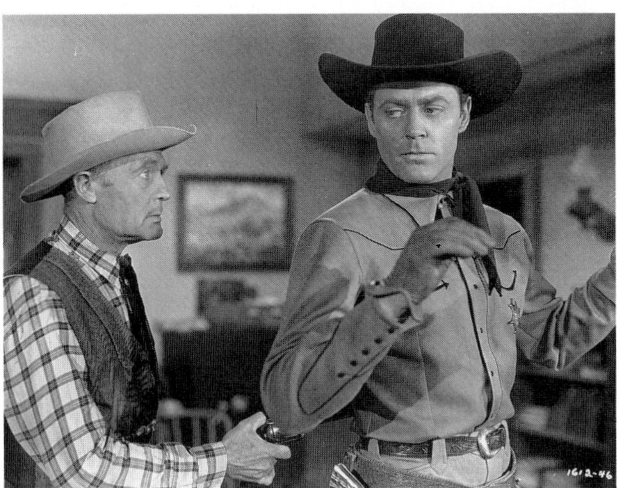

Forrest Taylor temporarily has the drop on Marshal Red Ryder in this scene from SANTA FE UPRISING.

Red (Allan Lane) is about to have a showdown with heavy Barton MacLane and his henchmen in the famous Republic cave set. The film is SANTA FE UPRISING.

The Ryder clan arrives in Bitter Springs shortly after Luke has informed Crawford of the Duchess' presumed accident. The Duchess spots Luke entering the saloon and points him out to Red, where upon her peaceable nephew goes to question him. Luke resents Ryder's implications and tells him so with his fists. The wild slugfest ends with Red the winner and the saloon in shambles. To uphold his image of respectability, Crawford arrives and commends Red for besting the ruffian and, once in his office, tries to encourage the Duchess to sell the toll road because of all the trouble in the area. He fails but manages to get Red to take the job of marshal.

Bruce Jackson, a Crawford ally, tells the Duchess that he wants to drive his herd across her toll road. Red sends Hank and other men he has hired to guard the cattle and eliminate any trouble but also decides to scout the area for trouble himself. He spots a band of outlaws waiting to attack and rides back to warn his men. As he does so, he is fired upon by Sonny Dibble. Sonny has spotted the Dibble brand on the cattle and is certain that these are the cattle which were rustled the night that his father was killed. Red chases Sonny and captures him at the Dibble ranch.

Red brings Sonny to town amidst accusations by the youngster that Red rustled his father's cattle. Although he is brought in for attacking the herd, the charge is soon changed to murder as Red is informed by Jackson that during Sonny's attack, Hank was killed by the youngster. In reality it is Jackson who shot the old timer. Mr. Moore, a citizen concerned by the banditry, is outraged that Sonny has been jailed and plots to free him. Red foils the attempt and assures all that Sonny will get a fair trial.

Meanwhile, Little Beaver is kidnapped and held at Crawford's order. To alleviate suspicion the newspaper editor offers $1,000 reward for the safe return of Red's sidekick. To lay blame on others, a note is written by Crawford stating that Little Beaver will be released when Sonny Dibble is freed. Crawford then takes a map to Red showing where Little Beaver is, claiming it was delivered by a gang member in exchange for the reward money.

Suspicious of Crawford, Red devises a ruse in which his men quit him, purporting to be tired of looking for his Indian pal. Red gives Crawford a gun and asks that he accompany him to the mine located on the map. Red precedes Crawford into the mine and is shot by him. Crawford goes in to meet Jackson and Luke, and having no more use for Little Beaver, shoots at him several times. After failing to kill the lad, Crawford checks the gun and finds blanks, thus indicating that Red Ryder is not dead. The lanky cowboy comes in with guns blazing and routs the crooks with the help of the posse's timely arrival. Red confronts Crawford one-on-one and easily bests him in a brief fistic encounter.

With all settled and an end to the troubles of Bitter Springs now in sight, the Duchess decides to sell the toll road and head home.

STAGECOACH TO DENVER

56 Mins .... Dec. 23, 1946

ALLAN LANE .... Red Ryder
BOBBY BLAKE .... Little Beaver
MARTHA WENTWORTH .... The Duchess
ROY BARCROFT. .... Bill Lambert
PEGGY STEWART .... Beautiful
EMMETT LYNN .... Coonskin
TED ADAMS .... Sheriff
EDMUND COBB .... Duke
TOM CHATTERTON .... Doc Kimball
BOBBIE HYATT .... Dickie Barnes
GEORGE CHESEBRO .... Blackie Grubb
ED CASSIDY .... .Felton
WHEATON CHAMBERS .... Silas Braydon
FORREST TAYLOR .... Matt Disher

ASSOC. PRODUCER .... Sidney Picker
DIRECTED BY .... R. G. Springsteen
ORIGINAL SCREENPLAY .... Earle Snell
PHOTOGRAPHED BY .... Edgar Lyons
MUSICAL DIRECTOR .... Mort Glickman

Emmett Lynn (Coonskin) has plenty to say to Allan Lane (Red), Martha Wentworth (the Duchess), and Roy Barcroft (Bill Lambert) in this street scene from STAGECOACH TO DENVER.

You are in bad company, Red. It doesn't take the audience long to figure out that Roy Barcroft and Ted Adams are probably up to no good—even if Adams is wearing that sheriff's badge. The scene is from STAGECOACH TO DENVER.

Red Ryder, driving his aunt's stagecoach, is headed for Elkhorn with a youngster named Dickie his only passenger. Dickie is to be sent to his aunt Mae in Denver because of the recent death of his parents. Since the Duchess' stage does not go to Denver, Dickie is transferred to the Overland Stage Lines in Elkhorn, where Felton, the land commissioner, is also Denver bound.

The stagecoach to Denver is stopped shortly after it leaves town by Duke, claiming to be delivering a mail bag left in town. As the driver puts the mail away, Duke tampers with the stage, causing it to wreck when the journey is resumed. Red's friend Coonskin finds the wrecked stage and its survivor Dickie, who is taken to Coonskin's ranch. Doctor Kimball checks Dickie and diagnoses him as being paralyzed. In need of a delicate operation, Dickie remains at the ranch until permission can be gotten from his aunt in Denver.

Bill Lambert, who ordered that the stage be tampered with hoping that Felton would be killed, is secretly trying to acquire lands in the area so that he can control all communications between Elkhorn and Denver. Learning that Red plans to send a telegraph, Lambert orders his men to stop him, since he wants to alter the report Felton filed before his death is known.

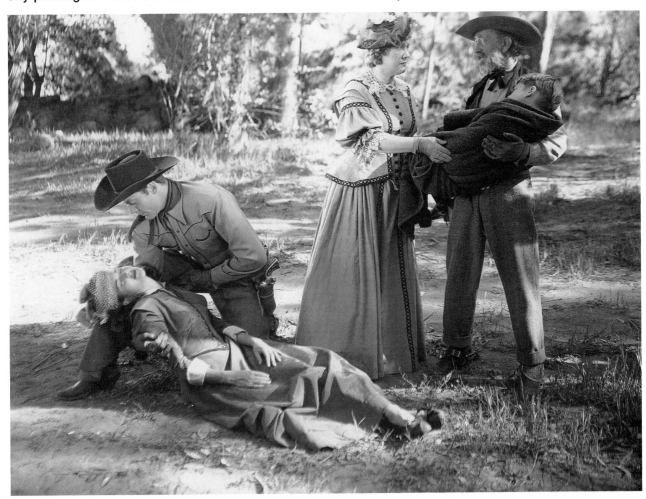

Peggy Stewart has just been gunned down by the bad guys in this scene from STAGECOACH TO DENVER. Allan Lane comes to her assistance as Martha Wentworth and Emmett Lynn help Bobbie Hyatt.

"I've been wanting to do this for a long time," Red tells Lambert (Roy Barcroft) in this scene from STAGECOACH TO DENVER.

The plan is foiled as Red routs the henchman with his blazing sixshooters. Red informs the Elkhorn sheriff, a Lambert sympathizer, of the trouble and vows to find out who is behind it.

Lambert's next move is to substitute two of his Denver cronies, Beautiful and Wally, for Dickie's aunt and the new commissioner. After the switch is made, Lambert greets his friends and is assured of their help. Beautiful makes it known that she wants no part of murder. Wally, a forger by trade, is told by Lambert to alter the reports of the land commissioner.

Beautiful is taken to Coonskin's where she falls for Dickie, who pitifully asks the aunt he has never seen for a pony. Beautiful does not want to assume responsibility for his operation but concedes. After the operation appears successful, she goes into town and informs Lambert that she plans to leave town.

The sheriff helps Lambert in his plot to acquire the ranchers' lands by ordering them off. Red confronts him and informs him that the doctor advised that Dickie not be moved, so they can't leave. The landowners are run off and burned out by the evildoers, prompting one of them, Matt Disher, to seek Lambert's aid in preventing the sheriff from furthering his crusade. Disher offers that the ranchers will fight back if necessary. Lambert offers to try to help.

Dickie takes a turn for the worse. A concerned Beautiful asks Lambert to get a specialist or she will start talking. Feeling threatened, Lambert refuses at first but changes his mind.

Red, Coonskin, and Little Beaver do a little surveying and find a few peculiarities. As Red surmises that the old commissioner was killed and a phony brought in, the echo of a discharging rifle stops the trio. Red spots Blackie after he has failed in an attempt to ambush Beautiful. He wings the gunman and then rescues Beautiful, whose wagon has run away.

Red questions the woman about the new commissioner, since they arrived on the same stage. She admits to knowing nothing and tries to discourage Red from going to Lambert's. He refuses her warning and goes to Lambert's for a confrontation. Red spots the purse that Beautiful dropped during the attempt on her life and accuses Lambert. Fists fly with Red emerging the winner.

Beautiful waits on the stage road the next day at Lambert's orders to secure a ride on top with the driver, unaware that Dickie, whose condition has worsened, and the Duchess are inside and on the way to Denver to see a specialist.

Red learns that Dickie and the Duchess are on board the Denver stage. He takes off in pursuit, but Lambert and the sheriff are not far behind.

Red stops the stage after knocking off Duke and two other henchmen with smoking guns. Beautiful rushes to see Dickie when she learns that he is inside but is shot in the back by Lambert. Red guns down Lambert, bringing an end to his scheme.

Dickie's real aunt is discovered safe and sound. Dickie's health improves quickly, so Red gives the youngster the pony he so desperately wanted.

Red (Allan Lane) gets a few lessons in the Marquis of Queensberry rules in this scene from VIGILANTES OF BOOMTOWN.

VIGILANTES OF BOOMTOWN

56 Mins .... Feb. 15, 1947

ALLAN LANE .... Red Ryder
BOBBY BLAKE .... Little Beaver
MARTHA WENTWORTH .... The Duchess
ROSCOE KARNS .... Bill Delaney
ROY BARCROFT .... McKean
PEGGY STEWART .... Mollie McVay
GEORGE TURNER .... Jim Corbett
EDDIE LOU SIMMS .... Player
GEORGE CHESEBRO .... Dick
BOBBY BARBER .... Player
GEORGE LLOYD .... Thug
TED ADAMS .... Sheriff
JOHN DEHNER .... Bob Fitzsimmons
EARLE HODGINS .... Governor

ASSOC. PRODUCER .... Sidney Picker
DIRECTED BY .... R. G. Springsteen
ORIGINAL SCREENPLAY .... Earle Snell
PHOTOGRAPHED BY .... Alfred Kelly
MUSICAL DIRECTOR .... Mort Glickman

In 1897 in Carson City, Nevada, the governor of Nevada proclaims it legal that a boxing match between Gentlemen Jim Corbett and Bob Fitzsimmons be held. Although many are in favor of the exhibition, there are those who believe boxing to be a display of barbarism and are adamant in their belief that the fight not take place. Molly McVay is one of the main people against the fight, and her vehement disapproval causes a fight at the proclamation. Among those favoring the fight is Red Ryder, who is about to mail a letter to the Jim Corbett camp permitting him to stay at and train on property owned by his aunt, the Duchess. As he mails the letter, the sheriff deputizes him to break up the disturbance caused by Molly. As fists fly, Red breaks up the battle.

Jim Corbett and his manager Bill Delaney arrive in Carson City and head for the Duchess ranch. They make the mistake of stopping at Molly's for directions. Molly's dog causes their buckboard to run away, but Red, who is on the way to meet Corbett and Delaney, stops the runaway and leads them to the ranch where they enjoy a peaceful dinner.

Red gets a little chummy with Sheriff Ted Adams in this scene from VIGILANTES OF BOOMTOWN.

The next morning training begins. Fitzsimmons arrives at the training session and trades barbs with his opponent. Unaware that this is being done for publicity, Red becomes involved when the combatants begin to throw punches and decides to throw a few of his own. Later, against Delaney's wishes, Corbett goes horseback riding with Red. While Delaney searches for them, he happens upon McKean, an ex-con headed for Carson City with his men to try to steal the fight money. McKean, is not pleased to learn that Red Ryder is in the area but refuses to turn back after having traveled so far.

That night Red is being taught how to box by Corbett when a shot ends the jovial atmosphere. Red searches outside and finds that Molly's dog, who had been tied up outside, was no longer there. Red suspects that the woman fired the shot in her attempt to halt the fight.

The next morning, Red tells the sheriff what happened, but upon learning that Molly is heading for San Francisco, he refuses to press charges. Red and Corbett are out riding when Little Beaver informs them that the fences have been cut and the cattle about to be rustled. Red goes to confront the rustlers, but Little Beaver and Corbett are shot at by McKean, who has failed in his try to ambush Red. Red saves his friends and, in running the gunmen off, recognizes McKean as being among them. He figures that he is probably in town to try to steal the proceeds of the fight. Red believes that the sheriff is in league with McKean and advocates shipping the money out in a hay wagon. After he feels the sheriff has informed the crooks, he plans to alter the plan.

Molly returns from her trip to San Francisco still determined to put a stop to the fight. She has brought two thugs back with her and has paid them to kidnap Gentleman Jim Corbett. She describes Corbett to them and gives them directions to the ranch. However, that night Red allows Corbett to sleep inside the house rather than his customary spot in the barn. Since Red has changed places with him, it is he that is kidnapped. The kidnapping of Red Ryder also paves the way for McKean and his men to make off with the fight money.

On the day of the fight, Molly is in town and sees Corbett at the weigh-in. Aware that her plan has failed, she goes to see what happened, only to learn that Red was kidnapped and not Corbett. Red explains the urgency of being released and is untied by Molly. The wagon with the money has been stopped by McKean and men, but Red holds them at bay, allowing the driver to get away. Molly arrives with help, thus allowing Red to go after McKean who has escaped. He knocks him from his horse and uses a punch taught him by Corbett to put McKean down for the count.

In town, Corbett doesn't fare as well as Red because Fitzsimmons knocks him out. Back at the ranch, Red jokingly suggests a punch that Gentleman Jim use if a rematch is given, as the story comes to an end.

HOMESTEADERS OF PARADISE VALLEY

59 Mins .... April 1, 1947

ALLAN LANE .... Red Ryder
BOBBY BLAKE .... Little Beaver
MARTHA WENTWORTH .... The Duchess
ANN TODD .... Melinda Dill
GENE STUTENROTH .... Bill Hume
JOHN JAMES .... Steve Dill
MAURITZ HUGO .... Rufe Hume
EMMETT VOGAN .... Langley
MILTON KIBBEE .... A. C. Blaine
TOM LONDON .... .Rancher
EDYTHE ELLIOTT .... Mrs. Hume
GEORGE CHESEBRO .... E. J. White
EDWARD CASSIDY .... Sheriff

ASSOC. PRODUCER .... Sidney Picker
DIRECTED BY .... R. G. Springsteen
ORIGINAL SCREENPLAY .... Earle Snell
PHOTOGRAPHED BY .... Alfred Keller
MUSICAL DIRECTOR .... Mort Glickman

Red Ryder and his Indian sidekick Little Beaver are leading a group of homesteaders in a search for free government land on which they can settle. Unfortunately, Red finds that all of the free land has been claimed, but he is able to locate land in Paradise Valley near Center City for two dollars per acre. Upon informing them, they are, of course, disappointed but consider themselves fortunate—all, that is, except Bill Hume, one of the homesteaders who talks against Red. A vote is taken to settle the dispute between the two as to whether the land shoud be purchased or whether the group should depart. Red wins.

After much hard work, the homesteaders have their community built, but a severe brush fire has been set in an attempt to force them out. Red and his friends battle the blaze, but he leaves to release some water from a nearby dam to help extinguish the blaze. Before reaching the dam, Red is fired upon by a gunman concealed in the rocks. While Red swaps lead with the gunman, Little Beaver rides ahead to find that much of the water in the dam has been released into the river.

White, the gunman who fired upon Red, manages to escape to Center City to inform his boss, Langley, what happened. Langley and A. C. Blaine, the publisher of the *Center City Gazette*, who have attempted unsuccessfully to buy up the land in Paradise Valley, are the culprits behind the fire. It is their intention to secure the local water rights and thus make a fortune. Blaine suggests that one million dollars in bonds be promoted to build the dam and plans to use his paper to push them.

Blaine arrives in Paradise Valley to congratulate Red on the excellent job being done with the Paradise Valley Newspaper. Red is offered a job by him to write for the *Center City Gazette*, but Red turns down the job, preferring to stay in Paradise Valley and to continue helping to establish the community. A dejected Blaine leaves after failing to take Red away from Paradise Valley and is later seen at the Hume ranch talking to Bill and Rufe.

The settlers have fallen on hard times of late, and the dynamiting of the dam by the Humes makes matters worse. A band of outlaws under orders from Langley sets fires and instigates a reign of terror that causes many of the settlers to leave the once peaceful community. Red learns from one of the departing settlers that he was bought out by Bill Hume for a lot of cash. The discussion is ended by gunfire, and Red rides off to ascertain the problem. Masked gunmen, in reality the Humes, have held up a freight wagon. Red's gunfire runs them off.

After taking the wounded driver to town, Red learns of a meeting at the Hume ranch. He arrives to find Langley attempting to get money from the settlers to build a dam. Another topic of the meeting is the accusation by Bill Hume that Red's Aunt, the Duchess, is overcharging the settlers for their goods. Hume informs all that he is opening his own store and will give them better prices.

Red gets a job working for the Center City Stage Line, owned by Blaine. After being on the job only a short time, Red is given a raise by his boss even though the stage line is losing money. The newspaper editor informs Red of the water shortage and manages to get him to promote the sale of the bonds through his paper to help out.

Back at Paradise Valley, Bill Hume tells a gathering that a letter from Langley informs of a meeting of the Paradise Valley Development Assoc., about to be held in Center City. At the meeting Blaine offers to buy up the land of each settler but is accused by settler Steve Dill of being in league with Langley to gain control of the water rights. Bill Hume backs his bosses and suggests that Red caused the problems by advocating the sale of the bonds in his column. After the meeting ends, Blaine is about to pay Bill Hume off but is knocked out and robbed and has his record books stolen by him.

An angry Steve Dill confronts Red at the stage barn. Little Beaver prevents him from shooting Red, who then has to fight the young man, after not being able to calm him. While Steve leaves to inform the settlers that Red is going to blow up the dam, Red heads to confront Blaine at the *Gazette.* Blaine comes to and feigns a memory loss when told by Langley that the books are gone.

Allan Lane and Ann Todd enjoy a brief respite in HOMESTEADERS OF PARADISE VALLEY.

At Paradise Valley, Steve incites the settlers against Red and has them join him in a confrontation with the Humes, who he believes to be in league with Red. Red and Little Beaver head for the Hume ranch upon learning of the impending confrontation and arrive as an exchange of gunfire takes place. A frightened Rufe gives up and prepares to confess but is gunned down by his brother Bill, who then escapes in a wagon. Red mounts Thunder and chases down Bill Hume. Red tricks him into implicating his bosses and, after a brief fight, Hume is carted off to jail by Steve.

With all their troubles behind them, a life of peace awaits the homesteaders of Paradise Valley.

OREGON TRAIL SCOUTS

58 Mins .... May 15, 1947

ALLAN LANE .... Red Ryder
BOBBY BLAKE .... Little Beaver
MARTHA WENTWORTH .... The Duchess
ROY BARCROFT .... Bill Hunter
EMMETT LYNN .... Bear Trap
EDMUND COBB .... Jack
EARLE HODGINS .... The Judge
EDWARD CASSIDY .... Bliss
FRANK LACKTEEN .... Running Fox
BILLY CUMMINGS .... Barking Squirrel
JACK KIRK .... Stage Driver

ASSOC. PRODUCER .... Sidney Picker
DIRECTED BY .... R. G. Springsteen
ORIGINAL SCREENPLAY .... Earle Snell
PHOTOGRAPHED BY .... Alfred Keller
MUSICAL DIRECTOR .... Mort Glickman

After a season of fur trapping on the Snake River, Red Ryder, Bear Trap, and their men head to have a pow-wow with Chief Running Fox about acquiring the trapping rights on his land. Before they arrive, Bill Hunter talks to Running Fox about acquiring the land for himself in exchange for horses. Hunter is unsuccessful, as Mr. Bliss, the Indian agent, warns Running Fox of dealing with the shady character.

A dejected Hunter spots Red and Bear Trap watering their horses, so he and his ruffians prepare to gun them down. Red is alerted to the impending danger by his steed Thunder and manages to hold his own against Hunter and his men before being aided by Indians in the area. Red is then able to meet with Running Fox and secure exclusive rights to trap beaver and otter on the Willamette in exchange for providing food to the tribe.

Hunter learns from one of his men that the Judge, a medicine man and former ally, is in town and has possession of Little Beaver, the grandson of Chief Running Fox. The evil Hunter plans to kidnap the Indian lad and turn him over to his grandfather to further his aim to gain trapping rights on the Indian land. The Judge refuses to reveal to Hunter where Little Beaver is and is killed by him. Red arrives in town shortly thereafter and confronts Hunter about the attempt to shoot him earlier. A slugfest takes place with Red beating his burly adversary. The body of the Judge is found following the fight and, with no one now around to care for Little Beaver, Bliss takes him.

The Duchess arrives in Wild Horse and attempts to persuade Red to return East with her. Red informs her that he has acquired trapping rights on the Willamette and will soon depart on a fur trapping expedition. Not to be outdone by her nephew, the Duchess stows away on board one of the wagons and finds another stowaway—Little Beaver. After making camp, Red discovers his hidden passengers and prepares to take Little Beaver back to Wild Horse. On the way back, Red stops at a lighted cabin, hoping to get its owner to take Little Beaver back. Unfortunately the cabin is occupied by Hunter and his men, one of whom overheard Red tell the Duchess that he had acquired the trapping rights. Red is captured and held briefly by Hunter before Little Beaver helps him escape.

Red and Little Beaver head back to camp and, the next morning, join the wagon train as it heads for its destination. Hunter and his men are close behind the wagon train. Hunter attacks the wagon train with a bow and arrow, hoping to cause bad blood between Red and Running Fox. After Red and most of his men have left to chase their attackers, Hunter doubles back to kidnap Little Beaver so that he can hopefully use him to bargain with Running Fox.

Red and his men notice that the hoof prints of the horses they are chasing are shoed, so they hurriedly return to camp. Met by gunfire, Red and his men retaliate and fare well before being helped by some of Running Fox's braves. Hunter grabs Little Beaver in a last-ditch effort to bargain for the rights, but the badman is no match for the Duchess, who knocks him out with a frying pan.

Although happy to see his grandson, Running Fox allows him to decide if he wishes to remain with his tribe or go with Red Ryder. Little Beaver chooses to go with Red, and thus is born the partnership between the two.

RUSTLERS OF DEVIL'S CANYON

58 Mins .... July 1, 1947

ALLAN LANE .... Red Ryder
BOBBY BLAKE .... Little Beaver
MARTHA WENTWORTH .... The Duchess
PEGGY STEWART .... Bess
ARTHUR SPACE .... Doctor Cole
EMMETT LYNN .... Blizzard
ROY BARCROFT .... Clark
TOM LONDON .... Sheriff
HARRY CARR .... Tad
PIERCE LYDEN .... Matt
FORREST TAYLOR .... Doctor Glover

ASSOC. PRODUCER .... Sidney Picker
DIRECTED BY .... R. G. Springsteen
ORIGINAL SCREENPLAY .... Earle Snell
PHOTOGRAPHED BY .... William Bradford
MUSICAL DIRECTOR .... Mort Glickman

After having served his country for a year in Cuba, Red Ryder is discharged from the service and heads home to see his aunt the Duchess and his sidekicks Little Beaver and Blizzard. Upon his arrival, Red is informed by his aunt that cattle rustlers have moved in and taken advantage of the absence of the many cowhands away at war. Treating Blizzard for his rheumatism, new town physician Doctor Cole informs Red that he has many patients due to the lead-slinging rustlers.

As Cole prepares to leave, Little Beaver informs Red of a rustling attempt. Red is pressed into immediate duty as he drives the rustlers off with his blazing six-guns. The wounded are taken to the Duchess' ranch for treatment. A discussion of the rustling problem takes place, during which Cole suggests that all ranchers unite their herds and have one big cattle drive. Cole, the boss behind the rustlers, has ulterior motives.

Meanwhile, a group of homesteaders is headed for the Lava Basin area, site of all the rustling problems. The group, which is to be taken there for $100 per head by Clark, includes Tad, a recently discharged veteran, and his sister Bess. As they depart, they are warned that the area is cattle country and that cattlemen generally have no use for homesteaders.

As they approach the area, the homesteaders spot a sign announcing a meeting of the area cattlemen called by Red Ryder. Assuming that the meeting is in reference to them, Bess arrives with a chip on her shoulder and refuses to heed Red's warning of the extreme danger in the area due to rustlers. Red recognizes their guide Clark as being the man who located homesteaders in the area before the war and accuses him of being in it only for the money. The accusations spark a brutal fight in which the burly Clark is topped by Red.

Matt, the leader of the rustlers, under the orders from Cole, attacks the homesteaders. Clark is shot and killed in the ambush, but the rustlers are driven off by Red who, unknown to the homesteaders, was expecting trouble and followed at a distance. Bess spots Red and assumes him to be the reason behind the attack. She drives Red off.

Red asks Cole to go look after the wounded

Allan Lane, Bobby Blake, and Martha Wentworth in a scene from RUSTLERS OF DEVIL'S CANYON.

homesteaders. Cole informs them that he took it upon himself to aid them after hearing the cattlemen brag about creating trouble for them. Playing both ends against the middle, the scheming doctor returns and informs Red that he told the homesteaders that the cattlemen had nothing to do with the ambush.

With the big cattle drive scheduled for the next morning, a rock with note attached is thrown through the Duchess' window, warning that the homesteaders were about to start trouble. The Duchess' barn is set fire the next morning after the drive has started. As Red and most of the men return to fight the blaze, the rustlers attack and easily steal the cattle.

With the homesteaders blamed for the trouble, the sheriff prepares to take Tad in for questioning. They are stopped by masked bandits headed by Matt and a man dressed like Red. Tad's injury at the hands of the men causes the sheriff to bring Red in. Knowing him to be innocent, the sheriff allows Red to escape, so that he can find out what is going on.

Dr. Cole is summoned by the Duchess to the cave inwhich Red is hiding to treat the hand he injured fighting the fire. Bess follows Cole who has learned from and over anxious Little Beaver and Blizzard that Red was allowed to escape. Bess jumps Red after Cole leaves but is tied up and locked in a room at the cave.

Pretending to be knocked out from the pills given him by Cole, Red awaits Cole's return. Cole and henchman Matt return and prepare to do away with Red, who prepares to defend himself. Bess manages to get free and realizes she was wrong as Cole tries to shoot her. Red exchanges lead with the rustlers as Little Beaver and Blizzard arrive with the sheriff and a posse. Red takes the doctor on, bare-knuckles style, and comes out an easy winner.

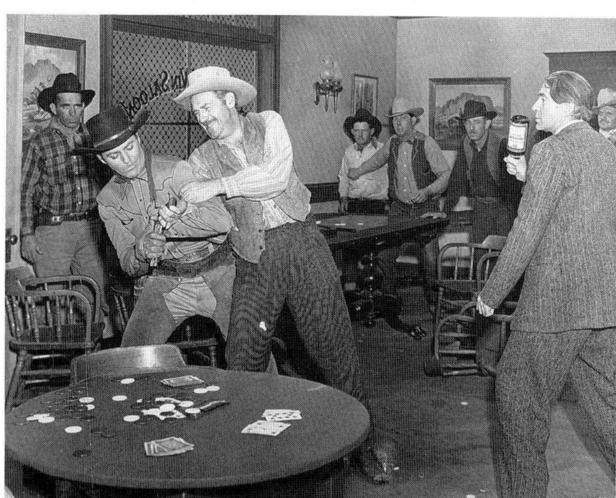

"Let go, I tell you; let go," Allan Lane says to Roy Barcroft as an angry Trevor Bardette approaches in a most menacing manner with a whiskey bottle in his hand. The tense scene is from MARSHAL OF CRIPPLE CREEK.

Bess and Tad prepare to settle down in the area after being offered help from Red, Little Beaver, and the Duchess.

MARSHAL OF CRIPPLE CREEK

58 Mins .... Aug. 15, 1947

ALLAN LANE .... Red Ryder
BOBBY BLAKE .... Little Beaver
MARTHA WENTWORTH .... The Duchess
TREVOR BARDETT .... Tom Lambert
TOM LONDON .... Baker
ROY BARCROFT .... Sweeney
GENE ROTH .... John Case
WILLIAM SELF .... Dick Lambert
HELEN WALLACE .... Mae Lambert

ASSOC. PRODUCER .... Sidney Picker
DIRECTED BY .... R. G. Springsteen
ORIGINAL SCREENPLAY .... Earle Snell
PHOTOGRAPHED BY .... William Bradford
MUSICAL DIRECTOR .... Mort Glickman

The discovery of gold in Cripple Creek has caused the town to be besieged by a lawless element bent on robbing the ore wagons and causing other troubles for the Cripple Creek Citizens. As Red and the Duchess discuss the outlawry, a bandit robs a local business and flees after killing the sheriff. Red mounts Thunder and gives chase.

Meanwhile, Long John Case, proprietor of the You Can't Win Saloon, is preaching about the death of legitimate business in the town if the lawlessness doesn't end. Some of the townsfolk advocate getting someone such as Bat Masterson to combat the bandits, while others feel a hired killer should be sought.

Red returns to town after successfully capturing the robber and is followed to the jail by Case, Baker, and other citizens. Case finds a badge at the jail and suggests that Red take the job vacated by the death of the sheriff. Red reluctantly accepts and advises that he will step down when someone more suited to the job is found.

Case and Baker head back to the saloon and encounter Tom Lambert, a newly-arrived man who makes known his desire to gamble until he makes his fortune. Lambert enters a poker game and loses all of his money to Sweeney, who has won by cheating. A

"I lost everything I had," Trevor Bardette tells Allan Lane in this scene from MARSHAL OF CRIPPLE CREEK. That's Tom London looking on with concern.

fight breaks out whereupon Red, the peaceable man, intervenes and breaks it up. Red sides with Lambert and offers him a job at the Duchess' ranch, since his wife and son are due to arrive soon. Wanting to make his bundle quickly, Lambert refuses the job offer.

Lambert returns to the saloon to get his money back after midnight when all have gone. Baker prevents Lambert from robbing Case, who informs the newcomer that he will help him make his bundle by hiring him to help hijack ore wagons. Lambert accepts the offer after being paid back the money he lost to Sweeney.

Taking a short cut into town to pick up a package, Little Beaver happens upon the hijacking of an ore wagon. He rides on to tell Red, who organizes a posse to capture the culprits. Sweeney escapes with the ore wagon, but Lambert is wounded in the gunbattle and apprehended by Red. Lambert is sent to state prison after refusing to name his accomplices in the crime for fear that Case will harm his wife and son who are due to arrive soon.

Red informs Mrs. Lambert and her son Dick about Lambert's musfortune when they arrive and takes them to the Duchess' ranch to live. Dick becomes bored with life at the ranch and manages to get a job from Case at the saloon. Red arrives to take the youngster home but has to fight off an attack by Sweeney, who has caught Dick cheating at cards. To prevent Red from taking Dick away, Case pays Sweeney back the money he has lost.

The not-too-pleased Sweeney, after having had a few drinks too many, tries to gun Red down for the beating he sustained at the hands of the marshal. Sweeney is sent to prison where he is coincidentally jailed next to Lambert. Not giving up in his attempt to get Red, Sweeney informs Lambert that Red is mistreating both Dick and his mother.

Lambert escapes with vengeance on his mind and heads to the Duchess' ranch to confront Red. Red manages to subdue and tie up his assailant with a capable assist from his sidekick, Little Beaver.

Afterwards, Red hides in an ore wagon that he expects to be hijacked so that he can find out who is behind the raids. After learning that Case, not Red, is the one mistreating Dick, Lambert gets free and goes to the cave hideout to assist the marshal. Lambert dies trying to help Red, who then heads for a confrontation with Case, whom he has discovered to be leader of the bandits. Red engages Case in a brutal fight that wrecks the saloon and then hauls him off to jail.

Having cleared up the hijacking problem, Red resigns as marshal and returns to the Duchess' ranch, where Dick is now hard at work.

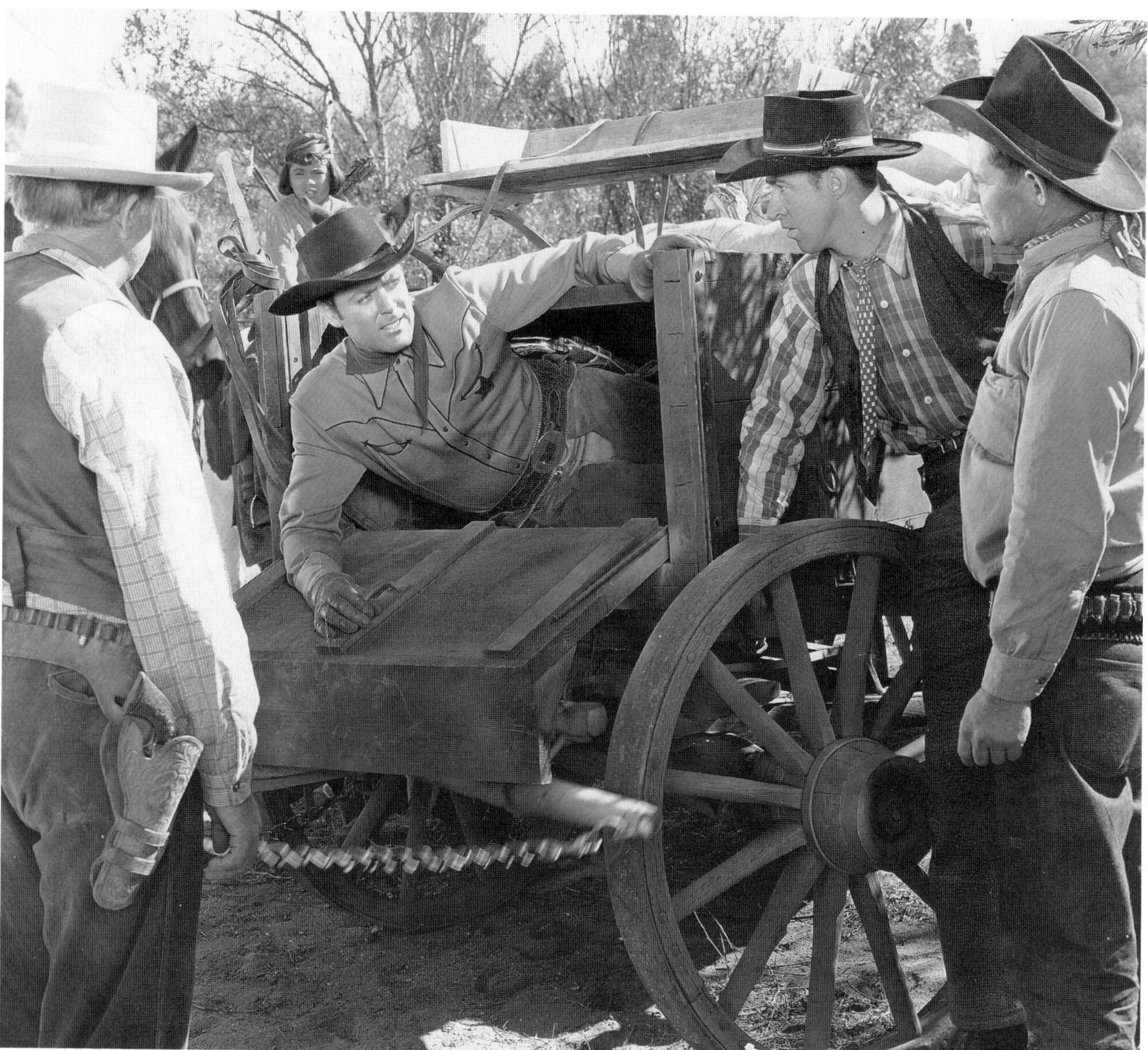

Red (Allan Lane) has a plan which calls for him to go undercover. He sure has the attention of these three men. Little Beaver looks on in the background. The scene is from MARSHAL OF CRIPPLE CREEK.

CHAPTER 4

"ROCKY" RIDES THE RANGE;
THE THIRD ALLAN LANE WESTERN SERIES

When Republic Pictures closed out the Red Ryder series in mid 1947, they were all set to initiate the new Allan "Rocky" Lane series. Lane had earned the right to prove himself in a series of his own. He had proven his ability to handle the acting demands of all kinds of roles through almost twenty years of film acting. His skill as an action performer had been amply demonstrated in serials, features, and, most recently, the popular Red Ryder series. He was a known commodity with the action Western film market—both film exhibitors and the fans who frequented their shoot-em-up picture theaters.

Rocky's series was planned as a low-budget enterprise by the studio. As a matter of fact, it was budgeted lowest on a four-tier scale of picture budgets. The budget for Rocky Lane pictures seldom rose much above the $50,000 level.

This might be a good place to examine Republic's financing of films to get a gauge on where Rocky's pictures fell in the Republic scheme of things. The studio was organized into four divisions of motion pictures. The divisions were classified as Jubilee, Anniversary, Deluxe, and Premiere grade. A Jubilee

Rocky, Eddy Waller, an unidentified actor with a gun, and Lyle Talbot play a scene in front of the Duchess' ranch house. This set was used over and over in Rocky's pictures. This scene is from DESPERADOES' OUTPOST (1952).

was the lowest budgeted picture; Premiere the highest. To give the reader an idea of the difference in budgets for the four categories, Rocky's 1951 picture, NIGHT RIDERS OF MONTANA was budgeted as a Jubilee picture at $55,200. An Anniversary film such as Roy Rogers' IN OLD AMARILLO (1951) was budgeted at $184,686. FIGHTING U. S. COAST GUARD (1951), a Deluxe picture, was budgeted at $532,111. The John Wayne/John Ford production of RIO GRANDE (1950) was one of the studio's Premiere pictures and was budgeted at $1,214,899.

Probably the most interesting piece of information regarding the Republic output and its budgeting is that the Jubilee and Anniversary pictures, the lower-budget series Westerns, were considered the bread-and-butter pictures of the studio. They had an established audience that would come back for each episode in the series and could be counted on to gross about $500,000 each. The big-budget Deluxe and Premiere pictures were a tough gamble for the studio because they were a one-time throw of the dice, and a lot of money could be lost on them. Without the "little" pictures the studio would have gone belly up many years earlier than it did.

It can be said pretty accurately that when you have seen one Allan "Rocky" Lane picture, you have seen them all. That line is not meant to be a putdown; it is just that the pictures have a sameness in casting, visual appearance, and scripting. All of them were shot on Republic's Western street and backlot and at Iverson's movie location ranch. The backlot house and barn commonly referred to as the "Duchess' Ranch" (from the Red Ryder series) can be seen in a raft of the Rocky Lane episodes with practically no modification from one picture to the next. Four of the five randomly-spaced Lane films I re-viewed immediately prior to writing this chapter utilized the Duchess' ranchhouse and barn. Those films were BANDITS OF DARK CANYON (1947), THE BOLD FRONTIERSMAN (1948), NIGHT RIDERS OF MONTANA (1951), and MARSHAL OF CEDAR ROCK (1953). SHERIFF OF WICHITA (1949) was the only one of the five not to

Rocky made a guest appearance in Roy Rogers' 1950 film TRAIL OF ROBIN HOOD. They are seen here chatting between takes on the Republic back lot.

utilize the Duchess' Ranch.

Iverson's movie location ranch was located a few miles out of Los Angeles and was the favorite outdoor Western location for the studio. It had a rugged hilly terrain with huge boulders that bespoke the old West to picture-goers, and there were great trails for stage-coach and buckboard chases. Because of this sameness in the filming locations and settings, often times horse chase footage, for example, could be utilized in several different films, thus saving dollars for the studio. One piece of stock footage from Iverson's that comes to mind is the one where Rocky runs up behind Black Jack and does a crupper mount up over the horse's rump into the saddle. That same piece of film was utilized every time the director wanted a flashy mount by the star—and it wasn't even Rocky doing the stunt!

The Rocky Lane pictures were geared by the studio to be a totally self-produced, assembly-line entity. The star was under exclusive contract to the studio. The casts, associate producers, and directors were in-house Republic employees, for the most part, who roamed from one Republic Western or melodrama to another, working regularly and making a modest but

The true B Western fan would immediately recognize this rocky terrain as being from Iverson's movie location ranch, situated only a few miles outside of Hollywood. Rocky and Clayton Moore are fending off the bad guys in this scene from SHERIFF OF WICHITA (1949).

comfortable living.

There were only five directors who worked on the thirty-eight episodes over the seven years. Philip Ford, Harry Keller, R. G. Springsteen, and Fred C. Brannon were used most often. Former stunt man Yakima Canutt directed two of the pictures but found working with Rocky not to his liking and so moved on to second unit direction of bigger-budget action pictures.

The casts had a familiarity about them that sometimes made one wonder if he had already seen the new Rocky Lane picture because he remembered seeing those same characters before. Roy Barcroft always seemed to be around and up to his usual dirty work. In one episode he would be the slick, crooked banker; in another he was the dirty, brainless dog heavy who would just as soon cut your throat as look at you. (Rex Allen once commented to me that "every kid in the movie theater knew immediately that Roy Barcroft was the bad guy, but it took that smart cowboy star about sixty minutes of film time to figure it out. " Ah, but that was part of the fun of Republic Westerns—recognizing the "old friends" who were the good guys and the bad guys.)

Other regulars were John Hamilton, Robert Shayne, Trevor Bardette, I. Stanford Jolley, Grant Withers, Clayton Moore, Kenneth MacDonald, Lane Bradford, George Chesebro, Forrest Taylor, Dick Curtis, Marshall Reed, Steve Clark, Rand Brooks, House Peters, Jr., Tom London—all the old standbys we had grown accustomed to in the Republic Westerns. The leading ladies, for the most part, were in a revolving door that seldom brought them back for return engagements. Only three actresses made as many as three appearances in Rocky Lane pictures (Mildred Coles, Claudia Barrett, and Mary Ellen Kay). Another three actresses appeared in two pictures each—Gail Davis, Martha Hyer, and Phyllis Coates. The rest appeared once and, for the most part, were never seen again in pictures.

Probably the element that raised the Rocky Lane pictures above most of the other B Westerns of that era was the excellent scripting. The stories for his films

Most B Western fans would probably award Roy Barcroft (seen here with Rocky) the title of "King of the Villains." He played all kinds of heavies in the B Westerns—everything from the slick "dress" heavy to the scummy "dog" heavy. He was foiled twenty-eight times by Rocky in his series of thirty-eight films. The scene here is from SHERIFF OF WICHITA (1949).

were generally taut little Western melodramas that contained a good deal of suspense, detection, and then resultant action. Rocky was usually a special agent, U. S. Marshal, or sheriff trying to uncover the chief bad man in the story. Through events and clues he would deduce who the villain was. Generally it was a civic official, bank president, or some other highly respected local townsperson who was covertly conducting the villainy. Quite often Rocky was not the focal point of the story. In many of the films the main plot situation was established during the first ten minutes without Rocky and then he entered the story in a lawman role through which he strove to resolve the established problem. Bob Williams was one of the script writers who added much to the word power of the Rocky Lane films, and BANDITS OF DARK CANYON (1947) is a good example of his work.

The plot for this film starts with the emphasis on the Bob Steele character, an escaped convict who strives to reestablish his relationship with his young son and also prove himself innocent of the crime he has been serving time for. Williams' script gave Bob Steele one of his finest character roles after a long career of playing cowboy heroes, and the actor delivered a controlled, sensitive acting performance, particularly in the scenes with the youth playing his son. Rocky doesn't enter the plot until the Steele character and his problems have been adequately established. Then he goes about the business of helping Steele clear up the mystery of who framed him years ago. We in the audience do not find out who the ringleader of the outlaws is until late in the story.

An attention-getting script gimmick in BANDITS OF DARK CANYON was the habit of dog heavy Roy Barcroft to eat shell peanuts and leave the shells around wherever a crime has been committed. In the 1949 film THE BOLD FRONTIERSMAN, again scripted by Willaims, he gave the slick heavy, saloon-owner Roy Barcroft (again), the fascinating trademark of flipping a coin as he was about to have a shoot out with someone. You quickly learned that when Barcroft started flipping that coin, it was time to dive under the tables. There was going to be action galore momentarily.

Here is a good example of Republic's use of rear-screen projection. The action part of this scene (roping the heavy on horseback from horseback) was done at Iverson's movie location ranch. The dialogue portion of the scene is now played on a sound stage in front of a projection of Iverson's. The technique saved money, but it never fooled anybody. The scene is from DESPERADOES' OUTPOST (1952).

Here is another example of a Republic "green set," an in-studio set made to appear as an outdoor scene. The fake rock in the foreground and rear-screen projection of an outdoor scene in the background are immediately obvious and distracting to most filmgoers. The scene is from DESPERADOES OF DODGE CITY (1948).

SHERIFF OF WICHITA, also scripted by Bob Williams, was a neat little mystery set in a deserted fort. As in so many classic mysteries, a group of people are invited by letter to a rendezvous where they will learn some valuable information they all seek. It was quickly established in the film that some years before a murder occurred in the fort and a payroll was stolen and never recovered. Now the participants of that occurrence are mysteriously invited back to the fort. Sheriff Rocky Lane finds out about the gathering and hopes to locate the missing payroll.

Of the five episodes I revisited for this chapter, 1951's NIGHT RIDERS OF MONTANA was the weakest in my estimation—but only by a little bit. Chubby Johnson was subbing for Lane's usual sidekick Eddy Waller, and although he was a competent actor, the chemistry with Rocky did not work as well. All of the usual ingredients (Republic stock company, same locations, a reasonably good script, etc.) were in place, but the capricious spark that ignites a story fizzled somewhat this time. One mitigating factor that hurt the film was the more blatant use of a studio "green set" (with human-manufactured trees and rocks and rear-screen projection), which gave the production a claustrophobic feel at times. (A disturbing green-set trend had become rampant in Western films at Republic and elsewhere during this period and greatly took away from the "reality" of the films. Most of the later Roy Rogers films suffered from this cost-saving and too-convenient device. Even an epic such as John Ford's THE SEARCHERS (1956), where cost was not really a factor, was seriously damaged by the use of studio green sets.)

There was more stock footage used in NIGHT RIDERS OF MONTANA than in the three earlier films I examined, but the inclusion was carefully handled and vital to the story. At the start of the picture a stock footage montage of horses being rustled was utilized to initiate the story. More stampeding horse footage was used at the climax. Rocky and his men and the outlaws were seamlessly inserted into the stock footage so that the good guys and bad guys appeared to be a part of the horse action.

MARSHAL OF CEDAR ROCK (1953) was made during the last year of Rocky's Western film career; he starred in only three more Republic pictures. Though the end was near, this film compares very favorably with the four other films I re-viewed for this chapter and, for that matter, it's on a par with all of the other Rocky Lane films I have seen over the years—probably the majority of them. Rocky was still in great physical condition even though he was now forty-nine years old (not exactly ancient but a time when many men put on weight and lose their youthful look—but not Rocky). For those in the know, Rocky's hairpiece (which he had used for years) did appear more evident for some reason.

The nifty, taut script by Albert DeMond concerned the "planned" escape of a prison convict by U. S. Marshal Rocky Lane so that the young man could either clear himself or lead the law to unrecovered stolen money. Rocky eventually cleared the fellow and pinned the crime on the town banker (guess who?), Roy Barcroft. The interesting plot was intelligently handled by director Harry Keller and has appeal to both youngsters and adults. All of the standard Rocky Lane film ingredients were present for this episode—stock cast, same locations, etc. This late episode was as good as any in the series, as indicated above, and there was no apparent letdown in the quality of the series as the end was drawing near.

The camera work in the Republic Westerns was always good (especially the horseback footage done with the camera truck) and in MARSHAL OF CEDAR ROCK the climactic fight in the barn between Rocky and Barcroft was particularly noteworthy. The interesting angles gave the fight an intensity that it would not otherwise have had. Speaking of fight scenes, the Rocky pictures always featured exciting, well-staged fights, and it was practically impossible to detect the use of a double for Rocky. Roy Barcroft once com-

This publicity photo was taken late in the final Rocky Lane series in front of one of Republic's manufactured rock sets.

mented in an interview that he did not much like doing fights with Rocky (and he did a lot of them) because Rocky didn't always pull his punches and then he would laugh at the damage he had inflicted on his opponent. To the fans in the movie theaters it was always pretty thrilling stuff.

One area in which the studio did not show great care (and revealed the films' low budgets) was in the use of stock footage utilizing a stunt double's action. In MARSHAL OF CEDAR ROCK there is a bulldogging stunt where Rocky supposedly jumps from Black Jack to another horse and rider and knocks the rider to the ground. The scene is, in reality, stock footage. Regrettably, the costume on the stunt man in the stock footage does not match Rocky's clothes. Another example of this sort of costume mismatch can be found in a bulldogging scene in the earlier film, BANDITS OF DARK CANYON, and elsewhere in the series.

Rocky's peculiar style of horseback riding has been the subject of comment by fans over the years, and perhaps mention should be made of it here. While there is no question that Rocky sat a saddle very nicely, his disturbing habit of slapping his legs against his galloping horse's side was most distracting and not a little funny looking to properly trained riders. Rocky also allowed his elbows to flap distractingly during chase scenes—again a no-no to trained riders. So why did he do it? Perhaps the leg slapping and elbow flapping were done intentionally to convey to juvenile audiences a greater sense of excitement through the movement. Who knows? It certainly was distracting though.

There is no question that Rocky Lane was a fine action star who was able to carry off the acting demands of his roles with aplomb. His voice quality was rich and apppealing; his handsome physical appearance made him a natural as the cowboy hero. The one human ingredient that I find missing from his screen character (and some say missing from him personally) is a sense of humor. I cannot remember a scene in any of his films where a genuine sense of humor is displayed. Cowboy heroes such as Gene Autry, Bill "Hopalong Cassidy" Boyd, and Roy Rogers displayed a vigorous sense of humor in their screen roles and thus added warmth and likeability to their characters. Rocky was always businesslike and serious in his roles—and that was okay—but a lightening up occasionally (as we say today) would have made his screen persona even more appealing.

With the cancellation of his Republic Western series in 1953, Allan Lane's starring film career came to an end. He would take an occasional supporting role in films or on television, but there were to be no more hero roles in which he could ride across the plains on Black Jack. His future in show business was to be behind the scenes with another horse—Mr. Ed.

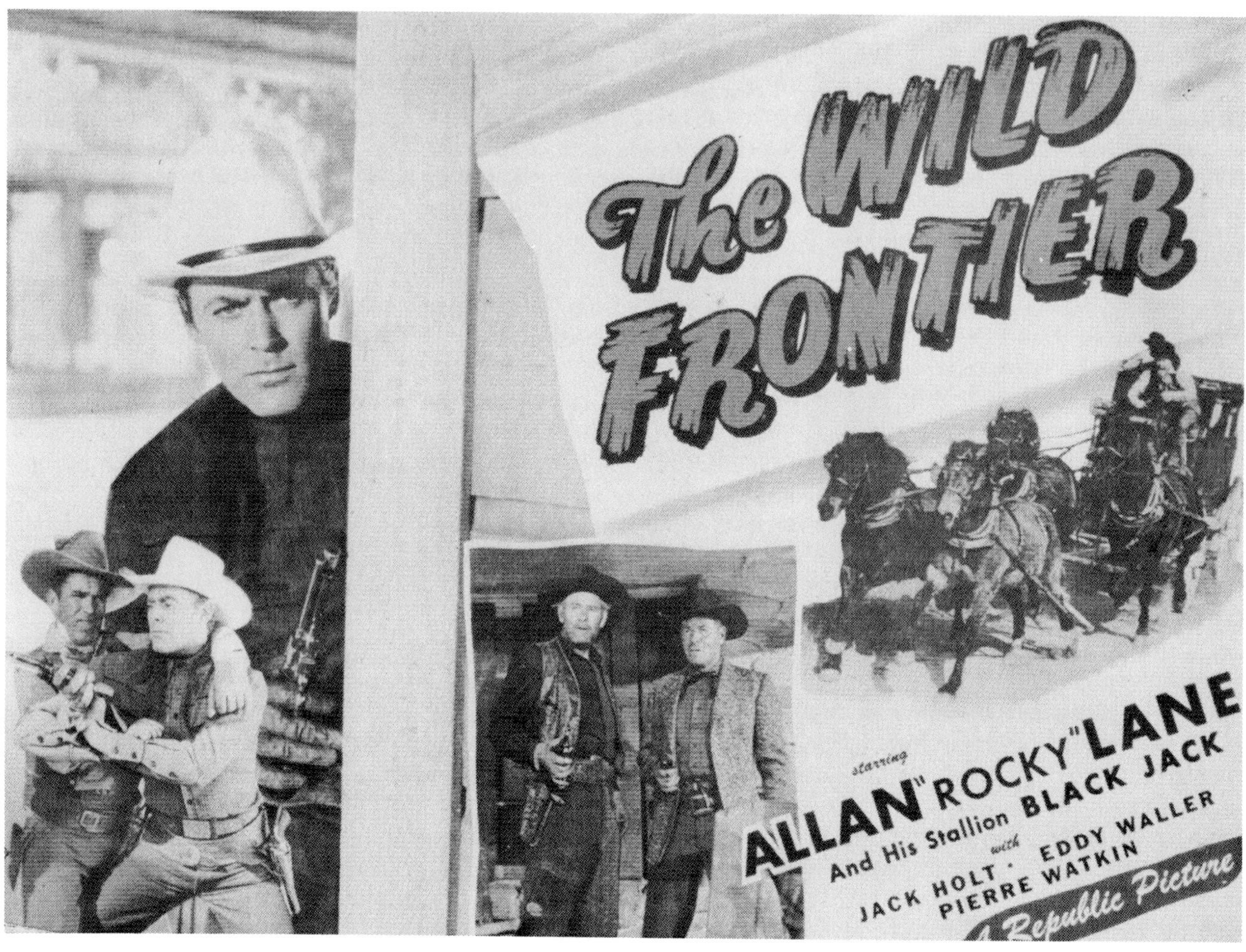

THE WILD FRONTIER

59 Mins .... Oct. 1, 1947

ALLAN LANE .... "Rocky" Lane
BLACK JACK .... His Stallion
JACK HOLT .... Saddles Barton
EDDY WALKER .... Nugget Clark
PIERRE WATKIN .... Marshal Frank Lane
JOHN JAMES .... Jimmy Lane
ROY BARCROFT .... Lon Brand
TOM LONDON .... Patrick MacSween
SAM FLINT .... Steve Lawson
TED MAPES .... A Gunman
BUDD BUSTER .... Sam Wheeler
WHEATON CHAMBERS .... Doc Hardy

ASSOC. PRODUCER .... Gordon Kay
DIRECTED BY .... Philip Ford
ORIGINAL SCREENPLAY .... .Albert DeMond
PHOTOGRAPHED BY .... Alfred S. Keller
MUSICAL DIRECTOR .... Mort Glickman

The town of Clayton City suffers from lawlessness resulting in the departure of many citizens. Jimmy Lane, one of its citizens, is very much in favor of establishing vigilantes. However, Jimmy proudly announces that his father Marshal Frank Lane is on his way to deal with the lawless element.

Saddles Barton, Clayton City's gunsmith and saddlemaker, thought to be respectable and above reproach by the townsfolk, is really the leader of the outlaw gang. Determined to prevent Marshal Lane from arriving, Barton dispatches masked gunmen to eliminate him.

Marshal Lane is accompanied by his eldest son Rocky on the trip, and the two Lanes give a ride to a stranger headed to town. Once inside their buckboard, the stranger turns gunman and orders them to pull over. The gunman is foiled by the Lanes who then outrun and out shoot his masked partners with the aid of Jimmy, who has ridden out to meet them. Though glad to see his youngest son, Marshal Lane chastises him for apparently revealing to someone that he was on the way.

Patrick MacSween proudly announces the arrival of Marshal Lane, and all are happy except Saddles Barton, who goes to his back office to order the gunman out of town who failed to eliminate Lane. Barton gives the gunman a gun loaded with blanks before his departure. Now that Lane is on the job, it is further announced that the insurance company handling the claims for the town in the amount of $50,000 will now send the money. Rocky and Jimmy are deputized to help their father.

In the saloon Nugget Clark, a secret deputy of Marshal Lane, brags to Lon Brand that Marshal Lane is afraid of him. Rocky enters the saloon and spots the discharged Barton gunman about to leave town. Recognizing him from the mishap on the road, Rocky confronts him and takes him in a vicious fight. The gunman pulls his blankloaded gun to shoot Rocky but is shot by Jimmy. Marshal Lane arrives and scolds his son for taking the law into his own hands. While at the saloon, Marshal Lane arrests Nugget for passing bad money.

Marshal Lane informs Rocky that Nugget is on their side and asks that he keep it a secret. The marshal goes to Barton's to question him and sees firearms in the shop identical to the blank-loaded gun carried by the deceased gunman. Barton is accused of being the gang leader and is taken to jail. Barton shoots the elder Lane at the jail, exits from the rear, and joins the gathering at the front of the jail. Aware that Nugget is no longer in jail, Barton blames the killing on him.

Barton orders his head henchman, Brand, to bring Nugget to his hotel room that night since the old timer claims to know when the insurance money is coming. While Brand brings Nugget in, he spots Jimmy and tries to shoot him only to be thrown off by Nugget. Rocky is riding nearby and trades gunfire with Brand and his men who are given the slip long enough for Nugget to inform Rocky that he is about to meet the boss that night.

Rocky waits at the jail until time for the meeting only to be surprised by Jimmy who comes in to offer help in any way possible. Not ready to divulge information to his younger brother, Rocky orders him away. A startled Jimmy later gums up the works when he sees Nugget at the saloon and tries to kill him, thus ending the chance for Rocky to learn the identity of the boss. Nugget returns later to talk with Rocky. Brand has followed him and sends for Barton. They overhear Rocky and Nugget reveal that the $50,000 is in the safe in the marshal's office.

The next morning Jimmy is at Barton's getting his gun fixed when he spots Nugget and tries to kill him again. Jimmy is wounded as the outlaws hit town and make off with the money. After the money is stolen, Barton tries to get the townsfolk to become vigilantes. Rocky confesses to Jimmy that Nugget is in league with them and that the stolen money is counterfeit. As they talk, one of the outlaws throws a rock with a note attached through the window.

Rocky locates the outlaws and along with Nugget trades gunfire with them. Brand dies in the hail of bullets as Jimmy arrives with a posse to help out. Rocky, astride his speedy horse Black Jack, chases Barton, who has escaped in a wagon. Rocky catches the wagon and fights Barton after jumping inside. The wagon overturns, but the adversaries continue their fight with Rocky topping his father's killer.

Jimmy is installed as Clayton City's sheriff, so, assured that the town is in good hands, Rocky and Nugget depart for further adventures in the wild frontier.

BANDITS OF DARK CANYON

59 Mins .... Dec. 15, 1947

ALLAN LANE .... "Rocky" Lane
BLACK JACK .... His Stallion
BOB STEELE .... Ed Archer
EDDY WALLER .... Nugget Clark
ROY BARCROFT .... Jeff Conley
JOHN HAMILTON .... Ben Shaw
LINDA JOHNSON .... Joan Shaw
GREGORY MARSHALL .... Billy Archer
FRANCIS FORD .... Player
EDDIE ACUFF .... Farraday
LEROY MASON .... Guard

ASSOC. PRODUCER .... Gordon Kay
DIRECTED BY .... Philip Ford
ORIGINAL SCREENPLAY .... Bob Williams
PHOTOGRAPHED BY .... John MacBurnie
MUSICAL DIRECTOR .... Mort Glickman

Ed Archer, a man imprisoned for the murder of his foreman Jeff Conley, is being transferred to a new prison when the stagecoach in which he is riding is set upon by masked horsemen with guns blazing. The stage wrecks and Archer manages to escape before the outlaws arrive. After the outlaws depart, Archer takes the clothes of a passenger named Farraday and, with the guard out cold, embarks on a journey to Placer City. After acquiring a horse from a nearby ranch, Archer forges ahead only to be trailed by Texas Ranger Rocky Lane. Archer is fired on from the rocks but is rescued by Rocky, who finds peanut shells at the site

The graveyard seems to have Nugget Clark (Eddy Waller) pretty spooked in this scene from BANDITS OF DARK CANYON.

from which shots came. Archer steals Rocky's stallion Black Jack and continues his journey.

Archer arrives at the ranch of Ben Shaw, his partner in a now defunct gold mine, and runs across his old friend Nugget Clark. Nugget is none too happy to see Archer because, not having heard of his escape, he believes him to be a ghost. Archer borrows money from Shaw to get across the border and is told by him and Nugget that after his gold mine petered out, the town of Placer City died and is now a ghost town. Rocky arrives to claim his stallion but has to defend himself against Shaw's foreman in a fight. The brawling Ranger is about to reveal the nature of his visit when Archer's son Billy awakens and sees his father. Not wanting to disappoint Billy, Rocky decides to wait until morning.

Rocky goes to bed down Black Jack and finds a note to Archer from a J. Cromwell asking that Archer meet him at midnight at Hangman's Ridge for some valuable information. Rocky goes back inside the ranch and learns from Nugget that Cromwell was the coroner of Placer City seven years ago when Archer was accused of killing Jeff Conley. Not revealing why he asked, Rocky slips away to keep Archer's appointment after Nugget falls asleep. At Hangman's Ridge Rocky finds Cromwell knifed and peanut shells at the scene.

The next morning Rocky, Archer, and Nugget leave the Shaw ranch. Rocky prepares to identify himself and place Archer under arrest, but their buckboard is the target of the bullets of three gunmen. Rocky chases them on Black Jack and shoots one of them, knocks another from his horse and bests him in a fight, then outdraws and shoots the third man. Rocky finds a poker chip from the Placer City Hotel and

Casino and asks Archer what he knows about it. Archer confesses to being an escapee sentenced for the murder of Jeff Conley, a murder he says he didn't commit. Rocky keeps his identity a secret and suggests that they go to Placer City to look around. Nugget feels that only a ding dang fool would go there since it is supposed to be a ghost town but reluctantly agrees to go. They return to Shaw's for supplies first.

As Nugget and Archer leave Shaw's for Placer City, they see a sheriff and deputy ride up. Believing that Black Jack belongs to his father, Billy places supplies in the saddlebag and finds Rocky's badge. He gives it to Shaw's niece Joan, who is now wary of Rocky's intentions. The Sheriff and deputy apprehend Rocky since Archer is not in site, and take him to the old Placer City Stage Co. where he meets a burly man standing in a sea of peanut shells. The man leaves for Placer City but not before instructing the bogus lawmen to dispose of Rocky. The two-fisted Rocky tricks them and mauls them in a fight before speeding off to Placer City.

Meanwhile Nugget and Archer look over the Casino at the deserted Placer City. Shaw and his niece arrive to inform Archer that Rocky is a Ranger. Rocky arrives and confesses but informs the gathering that he believes Archer to be innocent or else he would have arrested him. Rocky finds peanut shells at the Casino and then fights for his life as the man from the Placer City Stage Co. makes an appearance. A startled Nugget tells Rocky it's no use because he is fighting a ghost, Jeff Conley, the man Archer killed seven years ago.

Rocky and a reluctant Nugget leave for Boot Hill Cemetery to dig up Conley's grave. Meanwhile Conley goes back to the Casino to talk with Shaw, the man behind the plot to kill Archer. Joan overhears them talking and now knows the truth. Rocky and Nugget dig up the grave and find it empty. Rocky realizes that Archer is innocent. Suddenly, he and Nugget are shot at by a gunman. Rocky chases and captures the gunman, whom Nugget identifies as Ben Shaw's foreman.

Rocky and Nugget head for the mine after finding nothing at the Casino and arrive to find Shaw and Conley removing ore. Rocky takes Conley in a tough fight before chasing Shaw, who flees in an ore wagon with Archer and Joan tied up in back. Shaw tries to shoot the Ranger but is beaten to the draw.

Archer and Joan settle down, and Rocky departs but not before warning Nugget to look out for ghosts.

OKLAHOMA BADLANDS

59 Mins .... Feb. 22, 1948

ALLAN LANE	"Rocky" Lane
BLACK JACK	His Stallion
EDDY WALLER	Nugget Clark
MILDRED COLES	Leslie Rawlins
ROY BARCROFT	Sanders
GENE STUTENROTH	Oliver Budge
EARLE HODGINS	Jonathan Walpole
DALE VAN SICKEL	Sharkey
JAY KIRBY	Ken Rawlins
CLAIRE WHITNEY	Agatha Scragg
TERRY FROST	Sheriff
HANK PATTERSON	Postmaster
HOUSE PETERS JR	Passenger
JACK KIRK	Stage Driver

ASSOC. PRODUCER	Gordon Kay
DIRECTED BY	Yakima Canutt
ORIGINAL SCREENPLAY	Bob Williams
PHOTOGRAPHED BY	John MacBurnie
MUSICAL DIRECTOR	Mort Glickman

The Rawlins family, an honest, hard working family, has experienced much trouble with cattle rustlers. After his father is killed by rustlers, Ken Rawlins is left to take care of their ranch with the aid of Nugget Clark. The most recent attack on the Rawlins cattle causes Ken to wire for his best friend Allan "Rocky" Lane to come and help. Before Rocky arrives, Ken is killed by Sanders, a local ruffian who shoots Ken after he confronts crooked ranch hand Sharkey, when the latter calls his father a swindler.

Oliver Budge, editor of the *Grass Valley Tribune* and leader of the efforts to acquire the Rawlins property, writes a front page story of Ken's death, presuming him to be the last of the Rawlins clan. Nugget informs Budge that Ken was not the last of the family. Leslie Rawlins of St. Louis is coming in by stage.

Under orders from Budge, Sanders and his men attack the stage so that Leslie Rawlins will be eliminated. The outlaws' gunfire alerts Rocky, who is on his way to visit Ken. Rocky rides down on the outlaws and drives them off after they have shot the only male passenger, believing him to be Leslie Rawlins. Rocky is informed by one of the female passengers that she is Leslie Rawlins, Ken's cousin, and that she is on her way to care for the ranch after Ken's death. Shocked that his friend has been killed and determined to find the culprit, Rocky assumes the identity of Leslie Rawlins. He has the real Leslie pretend to be her house-

Rocky, looking like a big-city dude, comes to the rescue of Nugget in this scene from OKLAHOMA BADLANDS.

keeper, Agatha Scragg who has decided to return to St. Louis after the unfriendly reception given the stage.

Rocky arrives dressed as a dude and finds ranch foreman Nugget experiencing trouble with the ranch hands, who have not been paid recently. Sharkey is especially vocal in his disapproval and advocates taking the horses since no money is available. Rocky's intervention causes a fight with Sharkey. After topping him in a fight, Rocky pays him off and fires him. The remaining ranch hands give Rocky a week to pay them off.

Sharkey informs Budge of his fight. This causes Budge to wonder about Sanders' claim that the last of the Rawlins' family was a pantywaist. Budge has bought up the note on the Rawlins ranch in order to control the pass and charge ranchers for taking their herds through.

Leslie, posing as housekeeper Agatha Scragg, is being given a very bad time by Nugget, since she is anything but a housekeeper. She is so aggravated by him that she starts to reveal her real identity, only to be stopped by Rocky. Rocky then heads for Willow Creek Bridge in answer to a note left at the ranch asking that he come there. Rocky arrives and is confronted by a revenge-minded Sharkey. Alerted by his stallion Black Jack that a second person is hiding in the bushes, Rocky shoots and kills Sharkey and runs the other person, Sanders, off.

The postmaster delivers a package to Budge addressed to Miss Leslie Rawlins, hoping that the presumed comical misnomer will earn him a mention in the newspaper. Budge offers to deliver the package but not before opening it to discover women's clothing. Correctly assuming that the real Leslie Rawlins is the woman posing as Agatha Scragg, Budge hires actor Jonathan Walpole to pretend to be Leslie's uncle George Henry Black, the person who sent the birthday package. Budge delivers the package and informs Agatha that Leslie's uncle would arrive soon. Confessing to the truth, the woman is kidnapped by Budge and Sanders.

Rocky goes to pay off the note, but Sanders knocks him out and steals the money. Nugget finds an unconscious Rocky and returns him to the ranch. Rocky tries to tell Nugget and the sheriff that the missing housekeeper is in trouble as Walpole tells the sheriff that Rocky is not his nephew, causing him to be arrested. When Rocky admits to not being Leslie Rawlins and reveals that he is Rocky Lane, Nugget remembers the name to be that of Ken's best friend and helps him to escape.

Realizing that the man claiming to be Leslie's Uncle George is a phony, Rocky finds him on a stage being driven by Sanders, who is about to kill him. Rocky chases Sanders off and gets a confession from the phony uncle. Sanders goes to his shack, and Budge and Leslie get inside the stage. Rocky catches the stage and knocks Sanders off. Leslie disposes of Budge with a well-aimed shoe to the head.

With all the problems now behind, Nugget, believing that Leslie is still Agatha, suggests that the housekeeper take a couple of days off. He is dumbfounded to find that the woman he has given such a hard time is really Leslie Rawlins, his future employer.

THE BOLD FRONTIERSMAN

60 Mins .... April 15, 1948

ALLAN LANE	"Rocky" Lane
BLACK JACK	.His Stallion
EDDY WALKER	Nugget Clark
ROY BARCROFT	Smiling Jack
JOHN ALVIN	Don Post
FRANCIS MCDONALD	.Adam Post
FRED GRAHAM	Smokey
EDWARD CASSIDY	.Morton Harris
EDMUND COBB	Pete
HAROLD GOODWIN	Cowboy
JACK KIRK	.Rancher
KEN TERRELL	Judd
MARSHALL REED	Sam
AL MURPHY	Professor

ASSOC. PRODUCER	Gordon Kay
DIRECTED BY	Philip Ford
ORIGINAL SCREENPLAY	Bob Williams
PHOTOGRAPHED BY	Ernest Miller
MUSICAL DIRECTOR	Mort Glickman

Things are looking grim for Adam Post (Francis McDonald) and his son Don (John Alvin) as Rocky and Nugget check the murder evidence in this scene from THE BOLD FRONTIERSMAN.

Rocky Lane, a representative of the Atlas Drilling Company, is headed for the town of Cimarron Flats when he witnesses the attempted hold up of Sheriff Nugget Clark. Rocky's barking six-guns drive the outlaws off. Sheriff Clark reveals to Rocky that the men were trying to rob him of money collected from local ranchers to help solve the town's water shortage. There has been no rain in Cimarron Flats in six months.

Upon their arrival in town, Nugget heads to the saloon of Smiling Jack to buy water for Rocky's horse. A gambler accuses Jack of cheating and is shot by the saloon owner. Jack confesses to the killing but claims self-defense, so the cowardly Nugget does not arrest him. Also at the saloon is Don Post, son of Adam Post, the man entrusted with the monies collected for the water fund. Don, an habitual gambler, is celebrating his birthday and is given the money Nugget has collected to give his father. Don is asked to pay his gambling debt by Jack. Nugget loans the youngster three-hundred dollars to help.

After all depart, Smokey, a henchman of Smiling Jack, informs his boss that Rocky is the man who prevented them from robbing Nugget. Jack, the brains behind the plot to steal the funds, sends Smokey and other men out to prevent Rocky and Don from reaching the ranch with the money. Rocky engages the bandits in a blazing gun battle as Don rides ahead. Don turns over the money to his father and mistakenly drops the money on the floor that Nugget loaned him. Ashamed to tell his father where it came from, Don lets him think it is more money for the water fund.

Don returns to town to give Smiling Jack the money he borrowed from Nugget after removing it from the safe. Rocky has followed Don and prevents him from giving the money to Smiling Jack. However, he is too late to prevent him from losing a chiming watch given him by his father for his birthday.

The next morning Smiling Jack goes to Morton Harris, editor of the local paper and director of the water fund, and tells him that Don has stolen money from the fund to pay his gambling debts. He encourages Harris to go talk with Adam Post and follows him there. As the men talk, Jack knocks out and shoots Harris with his gun. Jack steals the money from Post's safe as the dazed man hears the chime of his son's watch. Rocky and Nugget arrive, but the elder Post refuses to talk and accepts the blame, fearing that Don is the culprit. Don confesses to the crime and is jailed.

Suspicious of Smiling Jack, Rocky goes to question him but has to fend off the fists of Smokey and Judd when Smiling Jack turns them loose on the cowboy. Rocky holds his own until Jack enters the fray and holds Rocky while his men finish their brutal assault. Rocky is thrown from the saloon.

Rocky goes to the jail to question Don, who has been sentenced to hang for Harris' murder. Rocky assures him that he believes him innocent and feels that Smiling Jack is behind it all. The next stop for Rocky is the Post ranch, where Post tells Rocky that he didn't see Don kill Harris, but he heard Don's chiming watch. Now Rocky knows that Smiling Jack is behind the shooting, and he informs Post that Don lost the watch to the saloon owner.

As Rocky and Post head for town, Jack has his men break Don out of jail so they can kill him. The murder attempt is prevented by Rocky, who rescues Don and rides away with Smokey and a horde of his outlaw friends in hot pursuit. A clever ruse enables them to get away and proceed to the Post ranch.

After instructing Don to lay low at the ranch, Rocky leaves for town only to be again accosted by several gunmen. He manages to elude them and arrives in town to enlist the aid of Nugget in carrying out a plan to prove Don's innocence. Rocky and Nugget enter the saloon through a top floor but are captured and tied up when an over-zealous Nugget gives them away. Jack informs the men that Don has been recaptured and his hanging will go on as planned.

Rocky and Nugget manage to get free of their bonds and set out to prevent Don from being hung. Rocky avenges the earlier beating he suffered at the hands of Smokey by winning a bruising fight. Smiling Jack is then shot when he attempts to outdraw Rocky, who then frees Don from the gallows.

Don and his father reconcile their differences over Don's gambling, and the future of Cimarron Flats is bright thanks to the help of Rocky Lane.

There's action aplenty in CARSON CITY RAIDERS as Rocky disarms young Hal Landon while Beverly Jons, Nugget, and villain Dale Van Sickel look on anxiously.

CARSON CITY RAIDERS

60 Mins .... May 13, 1948

ALLAN LANE .... "Rocky" Lane
EDDY WALLER .... Nugget Clark
FRANK REICHER .... Razor Pool
BEVERLY JONS .... Mildred Drew
HAL LANDON .... Jimmy Davis
STEVE DARRELL .... Tom Drew
HAROLD GOODWIN .... Dave Starkey
DALE VAN SICKEL .... Brennon
TOM CHATTERTON .... John Davis
EDMUND COBB .... Sheriff
HOLLY BANE .... Joe
BOB WILKE .... Ed Noble
and BLACK JACK

ASSOC. PRODUCER .... Gordon Kay
DIRECTED BY .... Yakima Canutt
ORIGINAL SCREENPLAY .... Earle Snell
PHOTOGRAPHED BY .... William Bradford
MUSICAL DIRECTOR .... Mort Glickman

After the sheriff of Carson City is killed by outlaws, Tom Drew takes the vacated post. At first reluctant because he is a former outlaw, though unknown to the townsfolk, Drew accepts the job to bring law and order to a troubled Carson City.

Dave Starkey, a noted outlaw has come to Carson City to join up with Razor Pool, the source of the town's trouble. Razor points ou t the new sheriff and assigns Starkey to get rid of him. Starkey accepts but offers to kill Drew for free because he recognizes him as former partner Fargo Jack. Deeming this vital information, Razor orders Starkey to dress as Fargo Jack used to and employ the peculiar gun draw that his former associate was noted for.

Headed for Carson City to hire on with freight-line owner Nugget Clark, Rocky Lane, is stopped by Drew, who tries to take his gun as part of his approach to dealing with crime. Rocky tricks him and continues his journey. Jimmy Davis, who has quit college to come help his father, and Nugget are attacked by masked

Sheriff Steve Darrell confers with Rocky and Beverly Jons as Nugget keeps tabs on outlaw Dale Van Sickel.

bandits. Rocky cuts cross country to help out. With Rocky tossing lead from the rear and Jimmy from the wagon, the outlaws are run off. Rocky chases one bandit, Brennon, and whips him in a fight after knocking him from his horse. Drew arrives and handcuffs the bandit.

Nugget arrives in town and informs an inquisitive Razor about Rocky, the stranger who helped him out on the trail. Nugget describes the bandits who attacked him, and Razor claims the dress and mode fit that of Fargo Jack. Rocky and Nugget go to Nugget's office where Rocky informs the old-timer that he is a special investigator for the freight company.

As Drew questions Brennon, John and Jimmy Davis offer to watch the office while Drew, at Brennon's suggestion, rides out to Devil Rock Creek to search for clues. Starkey, dressed as Fargo Jack, and his men break Brennon out and shoot Davis. After identifying the gun wielder as Fargo Jack, Davis, Rocky, and Nugget chase but lose the men.

They return to town where Rocky rejects an offer to be deputy. Rocky reveals that he is there on a special investigation and that he knows quite well about Fargo Jack. Drew confesses his former identity but proclaims innocence in the current troubles. Rocky assures him that all is okay as he offers to watch the jail that night.

The next morning Rocky tells Drew that the old Fargo Jack needs to operate again. A plan is devised in which Nugget is to take Brennon to the jail at Twin Rocks so that Drew, as Fargo Jack, can intercept him on the trail, and Rocky can follow Brennon to his gang. The plan works until Jimmy, who was informed of the plan by Drew's daughter Mildred, arrives. His attempt on Drew's life, after shooting Brennon, results in him being roped from his horse by Rocky to prevent further confusion.

Jimmy goes to the barber shop looking for Rocky and informs Razor of what has happened and suggests that Rocky and Fargo Jack work together. The angry lad sees Rocky outside and tries to gun him down, but a clever Black Jack saves his master. Rocky, Nugget, and Drew temporarily calm him down, but he heads for the county seat to seek more information on Fargo Jack.

Rocky doesn't need a shave from slick villain Razor Pool (Frank Reicher).

The bad guys have Rocky and Nugget pinned down behind the watering trough in this scene from CARSON CITY RAIDERS.

Rocky and friends decide to try to trap the outlaws before Jimmy returns, so they move some ore wagons to help draw the bandits out. Razor doesn't bite but he, Starkey, and a henchman confront Drew and threaten to harm his daughter if he refuses to cooperate. They steal badges from the sheriff to outfit their men. The phony deputies catch up to Nugget and send him back to town, leaving the ore wagons at their disposal.

Rocky, who is driving one of the ore wagons, makes it to the mine and is joined by Drew, who with Nugget's help manges to escape from his captors. The outlaws go down in a hail of gunfire. Jimmy arrives to gun down the man disguised as Fargo Jack. Realizing that the now unmasked Starkey is an impostor and that Drew is innocent, Jimmy tears up the photo he acquired at the county seat and helps prevent Drew's past from becoming known.

Rocky's got the drop on some of the bad guys in the famous Republic cave set.

MARSHALL OF AMARILLO

60 Mins .... July 25, 1948

ALLAN LANE .... "Rocky" Lane
EDDY WALLER .... Nugget Clark
MILDRED COLES .... Marjorie Underwood
CLAYTON MOORE .... Art Crandall
ROY BARCROFT .... Ben Dolan
TREVOR BARDETTE .... Frank Welch
MINERVA URECAL .... Mrs. Pettigrew
DENVER PYLE .... Night Clerk
CHARLES WILLIAMS .... Hiram Short
TOM CHATTERTON .... James Underwood
PETER PERKINS .... Sam
TOM LONDON .... Mr. Snodgrass
LYNN CASTLE .... Matilda Snodgrass
and BLACK JACK

ASSOC. PRODUCER .... Gordon Kay
DIRECTED BY .... Philip Ford
ORIGINAL SCREENPLAY .... Bob Williams
PHOTOGRAPHED BY .... John MacBurnie
MUSICAL DIRECTOR .... Morton Scott

The Amarillo-bound stage is stopped along its route by prospector Nugget Clark who is seeking a ride to Amarillo. Stage Driver Ben Dolan, in an attempt to outrun masked gunmen who take after the stage, unhitches the team and the stage wrecks. Passengers Nugget, James Underwood, and Hiram Short are told how to get to Halfway House, a deserted stage coach inn, by Dolan. The masked gunmen then ride up and tell Dolan that they will retrieve the horses.

After a three-mile walk, the passengers arrive at the spooky inn in search of rooms. A somewhat frightened Nugget knows that he must leave when the night clerk summons and talks to his non-existent porter George. After leaving in a buckboard located outside the inn, Nugget discovers the dead body of Hiram Short in the back and his terrified reaction causes the team to bolt. Rocky Lane, Marshal of Amarillo, stops the team and orders Nugget back to Halfway House upon finding the body.

Returning to the inn the next morning, Rocky and Nugget are greeted by stage agent Art Crandall who informs the marshal that in spite of Nugget's claim there was no trouble with outlaws the previous day. The situation becomes even more confusing when inn manager Frank Welch informs Rocky that no one named Underwood is there and that there is no night porter. Nugget shows Rocky the room in which he visited Underwood, but the room is now a storage room. Rocky questions the inn's only guest, Mrs. Pettigrew, a cranky battleaxe who claims that Nugget resembles the man who killed her late husband.

As Rocky and Nugget talk outside, Ben Dolan drives up in the stage. Before delivering the mail, Dolan puts a letter in his pocket. Rocky observes this and questions him about Nugget's allegations of trouble the previous day. He denies that there was trouble. When asked his name and that of the person on the letter he stuck in his pocket, Dolan kicks Rocky and rides off. After running him down on the speedy Black Jack, Rocky takes him in a tough fight. Dolan is about to reveal pertinent information when he is felled by a rifle shot. Rocky checks the dead man's pocket and finds a letter addressed to James Underwood from his daughter Marjorie, who is on her way to visit him.

As Nugget demonstrates how he supposedly ran off the outlaws the day before, his gun discharges and frightens Marjorie, who is driving close by. Rocky chases the frightened woman and informs her of the disappearance of her father. She informs him that her father had $50,000 in cash with him to purchase a ranch and retire. Rocky has her write a letter addressed to her father informing that she has been delayed but will arrive that night.

The letter is given to Welch, who is asked to keep it in case Underwood arrives. Rocky tells Welch that he is leaving to take Nugget to the Amarillo jail but returns moments later pretending to look for a glove, and notices that the mail slot in which Underwood's letter was placed is now empty. After departing, Rocky and Nugget are the target of two gunmen, but the bandits are cut down by the fast-shooting marshal.

Marjorie arrives at Halfway House that night and is greeted by the spooky night clerk who offers to take her to her father. She arrives at the room but finds no one there and is then told that she will be taken to him to force him to tell where he has hidden the money he was carrying. Rocky and Nugget arrive and move to get the clerk, but he is killed when his fleeing buckboard crashes.

Rocky and Nugget initiate a search for the missing money and find it has slipped between the registration desk and a crack in the wall. Crandall enters and upon seeing the package exclaims, "50,000." Rocky realizes that he is the culprit since no one but Underwood, his daughter, Nugget, his abductor, and himself knew the amount. However, Rocky can't make a move since doing so now might jeopardize Underwood's life.

Rocky gives Crandall the money and asks that he keep it for him. Crandall leaves but is followed by Rocky and Nugget to where Underwood is being held. Crandall and a driver depart with Underwood inside the stage. Rocky gives chase in another stage and shoots Crandall's driver. Crandall jumps to the stage driven by Rocky and the two men battle atop it. Rocky jumps to the stage in which Underwood is tied, after which Crandall's stage plunges into the river below.

With his sanity now restored to some degree, Nugget thanks Rocky who now departs.

DESPERADOES OF DODGE CITY

60 Mins .... Sept. 15, 1948

ALLAN LANE .... Rocky Lane
EDDY WALLER .... Nugget Clark
MILDRED COLES .... Gloria Lamoreaux
ROY BARCROFT .... Homesteader
TRISTRAM COFFIN .... Ace Durant
WILLIAM PHIPPS .... Ted Loring
JAMES CRAVEN .... Calvin Sutton
JOHN HAMILTON .... Strockton
EDWARD CASSIDY .... Jim
HOUSE PETERS, JR .... Henry
DALE VAN SICKEL .... Pete
PEGGY WYNNE .... Mary
TED MAPES .... Jake
and BLACK JACK

ASSOC. PRODUCER .... Gordon Kay
DIRECTED BY .... Philip Ford
ORIGINAL SCREENPLAY .... Bob Williams
PHOTOGRAPHES BY .... John MacBurnie
MUSICAL DIRECTOR .... Morton Scott

Greg McBride and his army of bandits rule the Dodge City area and stop at nothing to prevent the influx of homesteaders into their dominion. Allowing

You can bet that Tris Coffin and James Craven don't have Rocky's best interests at heart in this gun-toting scene from DESPERADOES OF DODGE CITY.

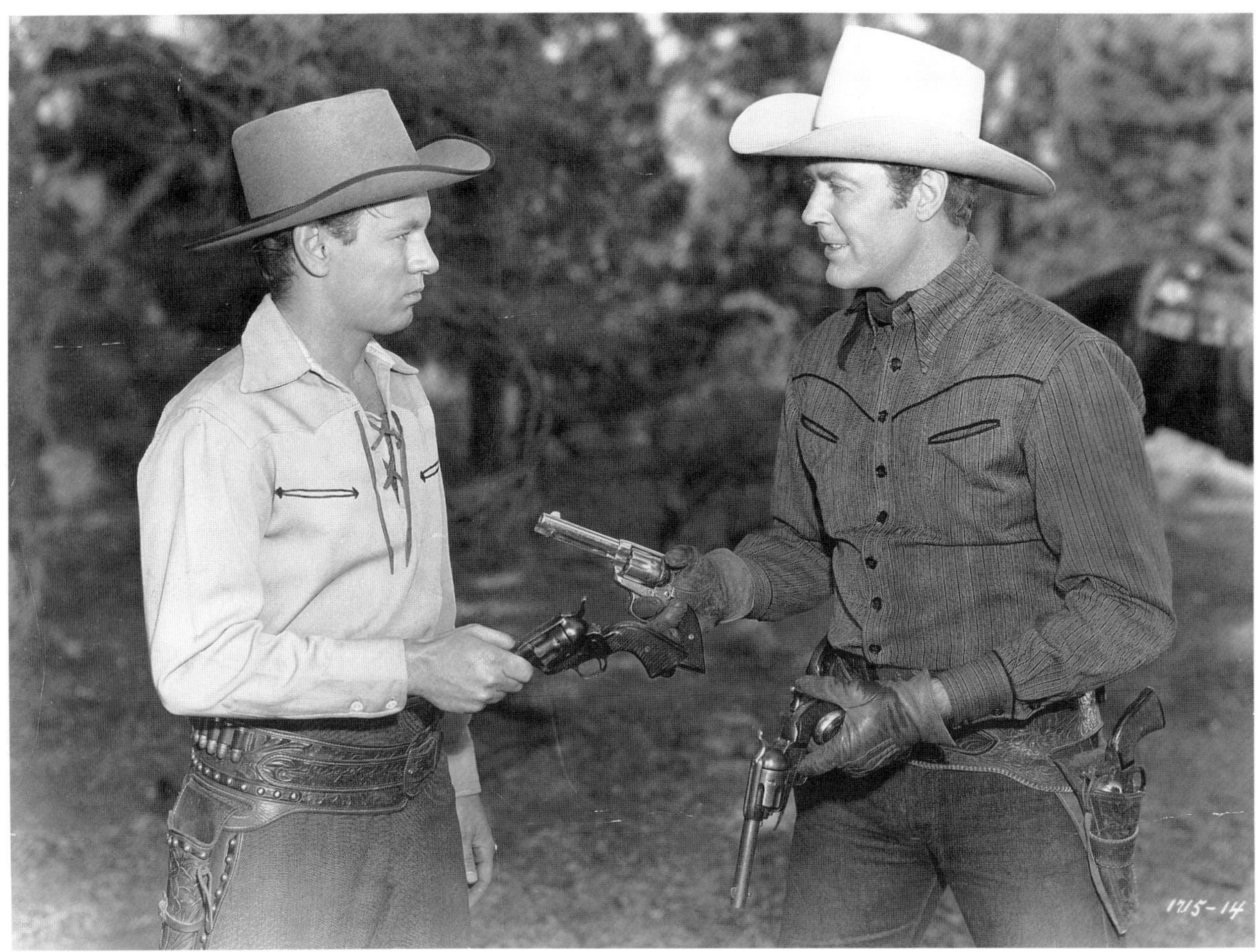

Baby-faced William Phipps hands over his gun to Rocky in this scene from DESPERADOES OF DODGE CITY.

them in would mean the coming of law into the territory and an end to McBride's rule. Tiring of the lawlessness, Dodge City Government Agent Stockton devises a plan involving a series of couriers to pass a message to the cavalry at Fort Henry to meet the next group of settlers and see to their safe arrival.

Rocky Lane, the last courier scheduled to receive the orders, is ready to do so when a shot rings out signaling the death of the courier from whom he was to get the orders. Rocky drops the bandit from his horse but not before the stolen orders have been dropped off at the Joshua Flats Relay Station, from which a stage is about to depart. Realizing that one of the passengers received the stolen orders, Rocky chases after the now-departed stage.

Rocky stops the stage and asks driver Nugget Clark, a secret courier himself, for a ride, since his horse has become lame. Rocky joins gambler Ace Durant, cowboy Ted Loring, rancher Calvin Sutton, and a homesteader who desires to be left alone as the stage continues its journey. The stage stops along the way to pick up entertainer Gloria Lamoreaux. Her arrival prompts Rocky to ride shotgun for Nugget.

Nugget is told to stop and water his horses by Rocky who plans to search the passengers for the orders. With gun drawn, Rocky identifies himself and prepares to search the baggage when lead is tossed in their direction. Rocky, Nugget, and the passengers seek refuge in a nearby vacant shack from the outlaws who drive the stage off. Rocky finds nothing in his search of the luggage, so he realizes that one of the passengers has the document on his person.

A rock is thrown through the window of the shack. The note attached to the rock indicates that the bandits' leader McBride is one of the passengers and that all will be freed if McBride is permitted to leave. With no one admitting to being McBride, the exchange of gunfire continues. Loring panics at being pinned down in the shack and runs out to face his attackers. The wounded man dies a short time later and is therefore eliminated as a suspect.

The next morning the owner of the shack rides up

and is gunned down by the hoodlums. Rocky finds a secret passage leading to the outside and decides that everyone should give their guns to him after which all will crawl through the passage and attempt to escape in the shack owner's wagon. The burly homesteader dies in the escape attempt as Rocky and the others ride away. Chased by McBride's men, Rocky mounts his stallion Black Jack and leads them away from Nugget, Gloria, Durant and Sutton.

Rocky returns to search remaining suspects Durant and Sutton but finds nothing. Believing that the orders were left at the shack, Rocky loosely ties up Durant and Sutton. After ordering Nugget and Gloria off to Fort Henry to warn the cavalry, Rocky leaves the men tied up and heads back to the shack, realizing that the real McBride will free himself from the loosely fitting bonds and try to prevent him from finding the orders.

Rocky finds nothing at the shack, so he waits for McBride to show. Durant arrives and starts to search the shack but is followed by Sutton who is revealed to be McBride. Sutton orders Jake, one of his henchman, to ride to Fort Henry and tell the cavalry to meet the wagon train at Indian Gap. He then leaves to lead an attack on the wagon train at Stovepipe Pass, the actual destination, but not before ordering Pete, another of his henchmen, to kill Rocky and Durant.

Rocky overpowers Pete after Sutton leaves. He then chases after Jake and manages to knock him from his horse. After defeating Jake in a fight, Rocky is off again. This time he manages to catch Nugget and give him the proper information to give the cavalry.

The hard-riding Rocky rides to warn the homesteaders to expect trouble. The trouble arrives in the form of McBride's Raiders who are held off by Rocky and the settlers until the cavalry arrives. McBride manages to escape but is caught by Rocky who outdraws the villainous man and sends him to his death.

The death of McBride and the safe arrival of the group of homesteaders signals the end of the desperadoes of Dodge City.

Rocky seems to have thrown quite a punch in this scene from DESPERADOES OF DODGE CITY.

Still clutching his gun, the wounded William Phipps gets treatment from Rocky as Nugget looks on.

THE DENVER KID

60 Mins .... Oct. 1, 1948

ALLAN LANE .... "Rocky" Lane
EDDY WALLER .... Nugget Clark
WILLIAM A. HENRY .... Tim Roberts
DOUGLAS FOWLEY .... Slit
RORY MALLINSON .... Jason Fox
GEORGE H. LLOYD .... Sheriff
GEORGE MEEKER .... Andre
EMMETT VOGAN .... Captain Roberts
HANK PATTERSON .... Sgt. Cooper
BRUCE EDWARDS .... .Fletcher Roberts
PEGGY WYNNE .... Mitzie

and BLACK JACK

ASSOC. PRODUCER .... Gordon Kay
DIRECTED BY .... Philip Ford
ORIGINAL SCREENPLAY .... Bob Williams
PHOTOGRAPHED BY .... John MacBurnie
MUSIC .... Dale Butts

Captain Stan Roberts of the Border Patrol sends a message to his son Fletcher by Sergeant Cooper, informing him where to deliver an incoming herd of cavalry mounts. After delivering the message, Cooper gives Fletcher a note supposedly from his younger brother Tim with his inscribed ring attached for identification purposes. Fletcher leaves to meet him but is instead met by Jason Fox, a debonair criminal who kills him and takes his clothes. Fox, who needs the horses to further equip an army of cutthroats, returns to steal the herd with his henchman Slit. The sleeping wranglers are mercilessly riddled with bullets.

Rocky Lane, a Border Patrol lieutenant, is riding to meet his best friend, Fletcher, when he is called upon to stop a badly wounded Cooper's runaway wagon. Taken back to town, Cooper tells Rocky and Captain Roberts that Fletcher killed the men. Rocky is shown the ring and letters but refuses to believe that Fletcher would murder his men. Rocky is granted permission to search for Tim in Cemetery Ridge, his last known address.

Because he must be extremely careful in the outlaw haven across the border, Rocky leaves his badge behind and has some of his men chase him to the border. Slit is on guard and sees Rocky shoot one of the men pursuing him. Slit, who pulls a gun of him, is tricked and disarmed by Rocky, who identifies himself as the Denver Kid.

Rocky, claiming to be in need of refuge from the law, is introduced to the crooked sheriff of Cemetery Ridge; pharmacist Nugget Clark, the towns only respectable citizen; Fox, owner of the Oasis Saloon; and Tim Roberts, who is using the name Tom Richards. After Slit informs his boss that he saw Rocky kill one of the Border Patrol men, Fox tells Rocky to help hijack a wagonload of gunpowder coming the next day.

As Rocky, Slit, and Fox's henchmen get ready to hijack the wagon, Rocky ropes Slit from his horse and knocks out the henchmen. Rocky, with the aid of his confidant, Nugget, takes the wagon for himself. When he informs Fox that he did this because he didn't want to split the money with anyone, Fox gives him all the money in front of a most unhappy Slit.

Rocky goes to thank Nugget for his help and infroms him that he believes that Tom Richards is really Tim Roberts, the man he is searching for. At the

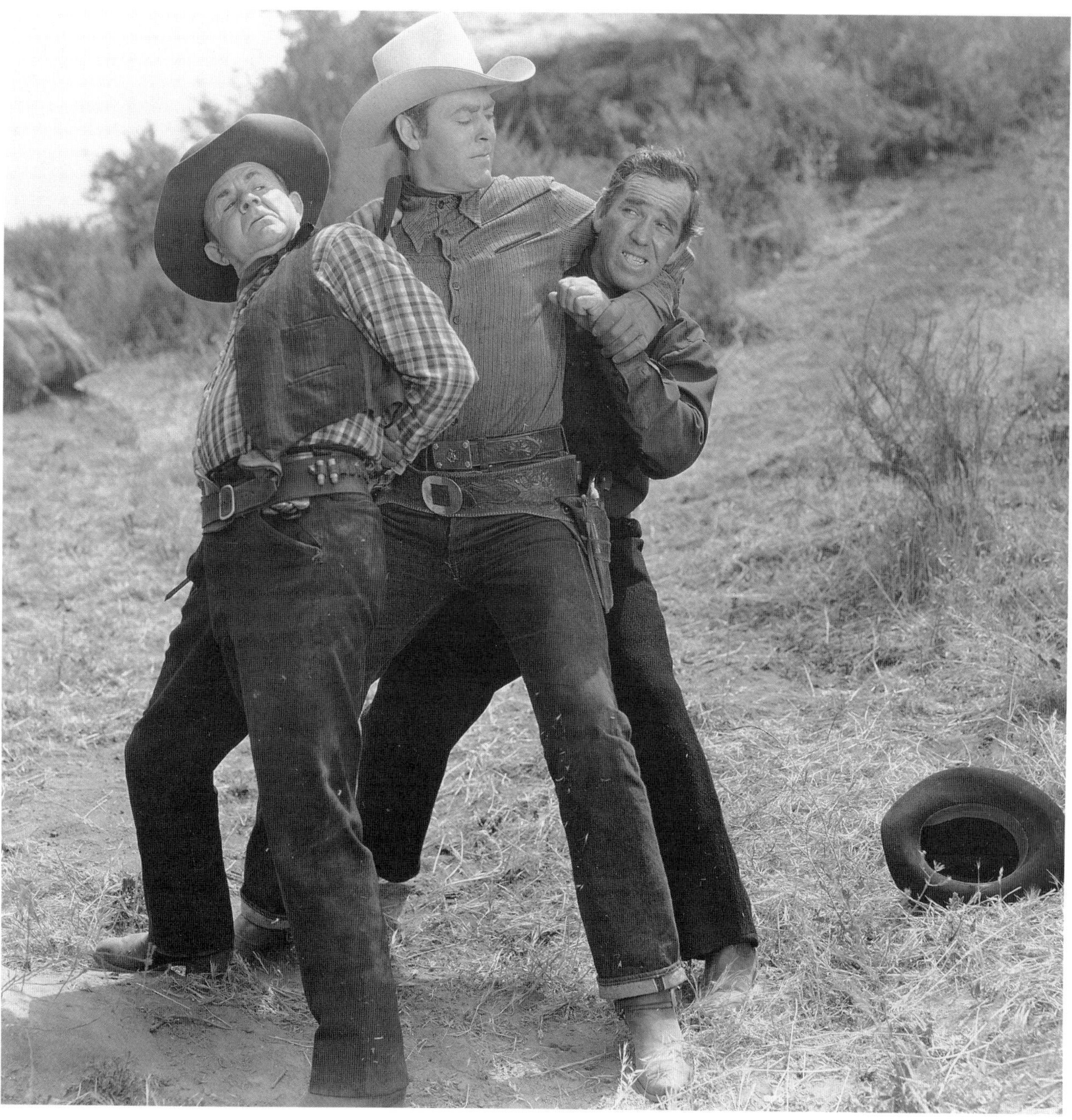

Rocky's got his hands full of problems in this scene from THE DENVER KID.

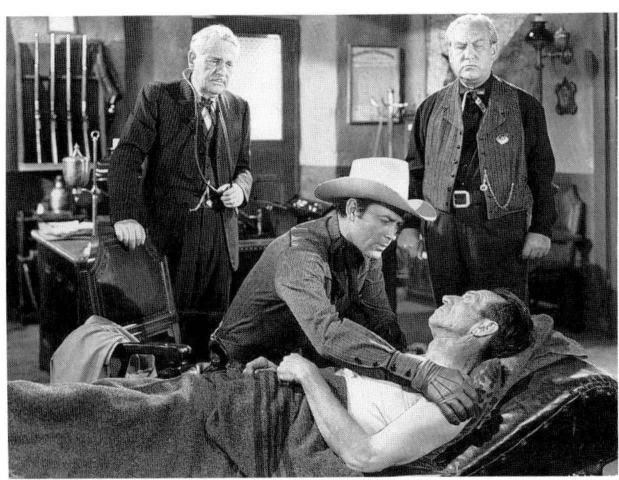

Rocky tries to get some information out of the poor victim as the sheriff and doctor look on.

Oasis, Rocky enters a poker game in which Tim is playing and baits him by making disparaging remarks about the Border Patrol. Tim leaves a winning behind when mention is made of the recent death of a Border Patrol member named Roberts. Realizing that Tim has taken the bait, Rocky leaves town believing that he will be followed. His hunch is right and he knocks Tim from his horse. He shows Tim the letter and ring but is assured by him that he lost the ring to Oasis dealer Andre in a card game.

Rocky goes to the saloon and gets Andre to leave with him. They meet Tim who questions him about the ring. After Andre admits that he gave it to Fox, he pulls a derringer from his coat but is shot and killed by Tim. Tim, who idolizes Fox, reveals that he is the only one who knows his true identity. Refusing to believe that Fox would cross him, Tim begins to wonder when Rocky asks where he thinks the horses will come from for the vast army he is forming.

Rocky decides that the time is right for Tim to know that he is with the Border Patrol. He also informs him that Nugget is on their side. The trio formulate a plan to reacquire the stolen herd and bring Fox to justice.

Rocky, Nugget, and Tim leave town under the pretense of checking on the herd. They are spotted by Slit and the sheriff who are bringing the hijacked gunpowder out. The sheriff discovers that coffee has been switched for the powder. After informing Fox of his discovery, the sheriff is joined by him, Slit, and others in an attempt to catch Rocky and the others.

Arriving at the canyon with guns blazing, Fox and his men cause the horses to stampede. Their attempt to turn them around fails, and they unknowingly cross the border to try to catch them. Fox is now captured by Rocky and taken to justice after a vicious fight.

Tim returns with Rocky to Border Patrol headquarters and joins up. Rocky asks Nugget to join also, but he can't because he is Cemetery Ridge's new sheriff.

SUNDOWN IN SANTA FE

60 Mins .... Nov. 5, 1948

ALLAN LANE .... "Rocky" Lane
EDDY WALLER .... Nugget Clark
ROY BARCROFT .... Tracy Gillette
TREVOR BARDETTE .... John Stuart
JEAN DEAN .... Lola Gillette
RUSSELL SIMPSON .... Sheriff Jim Wyatt
RAND BROOKS .... Tom Wyatt
LANE BRADFORD .... Bronc Owens
B. G. NORMAN .... Johnny Wyatt
MINERVA URECAL .... Ella May Watson
JOSEPH CREHAN .... Major Allen
.... and BLACK JACK

ASSOC. PRODUCER .... Melville Tucker
DIRECTED BY .... R. G. Springsteen
WRITTEN BY .... Norman S. Hall
PHOTOGRAPHED BY .... John MacBurnie
MUSIC .... Stanley Wilson

Armed robberies and killings around Sante Fe are all characterized by a dagger left at the scene bearing the Latin inscription Sic Semper Tyrannis, the same phrase shouted by John Wilkes Booth after his assassination of President Lincoln. Their discovery prompts Major Allen of military intelligence to assign Rocky Lane to the cases in an attempt to locate Walter Surratt, the fugitive leader of the Lincoln murder ring.

Printer Nugget Clark, who shared the stage ride with Rocky, gets a job with the local newspaper. John Stuart, editor of *The Guardian* and in reality Walter Surratt, is behind the trouble in the area and acts through rancher Tracy Gillette and his daughter Lola, Tom Wyatt's fiance.

After learning that troublemaker Bronc Owens is employed by Gillette, Rocky rides out to question the rancher to ascertain whether Bronc could be mixed up in the local robberies and killings. Rocky, who finds Tom and Lola at the Gillette ranch, is told by Gillette that Bronc is not involved in any robberies.

After Rocky leaves, Stuart, who was in a back

room, comes out to discuss a letter that Tom intercepted announcing the coming of a gold shipment. Stuart orders that the wagons be attacked. One of the drivers escapes and informs Sheriff Wyatt and Rocky of the attack. He asks why the sheriff provided no escort for them as they had requested by letter. The sheriff and Tom go to the post office to check on the letter which the sheriff believes was never received. Rocky stays behind and searches the office. He finds the letter in the trash.

Rocky has Nugget Clark print up an identical envelope and letterhead advising of another shipment. The letter is stolen by Tom and the wagons are attacked. Rocky and a few deputies are hidden in the wagons and drive the bandits off. Rocky and Nugget chase two of the masked men to a mine. The mask of a wounded bandit is removed by Rocky, who finds him to be the dying Tom. Tom asks that Rocky not tell his father of his involvement with the outlaws.

Rocky breaks the news of Tom's death to Wyatt but allows him to believe that Tom died while helping chase the outlaws. Wyatt tells Stuart to print in *The Guardian* that he will kill the man who murdered his son. Lola assumes Tom's office duties at the jail.

Stuart, Gillette, Lola, and Bronc surmise that Rocky sent the phony letter, since they know that he lied about Tom. Stuart orders that Rocky be watched. Bronc attempts to ambush Rocky but fails and is chased and knocked from his horse. Bronc comes up short in a fight with Rocky. Bronc is jailed and questioned by Rocky as Lola listens. After Rocky walks out, Bronc tells Lola to free him or he'll talk. Lola leaves the jail and then shoots and kills Bronc from the alley.

Rocky learns from Nugget that he saw Lola coming from behind the jail after the shots were fired. He and Nugget search her desk and find a letter indicating that wagons bearing a quarter of a million dollars are headed their way. Rocky rides to warn the wagons and succeeds in running off the bandits but not before they have gotten the money.

Rocky tells Nugget about the hijacking and shows him a dagger he recovered at the scene. Stuart intervenes and is questioned by Rocky about Gillette, whom he suspects of being one of the hijackers. Rocky leaves to search the mine on the Gillette property. Lola enters with gun drawn. Having told Wyatt at Stuart's order that Rocky killed Tom, Lola is told by Nugget that Stuart told Rocky where to find her father.

Rocky finds Gillette murdered with a dagger before Wyatt arrives to kill him. Rocky prevents a Stuart henchman from shooting Wyatt and chases Stuart who has fled in a wagon. He apprehends and subdues Stuart, whom Lola has identified as Walter Surratt, leader of the Lincoln murder ring.

RENEGADES OF SONORA

60 Mins .... Nov. 22, 1948

ALLAN LANE .... "Rocky" Lane
EDDY WALLER .... Nugget Clark
ROY BARCROFT .... George Keeler
FRANK FENTON .... Sheriff Jim Crawford
MAURITZ HUGO .... Pete Lasker
GEORGE J. LEWIS .... .Eagle Cloud
HOLLY BANE .... Jeff
DALE VAN SICKEL .... Brad
MARSHALL REED .... .Deputy
HOUSE PETERS JR .... Courier
and BLACK JACK

ASSOC. PRODUCER .... Gordon Kay
DIRECTED BY .... R. G. Springsteen
WRITTEN BY .... M. Coates Webster
PHOTOGRAPHED BY .... John MacBurnie
MUSIC .... Stanley Wilson

George Keeler, owner of the Stage and Freight Depot of Sonora, attempts to revive the feud between Indians and the white man to help him acquire the gold ore of the Sonora citizens and to acquire their land. His plan begins when he and a henchman murder Chief Blue Feather and steal his sacred tribal belt. The men split up when confronted, resulting in the death of the outlaw with the belt. The belt is sent by courier to Sheriff Jim Crawford of Sonora.

Keeler gets wind of the delivery of the belt and sends some of his gang to intercept the courier. Rocky Lane, on his way to Wyoming to settle down, is alerted to trouble by gunfire. He downs two of the gunmen and prevents the other from stealing the belt. Wounded by his attackers and seconds from death, the courier asks Rocky to deliver the belt to the Indian agent in Sonora.

Awakening from a night's sleep, old Indian scout Nugget Clark spots Rocky, whom he assumes to be the courier, riding into town before daybreak. Rocky takes the belt to the Indian agent and mistakenly gives it to Pete Lasker, a Keeler henchman who has killed the real agent and assumed his identity. Rocky mentions the trouble he encountered and offers to tell the sheriff, but Lasker volunteers to handle the task.

Rocky leaves town as Nugget arrives to find the body of the real agent. Assuming that Rocky is the culprit, Nugget notifies Crawford, who sends a posse

after him. Rocky rides hard to get away and later jumps a deputy from the rocks above. Informed of the situation, Rocky returns to clear himself, but is instead arrested when Nugget identifies him as the man he saw leaving the office. Rocky views the body and tells the sheriff that he gave the belt to someone else. He also suggests that the sheriff ride out of town where he will find the body of the courier and the dead outlaws. Keeler intervenes, claiming to have seen the courier ride in shortly before Rocky that morning.

Eagle Cloud, brother of Chief Blue Feather, arrives to get the belt. Nugget promises the hostile Indian that the belt will be there by sunrise. Fearing trouble from such a promise, Crawford asks Keeler to wire the marshal in Bancroft for additional help. The deceitful man informs him that the wires have been cut, probably by Indians, so Crawford sends a messenger to do the job. The messenger is chased and gunned down by Keeler's men.

After delivering the belt, Lasker prepares to leave town but is spotted by Rocky. Under intense questioning Rocky tells Crawford he will show him where to find the belt. Lasker spots Rocky and takes off. Rocky gives Crawford the slip and chases Lasker. Crawford and Nugget separate in their attempt to get Rocky, who is forced to stop by a wild shooting Nugget.

Rocky tells Nugget that Lasker is the man to whom he gave the belt. Aided by Black Jack, Rocky disarms Nugget but returns his gun to convince him that he can be trusted. They head for Lasker's ranch and are met by gunfire. Rocky shoots Lasker's men and chases him. Lasker runs straight into some hanging vines and strangles to death trying to extricate himself. The somewhat convinced Nugget informs Rocky that Keeler claimed to have seen the courier arrive before him. Believing him to be involved, Rocky and Nugget head for his shop. They discover his men moving out gold ore but are apprehended and held.

The next morning Rocky and Nugget are taken to be killed by henchmen Jeff and Brad, who argue over who gets Rocky's horse after they kill him. The smart animal frees his master as the men argue. Rocky then outdraws Jeff and knocks out Brad.

Rocky and Nugget prevent Eagle Cloud and his braves from attacking the town. Rocky rides into town to get a posse as the Indians follow Nugget to Bedrock Pass where they attack Keeler and the wagon train of stolen ore. As Rocky approaches with the posse, Keeler takes flight. Rocky runs him down and administers a sound thrashing to the villain. Keeler dies when he falls on a knife he had pulled to kill Rocky.

Sheriff Crawford asks Rocky to stay on as Indian agent, but the cowboy leaves for Wyoming after endorsing Nugget, who retorts, "Good man, that Lane. Of course, I knowed he was all along."

SHERIFF OF WICHITA

60 Mins .... Jan. 22, 1949

ALLEN LANE .... "Rocky" Lane
EDDY WALLER .... Nugget Clark
ROY BARCROFT .... Sam Stark
LYN WILDE .... Nancy Bishop
CLAYTON MOORE .... Raymond D'Arcy
EUGENE ROTH .... Howard Thornton
TREVOR BARDETTE .... Ira Flanders
HOUSE PETERS, JR .... Jack Thorpe
EARLE HODGINS .... Jess Jenkins
EDMUND COBB .... Marshal James
JOHN HAMILTON .... Warden
STEVE RAINES .... .Will
JACK O'SHEA. .... Joe
and BLACK JACK

ASSOC. PRODUCER .... Gordon Kay
DIRECTED BY .... R. G. Springsteen
WRITTEN BY. .... Bob Williams
PHOTOGRAPHED BY .... John MacBurnie
MUSIC .... Stanley Wilson

Clayton Moore holds a gun on Roy Barcroft and Gene Roth as Rocky and Nugget frisk them. The scene is from SHERIFF OF WICHITA.

Raymond D'Arcy, court martialed and imprisoned because it is believed that he was involved in the theft of an army payroll of some $25,000, escapes from prison after serving all but two months of a five-year sentence. Jack Thorpe is assigned to the mysterious case which saw D'Arcy escape after receiving a letter from Major Alvin Bishop, the leader of the payroll detachment who vanished after the theft.

Thorpe goes to see Nugget Clark, a civilian scout with the payroll detachment, and trails Nugget after the oldtimer has picked up a letter from Major Alvin Bishop but his not-so-subtle attempt at following Nugget results in him being discovered. Thorpe is replaced by Rocky Lane, the sheriff of Wichita County.

Rocky follows Nugget and manages to gain his confidence when he rescues him from three gun-toting bandits. He then trails him to Fort Borden, a deserted army post, and claims to have come there because he too received a letter from Bishop. As they talk, a human figure obscured by shadows lurks in the darkness.

D'Arcy arrives at the deserted fort and is captured by Rocky, who then reveals himself to be a sheriff sent there to bring him in. A scuffle breaks out, but the lawman prevails in spite of an attempt by Nugget to aid his friend. D'Arcy reveals that he only escaped because of the letter he received, hoping that Bishop would clear him of the unfair charges. The mysterious figure lurking in the shadows watches as Rocky de-

A short time after they leave the fort, Rocky and D'Arcy are shot at by outlaw Sam Stark and his bandits. Stark orders them back to the fort where he reveals that he also has a letter from Bishop. His letter belonged to a friend, Mike Bravers, whose untimely death, actually at the hands of Stark, resulted in his gaining possession of the letter. Bravers, a member of Stark's gang, was a member of the ill-fated detachment.

The still-concealed figure watches as two more members of the detachment arrive: ex-privates Harold Thornton and Ira Flanders. Thornton takes exception to Rocky's presence at the fort and makes the mistake of letting his displeasure be known with swinging fists. Rocky easily bests the outspoken man in a bruising battle.

The group discusses the payroll detachment of five years before, whereupon it is learned that D'Arcy had possession of the money but handed it to Bishop when they were attacked by a gang of outlaws. When D'Arcy awakened after being knocked out, both the money and Bishop were gone. Stark reveals that his men attacked the detachment to steal the payroll money and that he still wants it. He informs all that the fort is surrounded by his men.

The next morning cannon fire awakens the gathering. All run to the Field of Honor where footprints and an indentation left by a cane are found. Rocky looks around after the others walk away and stumbles upon Nancy Bishop, the major's daughter, who reveals that she wrote the letters to hopefully find her father's killer and the culprit who stole the army payroll. Rocky agrees to aid her in her quest if she will write another letter ordering that the culprit confess.

After the letter is received, Flanders panics and runs from the fort forgetting that it is surrounded by Stark's men. He is shot but confesses to Rocky before dying that D'Arcy and Bishop were innocent victims of a plot by him, Thornton, Bravers, and Stark to hijack the money. He goes on to reveal that Thornton knocked D'Arcy out but that no one saw the money or the major after that time.

Rocky and D'Arcy tie up Stark and Thornton at the fort. The outlaws are then drawn in by Rocky's gunfire so that he, D'Arcy, Nugget, and Nancy can escape and head for Little Horse Canyon, the scene of the attack on the payroll detachment.

They arrive at Little Horse Canyon and find marks caused by the major's cane leading to a cave. The payroll and the remains of Bishop are discovered in the cave as Stark and Thornton arrive. Taking Nancy hostage, they trade her for the payroll and flee the scene. Rocky mounts Black Jack and chases the villains. After transferring to their buckboard, Rocky overpowers them in a jaw-breaking fight.

Eugene Roth has just received a violent pummeling from Rocky in SHERIFF OF WICHITA. You'd think Roy Barcroft (right) would learn not to mess with Rocky from watching scenes like this.

Rocky and Gene Roth (billed Eugene in this film) have come to a dramatic facedown in this moment from SHERIFF OF WICHITA.

The War Department reinstates and promotes D'Arcy and gives Nugget a generous reward for his able assistance. Rocky Lane, the sheriff of Wichita, rides away to his next assignment.

DEATH VALLEY GUNFIGHTER

60 Min .... March 29, 1949

ALLAN LANE ...."Rocky" Lane
EDDY WALLER ....Nugget Clark
JIM NOLAN .... Shad Booth
GAIL DAVIS .... Trudy Clark
WILLIAM A. HENRY .... Sheriff Keith Ames
HARRY HARVEY .... Vinson McKnight
MAURITZ HUGO .... Tony Richards
GEORGE CHESEBRO .... Sam
FORREST TAYLOR .... Lester Clark
GEORGE H. LLOYD .... George
LANE BRADFORD .... Snake Richards
and BLACK JACK

ASSOC. PRODUCER .... Gordon Kay
DIRECTED BY .... R. G. Springsteen
WRITTEN BY .... Bob Williams
PHOTOGRAPHED BY .... Ernest Miller
MUSIC .... Stanley Wilson

The Lucky Brothers Mine, run by brothers Nugget and Lester Clark, has been anything but lucky of late as it has been under attack by outlaws determined to gain control of the quicksilver mine. A third brother was killed a year earlier by the marauding bandits. Aware of the recent troubles experienced by the brothers, Sheriff Keith Ames, who is in love with the brother's niece Trudy, guards the payroll brought to the mine. Nugget, who has very little confidence in the sheriff, asks him to leave. Outlaw Shad Booth and his gang rob the mine of its payroll and kill Nugget's brother Lester.

Nugget rides into Panamint Wells to inform Trudy of the death of her uncle. Although the mine was opened to raise money to send her East to study music, Trudy wants Nugget to give up the unlucky mine. Nugget refuses and seeks a loan from banker Vinson McKnight. McKnight, who is secretly in league with Booth, does not want to grant the loan but is called out by the sheriff and Trudy who ask that the loan be made since the townspeople have agreed to back it. The sheriff informs McKnight that he is sending for famous lawman Rocky Lane, known to him only by reputation, to help the town in its time of need.

Shad Booth arrives and expresses displeasure over the granting of the loan because he wants to gain possession of the mine valued at $250,000. Informed by McKnight that Rocky is on the way, Booth sends for Snake Richards, brother of his head henchman Tony Richards, to intercept Rocky and assume his identity since the sheriff has never seen the lawman.

Rocky is attacked on the trail by Snake, but he escapes on his swift horse Black Jack. After tricking Snake, Rocky shoots the hired killer in an exchange of lead and comes out the winner. Rocky finds an unsigned letter on Snake ordering that Rocky be killed. Rocky arrives in Panamint Wells and meets the sheriff and Trudy. He manages to get a job at Nugget's mine so he can secretly help him.

Rocky and Nugget arrive at the bank early the next morning to get the loan proceeds. Rocky is ordered by Nugget to ride back and inform the mine workers that the money is on the way. Rocky is alerted to impending danger when he finds a note in the same handwriting as that found on Snake attached to his saddle bag informing him to stay clear of Nugget on the way to the mine. The note has been placed there by Booth, who not knowing Snake Richards, assumes that Rocky is in fact the now dead killer. Rocky and the sheriff hide outside of town and rout the bandits. Rocky is called upon to save Nugget, who has been thrown from the wagon and dragged by the horses.

Booth and McKnight discuss the bungled attempt caused when the man they presume to be Snake Richards allied himself with the sheriff. Tony arrives and, upon seeing Rocky in town, he informs Booth that he is the real Rocky Lane and not his brother Snake. Aware that the sheriff has never seen Rocky and knows him only by reputation, Booth has Tony tell the sheriff that Rocky is his outlaw brother Snake Richards and that he does not want to be linked with any crime that he commits. The gullible sheriff swallows the bait and finds the note intended for Snake ordering Rocky's death.

Rocky tricks the sheriff and escapes when he learns that the sheriff has informed Tony of the routing of the quicksilver wagons across the desert. Rocky manages to warn Nugget before the bandits strike, but the sheriff arrests Rocky when Nugget tells him that Rocky suggested changing the route. Nugget also tells the sheriff that he saw no outlaws.

Nugget arrives at the bank that night and informs McKnight that a man will be buying his quicksilver in the morning, enabling him to pay off the loan. After Nugget leaves, Booth arranges for Rocky to be broken out of jail and blamed for robbing the bank's safe. Rocky escapes as Booth's men are about to kill him, and he heads back to town.

Rocky frees the sheriff from his bonds and convinces him that he is a lawman. Convinced that Rocky is telling the truth, the sheriff and Nugget join Rocky in preventing Booth and McKnight from robbing the bank's safe. Boothe escapes from Rocky, who manages to out fight him after a brief swap of lead.

With the job now finished and with Nugget exhibiting confidence in the sheriff, Rocky departs to find adventure elsewhere.

Gail Davis and William A. Henry enjoy a lull in the action as Rocky Lane and Eddy Waller look on in DEATH VALLEY GUNFIGHTER.

FRONTIER INVESTIGATOR

60 Mins .... .May 2, 1949

ALLAN LANE .... "Rocky" Lane
EDDY WALLER .... Nugget Clark
ROY BARCROFT .... Flint Fleming
GAIL DAVIS .... Janet Adams
ROBERT EMMETT KEANE .... Erskine Doubleday
CLAYTON MOORE .... Scott Garnett
FRANCIS FORD .... Ed Garnett
CLAIRE WHITNEY. .... Molly Bright
HARRY LAUTER .... Kenny Lane
TOM LONDON .... Jed
GEORGE H. LLOYD .... Milton Leffingwell
MARSHALL REED .... Outlaw
and BLACK JACK

ASSOC. PRODUCER .... Gordon Kay
DIRECTED BY .... Fred C. Brannon
WRITTEN BY .... Bob Williams
PHOTOGRAPHED BY .... Ernest Miller
MUSIC .... Stanley Wilson

Kenny Lane is on his way to see his brother Rocky and purchase a ranch when he is ambushed and robbed some ten miles short of his destination. The not-yet-dead youngster is discovered by Jed who is informed that Kenny's attacker had a rifle with a spy glass—a telescopic lens—on its barrel. An exuberant Rocky is reading a letter telling of his brother's pending arrival when Jed arrives with his body.

A dejected Rocky heads for Flagstaff, Arizona, the site of his brother's departure, to begin his search for his brother's killer. Rocky has no luck in Flagstaff, Prescott, or Phoenix and is off again when he is diverted by masked outlaws firing on a stage driven by Nugget Clark. Rocky drives the outlaws off and drives the wounded Nugget into town. Nugget offers Rocky a job with his stageline since he has had much trouble with outlaws recently but is turned down. About to head for Tuscon, Rocky is jumped by two men but holds his own in the unfair fight. A third man joins the fray and clubs Lane with his rifle before ordering that he stay away from the Square Nugget Stage Lines. Rocky comes to and discovers that his search has ended as the rifle with which he was hit bore a sight, which came off when he was hit.

Rocky checks into Molly Bright's Boarding House and informs Nugget that he has reconsidered and will accept the job offer. Rocky is introduduced to roomers Erskine Doubleday and Milton Leffingwell. Ed Garnett, owner of a stage line in competition with Nugget, is also a roomer at the boarding house. Garnett, who has been accused by Nugget of attacking his stages, is shown the telescopic lens by Rocky but says he knows nothing about it, nor does Scott, Garrett's son.

The next morning Doubleday pays a visit to town blacksmith Flint Fleming, the man who robbed and killed Rocky's brother. Doubleday, who made the telescope lens for Fleming, informs him that he is aware of his recent nefarious deeds but will remain quiet for $1000. Fleming reluctantly forks over the cash with the understanding that Doubleday will be named as an accomplice if he is apprehended. He also instructs his blacksmith friend to make him another telescopic lens, and to learn of shipments of the Garnett stage line.

Fleming and his masked accomplices attack the Garnett Stage the next morning after a tip from Doubleday. During the robbery, one of the gunmen informs Garnett that they were paid by Nugget to attack his stage. Garnett returns to town and confronts his competitor. He tries to get Nugget to sign a confession, but Rocky and Scott enter with both agreeing that if Nugget was behind it, why would they say so.

After picking up a package from Tucson, Doubleday goes to see Garnett and informs him that he is interested in investing money in his stage line for 10% of the line. He urges Garnett to take the bank draft he has given him to Tucson to be cashed. After Garnett departs, Doubleday informs Fleming that the old man is headed for Tucson. The blacksmith forges Garnett's signature to a note sent to Rocky and Scott in which he claims to know who killed the stage guard for the Garnett line in the previous holdup. Fleming then wires a telegram to Garnett in care of the Tucson Bank with the same information but has Rocky's name to it. Fleming ambushes Garnett on the way back and robs him of the money.

Rocky rides into town and is shot by Scott, who feels he wounded his father. With the Sheriff and Scott hunting for him, Rocky is on the run, but slips in to see Garnett under darkness of night. Rocky informs him that he didn't shoot and kill his guard nor him. He then learns from Garnett that the money which was stolen from him was a draft he had cashed. Rocky is also told that Doubleday now takes control of the stage line since he lost the money the watchmaker had invested. The Sheriff and Scott ride up causing Rocky to flee.

The next morning a race is to take place between the rival stage lines with the winner to receive a valuable mail contract. After Rocky tells Nugget that he believes the man behind the stage troubles and his brother's killer are one and the same, he corners Doubleday and orders him to ride inside Nugget's stage. The reluctant Doubleday agrees but panics as they near Suicide Band, the point at which Fleming is to attempt an ambush. Doubleday confesses and implicates Fleming. Rocky jumps from the stage onto Black Jack and follows Fleming to town. The blacksmith is trailed to his shop and beaten from pillar to post by Rocky before being slain after failing to outdraw his adversary. Having avenged his brother's death, Rocky then breaks the rifle with the telescopic lens.

Allan Lane and Clayton Moore in a scene from FRONTIER INVESTIGATOR.

THE WYOMING BANDIT

60 Min .... July 15, 1949

ALLAN LANE .... "Rocky" Lane
EDDY WALLER .... Nugget Clark
TREVOR BARDETTE .... Wyoming Dan
VICTOR KILLIAN .... Ross Tyler
RAND BROOKS .... Jim Howard
WILLIAM HAADE .... .Lonnegan
HAROLD GOODWIN .... Sheriff
LANE BRADFORD .... .Buck
BOB WILKE .... Sam
JOHN HAMILTON .... U.S. Marshal
EDMUND COBB .... Deputy Marshal
and BLACK JACK

ASSOC. PRODUCER .... Gordon Kay
DIRECTED BY .... Philip Ford
WRITTEN BY .... M. Coates Webster
PHOTOGRAPHED BY .... John MacBurnie
MUSIC .... Stanley Wilson

The town of Dry Wells has recently been the scene of many violent attacks and killings. On the watch for future problems, a deputy marshal spots the theft of a horse taking place. He gives chase but loses his quarry and returns to the scene of the crime. The man from whom the horse was taken identifies the bandit as Wyoming Dan, a bandit known for carrying his gun in his left hand.

Rocky Lane is dispatched by a U.S. Marshal to Dry Wells to bring Dan to justice. On his way there, Rocky spots the holdup of a stage by masked outlaws. The bandits gunfire causes driver Nugget Clark to lose control of the stage resulting in the need for Rocky to save him. In the wrong place at the wrong time is Wyoming Dan, who is spotted and apprehended by Rocky and blamed for the shooting of Nugget's Stage guard. Dan is innocent of the shooting; the guard was his son Tom.

The trio take a badly wounded Tom to Nugget's ranch where he later dies. Nugget has raised Tom and his brother Jimmy from kids with neither knowing their father to be the infamous Wyoming Dan. Dan confesses to having returned because he heard the area was beset by bad men, one of whom is Lonnegan, a former partner in crime. Dan believes him to be involved in the town's troubles, but feels that he is not the boss. He vows to get the man who killed his son after which he will turn himself in. Convinced that he is sincere, Rocky allows him to hide when the sheriff rides up and agrees to help him if he does not try to escape.

Rocky goes to town to look around and asks Ross Tyler, the town saddlemaker, if he knows anything about a gentleman named Lonnegan. Tyler, the man secretly behind the lawless element in the area, tells Rocky no, only to have his head henchmen come out of a back office when Rocky departs. Tyler orders Lonnegan to follow and eliminate Rocky. The hunter becomes the hunted as Rocky gives him the slip and captures him. He informs Lonnegan that his old friend Wyoming Dan wants to see him and that he and Dan want to join him because they are aware of a $50,000 currency shipment coming through. He advises the henchman to tell his boss that he and Dan plan to operate in this area.

Lonnegan passes the information along to his boss Tyler, who informs the sheriff of Dan's presence in the way. Nugget joins the posse to bring Dan in. The smart oldtimer alerts Dan and Rocky to the posse's presence by discharging a shot once near their cabin. They manage to escape and, figuring that Lonnegan alerted the sheriff, they hold up the currency shipment. Lonnegan and his men arrive and chase them, but a clever ruse permits them to escape. The holdup is a success except that Jimmy, the lone passenger on the stage, is told by the sheriff that one of the robbers was Wyoming Dan, the man he suspects of having killed his brother.

Tyler orders Lonnegan to get the money so that he can buy up the notes of the ranchers, but when Lonnegan and henchmen Buck and Sam meet with Rocky, they are told by him that he will do business only with their boss. Rocky and Dan chase Jimmy, and once they catch the young man, Rocky identifies himself as a marshal. He also tells Jimmy that Wyoming Dan, his father, did not kill his brother Tom. Before pretending to kill Jimmy for the benefit of Lonnegan, Rocky instructs him to have Nugget tell the sheriff to meet him at Willow Creek. After delivering the message to Nugget and having Rocky's story about Dan confirmed by Nugget, Jimmy straps on a gun to help out.

Rocky and Dan meet with Tyler and discuss splitting the take, but Tyler sees the presumed dead Jimmy ride into town. Threatening to gun Jimmy down, Tyler is told by Dan that Jimmy is his son. Rocky tells

Tyler that the money is at Nugget's, whereupon he and Dan are tied up by the departing boss and Lonnegan. Jimmy spots Black Jack outside Tyler's shop and goes in to free his father and Rocky. Rocky heads for Nugget's to stop Tyler and Lonnegan and once there, beats Lonnegan in a fight. Dan arrives and shoots Tyler to prevent him from shooting Rocky. Tyler's death has broken Dan's long-standing rule never to shoot to kill.

Wyoming Dan, having avenged the death of his son, Tom, prepares to disappear across the border when informed by Rocky that he has been pardoned by the governor. Dan settles down at Nugget's while Rocky rides away to further adventures.

BANDIT KING OF TEXAS

60 Mins .... August 29, 1949

ALLAN LANE .... "Rocky" Lane
EDDY WALLER .... Nugget Clark
HELENE STANLEY .... Cynthia Turner
JIM NOLAN. .... Dan McCabe
HARRY LAUTER .... Tremm Turner
ROBERT BICE .... Gus
JOHN HAMILTON .... Marshal John Turner
LANE BRADFORD .... Cal Barker
GEORGE H. LLOYD .... Fats Dobson
STEVE CLARK .... Tom Samson
I. STANFORD JOLLEY .... Willets
DANNI NOLAN .... Emily Baldwin
RICHARD EMORY .... Jim Baldwin
and BLACK JACK

ASSOC. PRODUCER .... Gordon Kay
DIRECTED BY .... Fred C. Brannon
WRITTEN BY .... Olive Cooper
PHOTOGRAPHED BY .... John MacBurnie
MUSIC .... Stanley Wilson

Jim and Emily Baldwin, a homesteading couple, head for the town of Elko when they, like many before, are attacked by the masked marauders. Jim is shot and the wagon wreck kills Emily. One bandit, Gus, removes a brooch from Emily and takes it to his boss Dan McCabe, head of the Jewell Land Co., an organization which sells free government property to homesteaders. Once the homesteaders near Elko, McCabe's men kill and rob them. The homesteaders that manage to get through are given phony deeds and later ambushed.

Rocky Lane is on his way to Elko to meet Jim and Emily when gunshots alert him to trouble. A wagon of homesteaders is being shot at by McCabe's men, but it's Rocky to the rescue as the outlaws are sent packing. Rocky is thanked by the homesteaders, U.S. Marshal John Turner, his son Tremm, and Tremm's new bride, Cynthia. Rocky rides on to town with Tremm to pay for their new property.

They arrive in town and are spotted by McCabe, who is not worried about this group as Tremm is a former partner in crime. Rocky pays the money to claim clerk Fats Dodson and is given a deed. While there, Rocky asks for and is given information concerning the Baldwin's land.

Rocky rides back to meet the marshal and Cynthia, but is assaulted by masked men along the way. He pulls the mask from Cal Baker but is hit from behind by one of his accomplices. They steal the deeds and prepare to shoot Rocky, but Black Jack saves his master. Rocky finds Marshal Turner and tells him of his misfortunes.

Marshal Turner returns to town with Rocky but doubts him when the claim clerk, a different man who purports to be the only one who handles claims, knows nothing of Rocky and shows that no deeds have been issued to him for the Turners or to the Baldwins that he claims to know. About to be jailed, Rocky spots Cal Barker, the bandit he unmasked, and chases him down. Marshal Turner and Tremm arrive at the end of a fight between Rocky and Barker. The marshal decides to jail both men.

McCabe discusses Barker's fate with Gus as Tremm arrives. McCabe threatens to reveal Tremm's tainted past to his father if he does not help free Barker. Tremm agrees when McCabe threatens to kill his father. Tremm and Cynthia arrive at the jail as Nugget Clark proclaims Rocky's innocence. Failing to relieve his father, Tremm takes the key to the back door of the jail.

Gus breaks Barker out of jail (and Rocky too) in an attempt to silence him. Nugget manages to get Black Jack to Rocky, enabling him to get away. Pursued by his rescuers, Rocky rides hard to dodge their bullets. He later returns to thank Nugget. Nugget tells Rocky that he believes him innocent and shows him a brooch given him by McCabe to make into a tie pin. The brooch was a gift from Rocky to Emily. They discuss Tremm's presumed participation in the jail break, and Rocky asks Nugget to tell him that McCabe wants to see him.

Tremm is anxious to see McCabe because he feels he is responsible for his father being wounded. Rocky and Nugget intercept Tremm on his way to visit

McCabe. Tremm informs them that McCabe holds a murder charge over his head. They promise to help get McCabe, with the first step being a search of the land office. The search turns up a map indicating that McCabe is selling free government land.

At Rocky's insistence, Tremm informs McCabe that he is leaving town, but he demands a cut of the take from the group of homesteaders on their way to claim their land. McCabe agrees, but plans to cross Tremm.

Tom Samson is given the deeds by Dodson, but turns them over to Tremm, who gives them to Rocky along with the money he was given as his share. Nugget is given the deeds and hides them in a cigar box in the store. Cynthia arrives, spots Rocky, and tells McCabe, Gus, and Barker of his presence. Rocky is apprehended but escapes.

The bandits attack, but Rocky arrives to help run them off. McCabe escapes but is caught by Rocky, who pounds him into submission.

Invited to stay by his new-found friends, Rocky, nevertheless, moves on but not before presenting Cynthia with the brooch that had once belonged to his friend Emily.

NAVAJO TRAIL RAIDERS

60 Mins .... Oct. 15, 1949

ALLAN LANE .... "Rocky" Lane
EDDY WALLER .... Nugget Clark
ROBERT EMMETT KEANE .... John Blanford
BARBARA BESTAR .... Judy Clark
HAL LANDON .... Tom Stanley
DICK CURTIS .... Brad
DENNIS MOORE .... Frank Stanley
TED ADAMS .... Sheriff Robbins
FORREST TAYLOR .... .Sam Byrnes
MARSHALL REED .... Jed
STEVE CLARK .... Larkin
and BLACK JACK

ASSOC. PRODUCER .... Gordon Kay
DIRECTED BY .... R.G. Springsteen
WRITTEN BY .... M. Coates Webster
PHOTOGRAPHED BY .... John MacBurnie
MUSIC .... Stanley Wilson

The town of Yellow Creek is experiencing trouble with outlaws raiding their freight wagons. The towns-people are on the verge of bankruptcy when Nugget Clark, owner of the Yellow Creek Freight Line, and Tom

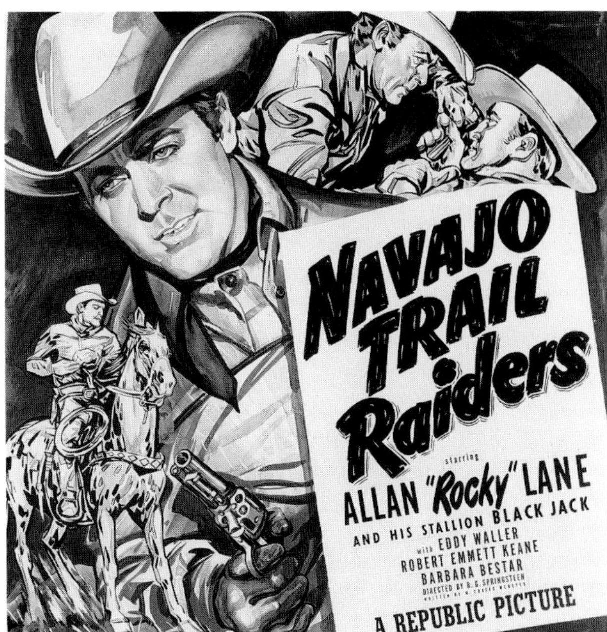

Stanley suggest that everyone pool incoming insurance monies due from their loses to help save the town. Since most believe that the bandits will hijack the incoming money, Tom advocates a plan whereby Nugget, who is going to get his own money, will be told by the insurance company the secret route by which the remainder of the money is to be brought.

Nugget picks up the money and is on the way back to Yellow Creek when bandits attack. Deputy Marshal Rocky Lane is enroute to Yellow Creek for the wedding of his friend Tom when he spots the old-timer having trouble. Rocky drives the bandits off and escorts Nugget into town.

Upon their arrival, Tom is given Nugget's money to put in the safe. Tom's outlaw brother Frank arrives and demands the money to keep quiet about Tom's time in prison for a stage holdup. Rocky arrives, but not before Frank has stolen Nugget's money and Tom's valuable watch. After hearing his friend's confession, Rocky suggests that Tom publicly confess so he can end Frank's blackmailing.

Frank shows up the next day for more money, but is turned down. Tom vows to confess his misdoings as he leaves to meet the messenger bringing news of the secret route. Undaunted, Frank goes to John Blanford, editor of the *Yellow Creek Star* and leader of the outway raids, and offers to sell a story concerning Tom. He tells Blanford that the money he has was given to him by Tom to learn the secret route. Seeing a way to further his plans, Blanford accepts Frank's offer and informs Nugget and the sheriff of Tom's past.

Blanford's men intercept the messenger and

Action was the hallmark of the Allan "Rocky" Lane films. These two shots from NAVAJO TRAIL RAIDERS show some of that action.

Eddy Waller was the perfect sidekick for the usually sober-sided Rocky Lane. Eddy as Nugget Clark could provide gently humorous scenes (he wasn't much for slapstick) or he could get involved with the action in a serious and believable manner.

split up when Rocky and Tom chase them off. Rocky rides after the men and manages to catch Jed while Tom remains at the side of the wounded messenger. The sheriff, seeing Tom standing over the messenger, begins to believe the allegations leveled against him and takes him to jail.

Rocky arrives in town with Jed in tow and turns him over to the sheriff. The sheriff questions Jed who is coerced by Blanford to name his co-conspirator. Jed names Tom as the man who paid him to kill the messenger. Rocky remains quiet so that he can investigate the case.

Frank goes to Blanford and, although already paid, offers to sell the message about the secret route for $25,000. Blanford refuses and orders Brad to follow Frank and take the watch in which the message has been hidden. Brad kills Frank, but Rocky gets to the watch first. Presumed by the sheriff to have killed Frank, Rocky becomes a wanted man.

Rocky sneaks back into town that night to talk to Nugget and a jailed Tom. Before leaving to prevent the sending of the insurance money, Rocky gives the watch to Tom after learning it belongs to him. Blanford arrives after Rocky departs and accuses Nugget of aiding the wanted man. To justify his actions, Nugget tells Blanford that Rocky is on his way to the insurance company.

Brad is dispatched to stop Rocky and succeeds. Rocky is tied up in a cave and beaten mercilessly by Brad as Blanford, hidden by the shadows, encourages the ruffian to find out where the watch is. Rocky is cut loose and taken to be killed but escapes after hearing that the message with the secret route is in the watch.

Blanford beats Rocky to town and frees Jed and Tom. After getting the watch, he plans to use Tom to help get the money and then kill him.

After alerting Nugget to his suspicions about Blanford, Rocky enlists his aid in a search of the newspaper office. The empty watch is found, so Rocky keeps an eye on Blanford and trails him the next morning after instructing Nugget to get the sheriff.

Rocky finds Tom being used to stop the stage carrying the money and trades gunfire with his captors. The posse arrives to rout the bandits as Rocky chases Blanford and Brad to the cave in which he was brutally beaten. Rocky avenges the earlier beating by besting Brad in a punishing brawl. Nugget arrives just in time to gun down Blanford, who is about to shoot Rocky. Tom and Nugget's niece Judy can now prepare for their wedding because Rocky, the best man, has ended the reign of the Navajo Trail Raiders.

POWDER RIVER RUSTLERS

60 Mins .... Nov. 25, 1949

ROY BARCROFT .... Bull Macons
FRANCIS MCDONALD .... Shears Williams
CLIFF CLARK .... Lucius Statton
DOUGLAS EVANS .... Devereaux
BRUCE EDWARDS .... Bob Manning
CLARENCE STRAIGHT .... Telegraph Operator
TED JACQUES .... Blacksmith
TOM MONROE .... Guard
STANLEY BLYSTONE .... Rancher
and BLACK JACK

ASSOC PRODUCER .... Gordon Kay
DIRECTED BY .... Philip Ford
WRITTEN BY .... Richard Wormser
PHOTOGRAPHED BY .... John MacBurnie
MUSIC .... Stanley Wilson

Nugget Clark, the tall-tale-telling old-timer of El Dorado, is driving the stage to town when he spots a holdup. He gives chase to help but loses control of the stage and is thrown off. Railroad agent Rocky Lane, on his way to El Dorado to meet friend and co-worker Bob Manning, spots the troubled Nugget and helps him out. Nugget exaggerates when he tells Rocky what happened, so the railroad agent is unconcerned after having heard no shots.

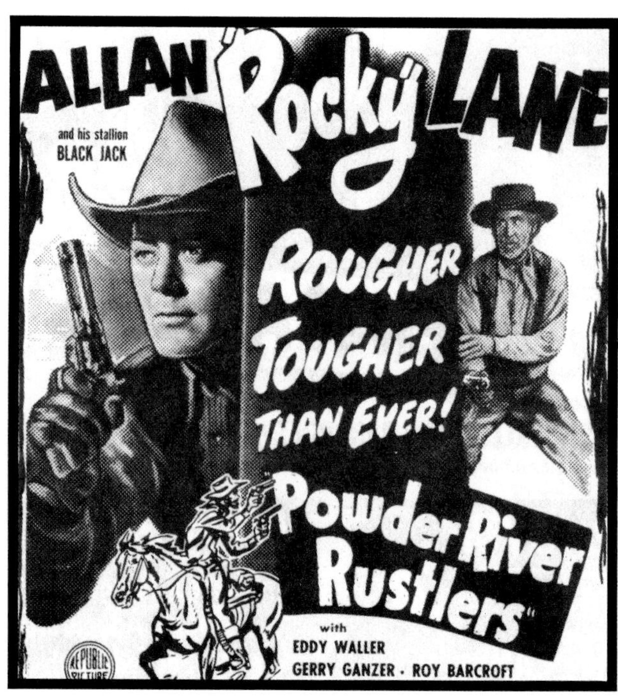

Nugget arrives in town and advocates the forming of a posse to search for the man that the outlaws kidnapped. He describes the buckboard and all details to the gathering who doubt him when the buckboard arrives intact. Devereaux, an actor hired to play the role of Bob Manning,refuses Nugget's claim, but Rocky knows the man is an imposter since Bob is a personal friend. The phony railroad man tells the gathering that they must raise and turn over to him within three days, $50,000, half the money needed to build the railroad.

A suspicious Rocky rides out to question Nugget who has left town for his shack. Rocky is called upon to save the old-timer again when he is dragged by his horse after being shot at. Rocky questions Nugget about his attacker and is told that he put six slugs in the assassin. After Rocky finds Nugget's gun full, Nugget tells him that he is fast on the reload and to wait and see who will be buried the next day.

Rocky identifies himself and tells Nugget he believes him. To find out if Bob is still alive, Rocky sends a telegram to him at the El Dorado telegraph office. An answer to the cleverly worded telegram will indicate that Bob is okay and alert him that Rocky is on the case.

Nugget gives the telegram to Deveraux, the man claiming to be Bob, and is told that he will answer later. Deveraux asks his boss, local tailor Shears Williams, what he should do, and is told that Bull Macons, a Shears henchman, will get the answer from Bob and bring it back.

Rocky trails Macons but loses him when Nugget rides up to tell him that the telegrapher revealed to him that Bob's wife is on the way. Fearing that she will be harmed, Rocky and Nugget intercept the stage. Rocky identifies himself to Louise and stage driver Lucius Statton before rigging a dummy to take Louise's place and driving off. The killers attack the stage and drive it off a steep embankment. Rocky rides back and instructs Statton, who is also town deputy, to advise Deveraux of Louise's death but to say no more.

Rocky rides into town after taking Louise to Nugget's. He advises Statton to wire the sheriff in Helmut for help and prepares to leave to meet him when Statton gives Rocky the monies collected to prevent it being stolen. Shears spots the departing Rocky and questions Statton. Believing that he can trust Shears, Statton tells all and is knifed in the back. Shears implicates Rocky.

Rocky arrives to meet the sheriff but finds two imposters. He trades punches with the henchmen and then departs for Nugget's.

Nugget learns that Rocky is being hunted and informs the townsfolk that he is innocent. Doubted as usual, Nugget tells Louise who comes out of hiding to help Rocky. She informs Shears of Rocky's innocence but is captured and taken to the hideout.

At Nugget's, Rocky finds that he must hit the trail again as Louise has left for town. He confronts Deveraux and obtains a confession. Shears knifes him but not before he has revealed where the Mannings are hidden.

Through a clever ruse, Rocky and Nugget free the Mannings. The ruse is discovered and a violent exchange of gunfire results. Rocky, Nugget, and Bob gain the upper hand before Rocky takes off after Shears and Macons.

At the tailor's shop, a donnybrook takes place in which Rocky is stabbed in the shoulder by Macons. Rocky out-fights the roughneck before Shears succumbs to a well-placed bullet.

With the violence and bloodshed over now, Rocky goes South for new adventures.

GUNMEN OF ABILENE

60 Mins .... Feb. 6, 1950

ALLAN LANE .... "Rocky" Lane
EDDY WALLER .... Nugget Clark
ROY BARCROFT .... Brink Fallen
DONNA HAMILTON .... Mary Clark
PETER BROCCO .... Henery Turner
SELMER JACKSON .... Dr. Johnson
DUNCAN RICHARDSON .... Dickie
ARTHUR WALSH .... Tim Johnson
DON HARVEY .... Todd
DON DILLAWAY .... Bill Harper
GEORGE CHESEBRO .... Martin
STEVE CLARK .... Wells
and BLACK JACK

ASSOC PRODUCER .... Gordon Kay
DIRECTED BY .... Fred C. Brannon
WRITTEN BY .... M. Coates Webster
PHOTOGRAPHED BY .... Ellis W. Carter
MUSIC .... Stanley Wilson

The town of Blue Valley has recently experienced a reign of terror the likes of which it has never seen. The town, unknown to its citizens except store owner Henry Turner, is situated above a rich gold vein. Turner plans to get the riches and has hired outlaw

Brink Fallon and his men to help him.

Nugget Clark, sheriff of Blue Valley for some twenty years, does what he can to combat lawlessness, but since he falls short of the town's needs, Deputy Marshal Rocky Lane is sent to help at the request of the citizens.

Dr. Johnson is returning on the stage after a trip to acquire help for the town when the stage is attacked. Nugget's son Jim and grandson Dickie are on board the stage. In earshot of the trouble and on the way to Blue Valley, Rocky rides down the outlaws and chases them off with the aid of his six-guns.

The doctor tries to save Nugget's son but fails. Not wanting to hurt Nugget's feelings, Rocky remains incognito with only Dr. Johnson aware of his identity. He turns over his badge and papers to the doctor and asks that he keep his identity a secret. Nugget's niece Mary overhears the discussion but also feels it best to keep Rocky's identity a secret.

Rocky manages to hire on as Nugget's deputy and learns that freight wagons heading into or out of town have been attacked. Rocky and Nugget ride out to check on incoming wagons and find trouble. The driver of the wagon they stop is most unruly. As they question him, Brink and his men ride up shooting, allowing the freight driver to escape. Rocky takes a sample of a substance he retrieved from the wagon to Dr. Johnson for analysis.

The doctor takes the substance to Turner's store as he prepares to buy testing equipment. Turner sends Brink to kill Johnson to prevent him from discovering that the substance is blasting powder they use in the abandoned mine which leads into town. The doctor is killed by Turner's henchman Todd. Turner is given Rocky's papers by Brink, who has found them on the doctor.

Rocky takes Todd to jail but Tim, Dr. Johnson's son, tries to kill his father's murderer. After questioning the prisoner and getting nothing, Nugget is convinced by Rocky to allow him to escape so they might trail him. The plan works until Tim, who alerts Turner of the escape, trails Todd and wounds him. Rocky ropes Tim from his horse, but Todd escapes into the mine fields.

Convinced that the escape was planned, Turner gives Rocky's badge and papers to Brink, who is to masquerade as the marshal. Brink arrives and spots Rocky, and in an effort to discredit him, identifies him as a criminal wanted for murder. Rocky escapes on Black Jack.

Rocky returns to find a dejected Nugget writing a farewell letter to his grandson. He informs Nugget that Brink is lying and tries to encourage him to stay. Nugget agrees to stay. Tim arrives and pulls a gun on Rocky. Since Mary is aware of Rocky's true identity, she reveals it to save him. Tim confides that Turner suggested that he look for Todd at the mine fields. Nugget then recalls that Brink, the man claiming to be the new marshal, rode into town earlier looking for Turner. They devise a plan to expose the crooks.

Tim goes to Turner's and informs him that he just saw Brink headed for the mine. Figuring that Turner will head there, Rocky follows him while Nugget tries to distract Brink, who is really in town. Nugget fails and Brink follows Rocky. Rocky arrives and gets the drop on Turner and Todd only to find himself captured by Brink. Turner orders Brink's men to ride in and shoot up the town and tells Brink to ask the citizens to leave until Rocky and his gang are run out of town. Turner plans to eliminate the citizens as they get to Rainbow Ridge, thus allowing him and his men easy access to the rich vein of gold.

Nugget heads for the mine field and spots Black Jack. The brilliant equine shows Nugget the entrance to the mine. Nugget helps Rocky escape, and they ride to prevent Turner and his cronies from dynamiting the fleeing townsfolk. They succeed in preventing the people from being killed but are spotted by Turner and his men. Dynamite is hurled to kill them, but Rocky trounces Brink in a fight atop a cliff. Turner falls with a stick of dynamite in hand causing a land slide which buries his men. With Nugget still unaware that Rocky was sent to replace him, he remains the sheriff and Rocky moves on.

CODE OF THE SILVER SAGE

60 Mins .... March 25, 1950

ALLAN LANE. .... "Rocky" Lane
EDDY WALLER .... Nugget Clark
ROY BARCROFT .... Hulon S. Champion
KAY CHRISTOPHER .... .Ann Gately
LANE BRADFORD .... Curt Watson
WILLIAM RUHL .... Major Duncan
RICHARD EMORY .... Lieut. John Case
KENNE DUNCAN .... Dick Cantwell
HANK PATTERSON .... Sgt. Woods
JOHN BUTLER .... Charlie Speed
FORREST TAYLOR .... Sandy Wheeler
and BLACK JACK

ASSOC. PRODUCER .... Gordon Kay
DIRECTED BY .... Fred C. Brannon
WRITTEN BY .... Arthur E. Orloff
PHOTOGRAPHED BY .... John MacBurnie
MUSIC .... Stanley Wilson

Eddy Waller and Allan Lane

Fred Gately, editor of the *Bolton City News,* makes a public appeal in the paper for the President to come to Arizona, a state terrorized by killers and plunderers. Gately's crusade causes his death at the hands of the killers, who are secretly led by Hulon S. Champion, gun salesman. Nugget Clark and Gately's daughter Ann carry on and print news that the President has accepted the invitation and that Duncan will bring details by stage.

The outlaws attack the stage after being forewarned by Charlie Speed, a worker in the newspaper office. Lieutenant Rocky Lane of U.S. Cavalry Intelligence is in the vicinity and captures one of the bandits after running off his partners. Rocky arrives in Bolton City but finds no sheriff to take his prisoner. Major Duncan asks Nugget Clark if Lieutenant John Case has arrived yet with supply wagons. Nugget is glad to hear that Case, known to him for many years, is on the way. Case is bringing in secret news of the President's arrival. Rocky is granted permission to ride out and meet his longtime friend. Champion henchman Curt Watson is sent to investigate the incoming wagons, since Champion, a ten year army veteran, knows of no army detachment in the area.

Dick Cantwell is given forged orders to take to Case announcing that he is to relieve him. Cantwell waits until Case leaves and requests that all firearms be brought to him for inspection. Case is intercepted and searched by Champion and Watson who knock him out, steal his orders, and substitute fake orders. Gunfire signals the extermination of Case's men but alerts Rocky to trouble.

Rocky questions his friend and returns to town with him. Major Duncan checks a personnel list and finds no Lieut. Cantwell. Case, still in possession of his orders, is arrested but is released on his own recognizance. The orders request that Duncan go to Fort Crain to receive a map of the presidential route from a Captain Mathews, but Rocky goes instead. He arrives at the deserted fort and is met by Cantwell pretending to be Mathews. Rocky asks for identification and is given a card which arouses his suspicion. He is then set upon by Cantwell and a hidden Watson. The attack ends when Nugget rides up and chases the men off. The real Mathews arrives and delivers the map.

Rocky takes the card to town and finds that the printing matches that on the envelope that Case brought in earlier. Charlie Speed is implicated and is about to tell all when he is cut down by a bullet from Watson's gun. Rocky chases Watson and brings him back. Champion arrives and offers to examine the bullet removed from the dead man for comparison with those in Watson's gun. His phony analysis exonerates Watson, but the henchman is held because of the Fort Crain incident. Watson implicates Case as the man who ordered him to Fort Cain.

Rocky learns from Ann that she saw Champion moments before the death of Speed. Rocky and Nugget search Champion's shop and find the manner in which he dispenses with his cigarettes, a manner common to a service man. They find the makings of a bomb and the type bullets with which Speed was killed, a type Champion claimed that he did not sell.

Gunfire ends the search as Champion has Cantwell and others break Watson and Case out of jail. Rocky and Nugget give chase while Duncan, who was wounded in the battle, reveals the presidential route to Champion and asks that he find Rocky and Nugget and give it to them. When they return and are told that Champion was given the route, they ride off to intercept the presidential party. They discover that Champion plans to assassinate the President but manage to help his stage blast its way through the waiting gunmen.

Rocky chases Champion back to his shop. A wild slugfest takes place before Champion becomes impaled on a sword with which he threatened Rocky.

With the death of Champion signaling an end to the terrorism in Arizona and the exoneration of Lieutenant Case, Rocky leaves a now peaceful Bolton City.

"ROCKY" DEALS JUSTICE WITH A FLAMING SIX-GUN!
ALLAN
Rocky
LANE
and his stallion
BLACK JACK!
SALT LAKE RAIDERS
with
EDDY WALLER · ROY BARCROFT · MARTHA HYER

SALT LAKE RAIDERS

60 Mins .... .May 1, 1950

ALLAN LANE .... "Rocky" Lane
EDDY WALLER .... Nugget Clark
ROY BARCROFT. .... Britt Condor
MARTHA HYER .... Helen Thornton
BYRON FOULGER .... John Sutton
MYRON HEALEY .... Fred Mason
CLIFTON YOUNG. .... Luke Condor
STANLEY ANDREWS .... .U.S. Marshal
RORY MALLISON .... Sheriff
KENNETH MACDONALD .... Deputy Marshal
GEORGE CHESEBRO .... Stage Driver
and BLACK JACK

ASSOC. PRODUCER. .... Gordon Kay
DIRECTED BY .... Fred C. Brannon
WRITTEN BY .... M. Coates Webster
PHOTOGRAPHED BY .... John MacBurnie
MUSIC .... Stanley Wilson

Fred Mason, a man imprisoned for the murder of Silver City banker John Thornton and the theft of $100,000 from his bank, escapes to freedom when the wagon in which he and other prisoners are riding wrecks. The wagon is enroute to a new prison when it is attacked by gun-wielding masked men. Mason, who is actually innocent of the crimes for which he has served six years, heads for Silver City to hopefully clear himself but stops for a fresh horse at the Overland Stage Relay Station run by his friend Nugget Clark.

Rocky Lane is hot on the trail of Mason and arrives at the relay station shortly after the escapee's departure. Rocky gains little information from Nugget, a Mason Sympathizer, but Nugget's ward Helen Thornton, the deceased banker's daughter, has little good to say of the man with whom she grew up. Rocky finds Mason in Silver City, now a ghost town, and prepares to take him back. Suddenly, Mason and Nugget (who has followed Rocky there) are fired upon from all sides.

Britt Condor and his brother Luke are responsible for preventing the departure of the men as well as the attack of the prison wagon. The Condors and their outlaw gang are searching for the missing $100,000 and promise to gun down anyone who tries to leave. Although very much aware that Rocky is a lawman, Mason refuses to reveal this fact to the Condors, thus sparing his life. Rocky convinces Britt to allow Nugget to leave to meet an incoming stage at the relay station to prevent Helen from becoming suspicious of his absence. Britt allows the old-timer to go but sends his brother Luke along to bring him back.

After slipping a message to the stage driver at the relay station, Nugget returns but is about to be eliminated by Luke who no longer feels it necessary to allow him to live. Rocky intervenes and prevents Nugget's demise by besting Luke and another outlaw in a fight. Rocky, Mason and Nugget begin a search for the missing money but are stopped when John Sutton, former attorney in Silver City, arrives hoping to find the money too. Rocky and friends overhear Sutton and Britt talk of their allegiance six years ago.

The ghost town gets crowded as Helen arrives. Helen is upset to find Mason there and attempts to shoot the man she suspects of killing her father. Rocky stops her and learns through questioning her that her father sent for Sutton, Mason, and the sheriff before he was killed. Sutton arrives to make an attempt at killing Mason but is foiled by Rocky, who accuses him of murdering Thornton and shifting the blame to Mason. Sutton confesses to having killed Thornton during a struggle for the possession of a gun. Sutton is then bound and gagged.

A diligent search is made by Rocky to find the money before sunrise. He succeeds but is heard telling Nugget of the discovery by Sutton, who also learns of the posse due to arrive at the relay station soon. Nugget is about to be permitted to leave to meet another incoming stage when Helen's presence is discovered and Sutton is found and untied. Threatening to harm Helen, Britt gives Rocky and his associates ten minutes to come up with the money.

An unlucky Sutton tries to escape but is gunned down by the Condor gang. Rocky, Nugget, Helen, and Mason have better luck as they are able to get away even though chased by Luke and his gun-toting partners. The arrival of the posse from nearby Overton spells defeat for the Condor gang, but Luke manages to escape.

Rocky chases Luke back to Silver City and captures him. Using Luke as a shield to draw out his brother, Rocky is shocked when the elder Condor, a man who asks or grants no quarter, guns down his own brother to prevent capture. Once his shells are spent, Britt is cornered by Rocky and topped in a vicious slugfest.

Britt Condor is sent to prison and Mason is vindicated. Amidst news that the town of Silver City is about to experience a rebirth, Mason is made president of Thornton's bank, and he and Helen announce their impending engagement.

COVERED WAGON RAID

60 Mins .... June 30, 1950

ALLAN LANE .... "Rocky Lane"
EDDY WALLER .... Nuggett Clark
ALEX GERRY ....Harvey Grimes
LYN THOMAS .... Gail Warren
BYRON BARR .... Roy Chandler
DICK CURTIS .... Grif Landers
PIERCE LYDEN ....Brag
SHERRY JACKSON .... Susie
REX LEASE .... Bob Davis
LESTER DORR .... Pete
LEE ROBERTS .... Steve
and BLACK JACK

ASSOC. PRODUCER .... Gordon Kay
DIRECTED BY .... R. G. Springsteen
WRITTEN BY .... M. Coates Webster
PHOTOGRAPHED BY .... John MacBurnie
MUSIC .... Stanley Wilson

Bob Davis, a settler bound for the Chandler ranch with his daughter Susie, is attacked by a band of masked gunslingers. Davis is wounded but orders Susie to hide. The bandits run the wagon off hoping that it will wreck. Rocky Lane, special investigator for the Mohican Insurance Company, stops the runaway while on his way to investigate the unusually high

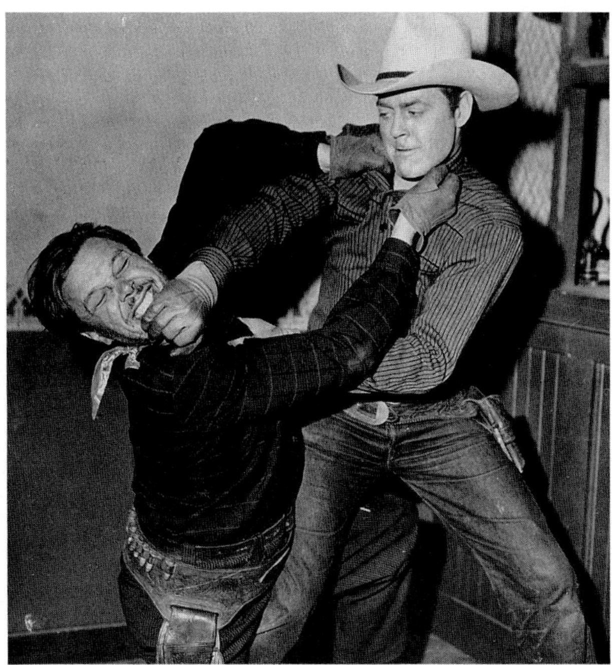

Dick Curtis (getting his jaw ripped off by Rocky) was one of the best of the B Western villains. He didn't appear in many Republic Westerns. You could usually find him giving Charles "Durango Kid" Starrett a hard time over at Columbia Pictures.

number of claims arising from the area. Before dying, Davis asks him to take Susie to Nugget Clark in West Bend, Colorado.

Grif Landers and fellow henchman Brag head for the Three Monkeys Hotel and Saloon in West Bend to inform it's proprietor, their boss Harvey Grimes, that they have taken care of another settler. Grimes, also known as the Deacon, receives valuables stolen from Davis and pays his henchmen off. Brag informs him of the stranger who rode down on them and saved the wagon from wrecking. The Deacon, who is also the local postmaster, receives and opens a letter intended for Nugget, foreman of the Chandler ranch.

Rocky arrives and asks about Nugget at the saloon. Grif and Brag inform the Deacon that Rocky is the stranger they spoke of and are ordered to follow and get rid of him. Rocky eludes the gunmen and arrives at the Chandler ranch, where he identifies himself to Nugget. Nugget informs him that the trouble began years ago when old man Chandler began selling parcels of land to bring honest citizens in.

Rocky returns to the saloon and finds Roy Chandler about to engage Grif and Brag in a game of cards. Rocky sits in and notices that a watch chain found at the scene of the shooting matches the fob worn by Brag. Rocky shows it to the frightened gunman and leaves only to hear a gunshot after his departure. Grif has shot and killed Brag in Roy's presence but the killing is blamed on Rocky, who hastily departs.

Roy confronts the Deacon after Rocky has set him straight but is accosted and beaten by Grif. The Deacon orders Grif to take Roy out and take care of him but Rocky and Nugget, who have learned Roy's whereabouts from Gail, arrive and swap lead with Grif and an accomplice. Rocky and Nugget chase the fleeting roughneck but lose the trail.

While discussing Roy with Nugget and Gail, Rocky learns of a large wagon train of settlers due to arrive the next day. Rocky suspects trouble, especially

Slick villain Alex Gerry has the drop on Rocky as henchman Dick Curtis looks on in delight. The scene is from COVERED WAGON RAID.

Rocky, Nugget, and Lyn Thomas take a moment from the action to confer on matters of the plot. The scene is from COVERED WAGON RAID.

after learning that Nugget's mail goes to the saloon before he gets it. Rocky returns to the saloon and searches the Deacon's office for clues while Nugget distracts him. Finding evidence to link the Deacon or someone to the holdups and learning that the incoming settlers will have problems, Rocky advises Nugget that they will meet the settlers.

As they prepare to warn the wagon train, shots ring out. Rocky jumps from Black Jack onto the lead wagon and stops it. With Nugget aiding him in a ruse, Rocky gets the drop on the outlaws and tells Grif that he will grab all incoming loot if the boss does not meet with him.

Grif informs the Deacon of the meeting at a deserted relay station as Gail comes by still in search of Roy. She makes the mistake of informing the presumed respectable Deacon that Rocky and Nugget have been searching for Roy all day and that Rocky is a special investigator. Rocky is knocked out by the outlaws but manages to hear the planned attack on the wagon train at Canyon Pass. After the Deacon and Grif leave, Rocky gets the drop on the henchman left to guard him, out draws and shoots him, and then escapes.

Rocky informs Nugget of the attack and sends him to get the sheriff and a posse, while he rides out to meet the wagon train. Rocky arrives and transfers to the last wagon in which he surprisingly finds a bound and gagged Roy. Rocky blocks the trail with his wagon as the gunmen begin to dispense lead. The posse arrives to help out, leaving Rocky free to chase the quickly departing Grif.

Rocky corners Grif at the saloon and questions him. The Deacon emerges from his office with gun in hand. Rocky tricks the Deacon before engaging Grif in a punishing fight. After toppling the head henchman, Rocky beats the Deacon to the draw with a well-placed bullet.

Rocky leaves West Bend content to know that the settlers are now safe coming there after the extermination of Harvey Grimes, the ruthless deacon.

VIGILANTE HIDEOUT

60 Mins .... .Aug. 6, 1950

ALLAN LANE .... "Rocky" Lane
EDDY WALLER .... Nugget Clark
ROY BARCROFT .... Muley Price
VIRGINIA HERRICK. .... Marigae Sanders
CLIFF CLARK. .... Howard Sanders
DON HAGGERTY .... Jim Benson
PAUL CAMPBELL .... Ralph Barrows
GUY TEAGUE .... Blackie
ART DILLARD .... Pete
and BLACK JACK

ASSOC PRODUCER .... Gordon Kay
DIRECTED BY .... Fred C Brannon
WRITTEN BY .... Richard Wormser
PHOTOGRAPHED BY .... John MacBurnie
MUSIC .... Stanley Wilson

Range Detective Rocky Lane, on his way to Cottonwood Springs, hears a sudden explosion. Riding in the direction of the explosion, Rocky finds Jim Benson, manager of one of Cottonwood Springs' freight lines, knocked unconscious. Rocky pulls him to safety and heads for town.

Upon arrival, Rocky attempts to get water for Black Jack and learns that the town is suffering from a severe water shortage. The townspeople have raised $25,000 for the erection of an aqueduct when water is found and have offered local inventor Nugget Clark $10,000 to help them find water. The Nugget Clark Earthbeat System is the cause of the explosion that almost killed Benson, so Nugget is asked to turn in his dynamite. Since Benson refuses to complain, the matter is dropped.

Rocky and Nugget head for the inventor's office to discuss Nugget's reason for having summoned the range detective.

At Nugget's, Rocky learns that the cattle rustling he has been called on to investigate concerns only three cows, Faith, Hope, and Charity. Feeling that he

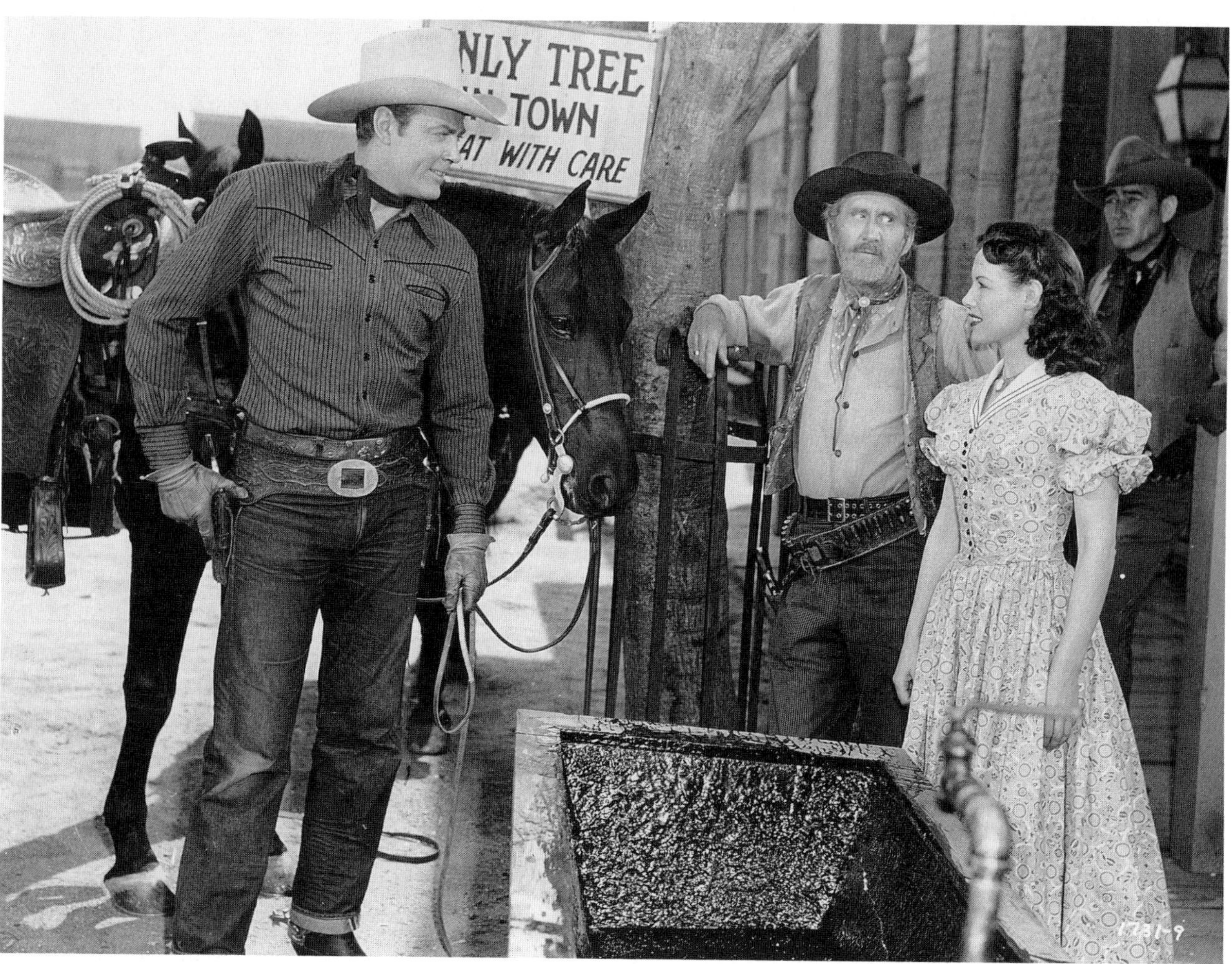

Rocky, Nugget, and leading lady Virginia Herrick have a chat next to the only tree in Cottonwood Springs. The scene is from VIGILANTE HIDEOUT.

This was a tough film for actor Don Haggerty. Here we see Rocky disarm him in a stern-looking scene.

Now Rocky tries to revive the unconscious Haggerty out among the Iverson movie location rocks.

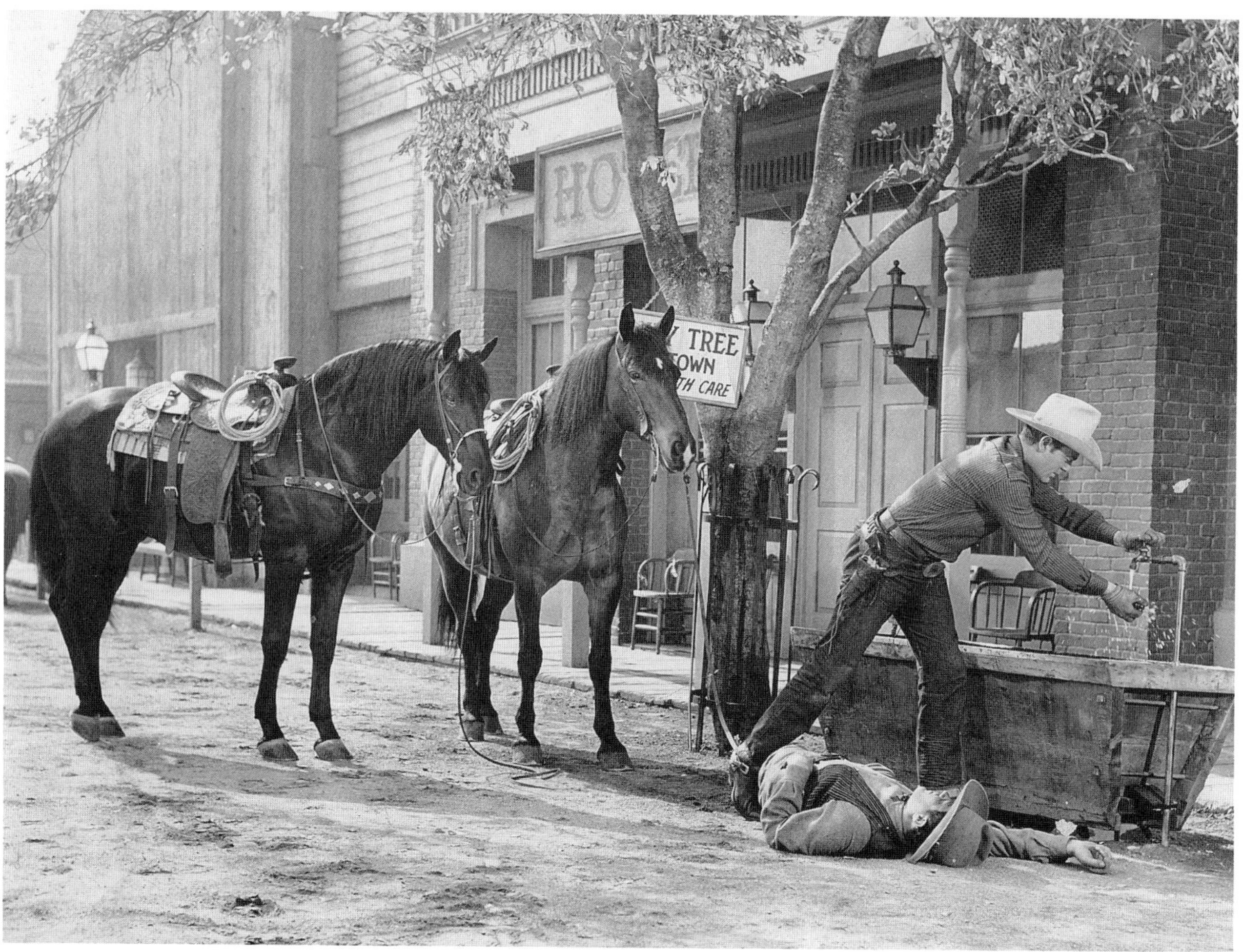

The still-unconscious Haggerty is about to get splashed by water provided by the faucet at the public watering trough. Things get worse. At the end of the film he is blown up by dynamite.

will be a laughing stock when his co-workers learn of his job, a stunned Rocky heads for dinner with Nugget.

Rocky and Nugget talk over the rustling of Nugget's experimental herd over dinner at Howard Sanders' hotel. Rocky surmises that there is more to the rustling than Nugget's scrawny herd, so he questions the old-timer about some Cottonwood Springs citizens. Nugget indicates that Price, who is also having dinner, has been in town each time his herd has been run off. Disliking the attention he is receiving, Price pulls out his bullwhip, but Rocky shoots the whip from his hands and trounces him in a room-wrecking brawl.

Price leaves and is practicing with his bullwhip out back when a masked figure walks up to him. Price is offered money to run Nugget's cows off. The man encourages him to do so because Rocky will surely follow, and Price will, therefore, be able to avenge the beating he received. Nugget's alarm alerts him to the rustling of his herd, and Rocky does indeed give chase. Price follows but is tricked and caught. He manages to escape when Nugget rides up to find out who has been rustling his herd.

Benson, the man behind the mask, now without his disguise orders Price to gather his men and make lots of noise in town. Price tries but fails again, thanks to Rocky. After another failure, Benson goes to Sanders and threatens to expose facts of the hotel owner's tainted past if he refuses to help him achieve his goal—the dynamiting of the bank vault and the subsequent theft of the $25,000 collected for building an aqueduct. Sanders is informed by Benson that the town is on top of an old copper mine and that he plans to get to the vault by digging a tunnel through the mine passage under Nugget's corral, the reason for the attempts to rustle Nugget's cows.

The next day an attempt is made to blow up the vault, but Rocky pulls the wagonload of dynamite away. The dynamite used was stolen from Nugget, so he is again asked to turn over his dynamite. The old-timer refuses and is about to be arrested by Benson, entrusted with upholding the law. Nugget decides to run. Benson tries to shoot Nugget, but Rocky stops him. Rocky is given fifteen minutes to leave town.

Having learned that Price has left town, Rocky returns to ask Sanders' daughter if she has heard such talk in the restaurant. Rocky's information is confirmed. Nugget advises him that he has a load of dynamite to get up north and that Price might be headed to hijack it. Rocky and Nugget are discovered and fired upon by Benson and the town vigilantes. Benson issues a shoot-to-kill order on Rocky. Sanders dissents and is killed by Benson. Rocky is blamed for the murder.

Rocky arrives in Sullivan to find Nugget's premonition correct. Price is hijacking the dynamite. He hides in one of the wagons but is discovered. A fight breaks out, after which Rocky chases the fleeing Price. He corners the mule-skinner and has him drive the rest of the way to the old abandoned Blue Bonnet Mine. Benson spots Rocky and runs into the mine upon his arrival. A blazing gun battle takes place with Benson being blown up when a stray bullet hits the dynamite near him.

Rocky returns to town and sees that the explosion has caused a big hole in Nugget's corral, a hole from which water is running. An artesian well has been discovered, and Rocky departs now that the town has gotten its water.

FRISCO TORNADO

60 Mins .... Sept. 6, 1950

ALLAN LANE .... "Rocky" Lane
EDDY WALLER .... Nugget Clark
MARTHA HYER .... Jean Martin
STEPHEN CHASE .... Jim Crail
ROSS FORD .... Paul Weston
MAURITZ HUGO .... Brad
LANE BRADFORD .... Mike Crystal
HAL PRICE .... Thompson
REX LEASE .... Mac
GEORGE CHESEBRO .... Guard
EDMUND COBB .... Stage Driver
and BLACK JACK

ASSOC. PRODUCER .... Gordon Kay
DIRECTED BY .... R.G. Springsteen
WRITTEN BY .... M. Coates Webster
PHOTOGRAPHED BY .... John MacBurnie
MUSIC .... Stanley Wilson

Nugget Clark, owner of the Bold Bluff Stage and Freight Line, has had more than his share of troubles-

recently as his stages have repeatedly been the target of outlaws. The incoming stage, now an hour late, proves no exception as Brad, an outlaw, hijacks it and kills the driver and guard after pretending to need a ride.

The horses arrive without the stage, causing further worry for Nugget. Nugget is given a telegram by Paul Weston, attorney for Jim Crail, secret leader of the gang behind the town's troubles. Nugget informs Crail, who makes his living by selling high-priced insurance to the worried citizens, that Marshal Rocky Lane is on his way to replace the recently killed sheriff. Nugget has yet to purchase the insurance offered by Crail, and it is his belief that this is the reason for the attacks on his stages.

Rocky is on his way to town when he is stopped by Mac, a Crail henchman. Mac examines Rocky's papers and summons his fellow henchmen to gun him down when his identity is discovered. Rocky gets away but without his papers.

Rocky reports to the sheriff's office and meets Nugget, the man who wrote for him to come. Having informed the old-timer of his encounter, Rocky suggests that his identity be kept secret in hopes of getting a lead. Nugget informs Rocky of his belief that Crail is behind the troubles and tells him that $50,000 is due in soon from the county seat. As they converse, outlaws ride in and shoot up the town. Rocky blocks the street with a buckboard and his flood of gunfire drives the gunmen off. A rock with a note attached is thrown into the sheriff's office urging the marshal to leave.

At the insistence of Nugget's niece Jean, Paul's girlfriend, Rocky rides to talk with Crail. He reveals that so far he has not had to pay a claim. A suspicious Rocky leaves and runs into Paul along the trail. Mike Crystal, a henchman of Crail's, prepares to shoot Rocky as he and Paul talk, but Rocky is warned by Paul in time to shoot the rifle from Mike's hand.

Paul continues on his journey to his boss's ranch

Eddy Waller as Nugget Clark appeared in thirty-two of the thirty-eight Allan "Rocky" Lane films. In this scene (as usual) Rocky and Nugget have their eyes peeled for the bad guys.

and, once there, threatens to quit after revealing that he saw one of his workers try to kill the marshal. Crail has the perfect alibi when he shows Paul Mac's body with Rocky's identification papers attached. Convinced that the dead man is Rocky and that the marshal is phony, Paul agrees to stay and report all to him.

Meanwhile Rocky suggests that he meet the incoming stage and change its route in an attempt to see to it that it gets through. Jean types an authorization letter for Rocky as Paul arrives to inform all that he no longer works for Crail. When Rocky leaves, Paul informs Crail of the plan to reroute the incoming stage.

Rocky takes over the stage at Willow Bend Road but is stopped shortly afterwards by Crail's accomplice Brad. Rocky gives him a ride but the devious Brad pulls a gun in an attempt to force him down the road where his friends are waiting. Rocky disarms Brad and eludes the outlaws hail of bullets.

Brad is questioned by Rocky about the hijack attempt, causing Paul to wonder why he would bother if he is indeed a phony. Questioned by Paul, Crail suggests that the interrogation is just a trick to prevent suspicion. The gullible attorney is convinced.

After learning through questioning Jean that Paul knew of the plan to reroute the stage and that Paul is guarding the jail while Nugget has dinner, Rocky rushes to the jail only to be met by gunshots. Rocky chases Brad but is himself chased by Paul who is tricked and captured. Rocky questions Paul and learns that Crail has accused him of being a phony. Crail listens outside the jail and learns the route that Nugget will use in bringing in the money from the county seat. Crail, Mike, and Brad enter the office and tie up Rocky and Paul. Rocky and Paul manage to get free with Jean's help after Crail and Mike depart.

Rocky rides hard to warn Nugget of the impending attack on the stage and in so doing encounters Mike, whom he bests in a fight. Rocky manages to warn Nugget in time, and Paul arrives with a posse to capture the bandits. Rocky pursues a hastily departing Crail to his ranch and tops him in a fight that wrecks the house.

With the troubles over and Paul now sheriff, Rocky can depart.

RUSTLERS ON HORSEBACK

60 Mins .... Oct. 23, 1950

ALLAN LANE .... "Rocky" Lane
EDDY WALLER .... Nugget Clark
ROY BARCROFT .... Leo Straykin
CLAUDIA BARRETT .... Carol Reynolds
JOHN ELDREDGE .... George Parradine
GEORGE NADER .... Jack Reynolds
FORREST TAYLOR .... Josh Taylor
JOHN CASON .... Murray
STURAT RANDALL .... Jake Clune
DOUGLAS EVANS .... Ken Jordon
TOM MONROE .... Guard
and BLACK JACK

ASSOC. PRODUCER .... Gordon Kay
DIRECTED BY .... .Fred C. Brannon
WRITTEN BY................................ Richard Wormser
PHOTOGRAPHED BY .... John MacBurnie
MUSIC .... Stanley Wilson

Deputy Marshal Rocky Lane, on the trail of accused murdered Jake Clune, has to rescue his quarry who has been thrown and dragged by his horse. Peddler Nugget Clark happens along and offers assistance. Rocky identifies himself but asks that his identity not be revealed when the unconscious man awakens. Rocky leaves Nugget to guard him while he goes off for firewood. Believing that he his dying, Clune confesses to murder and informs Nugget that he was headed for the Reynolds ranch to do a job.

Hired killer Murry, sent by Leo Straykin to meet Clune, a man only known to him by reputation, spots Rocky and Clune handcuffed together. Murry shoots Clune believing him to be the lawman since his left hand is cuffed and is gun hand is freed. Murry identifies himself to Rocky as being from the Reynolds ranch after being convinced that he is Clune. Nugget follows the men to the Reynolds ranch because he believes that Rocky is in trouble. Fearing that his cover is about to be blown as Nugget arrives, Rocky identifies him as his sidekick. Rocky is informed by Straykin that an army is being formed to attack the railroad's gold shipments and that a man on the incoming stage has the money needed to buy the horses needed.

Straykin and Murry prepare to attack the stage, with Rocky and Nugget to rob Josh Taylor, an Easterner bearing $125,000 to purchase the Reynolds ranch. The stage is allowed to pass when Straykin sees his boss, George Parradine, on board. Other passengers on board, all headed for the Reynolds ranch, are Ken Jordon, Taylor's lawyer; and Jack Reynolds, son of the deceased owner who is arriving bent on vengeance since he suspects that his father was killed. Jack, using the name Bob Bennett, pretends to be a surveyor hired by Taylor.

The stage is met later by Straykin, who is told by Taylor that he didn't want to bring that much cash, so he has told his brother, the sheriff of a nearby town, to send the money if he sends him the proper piece of a group of some five pieces of metal. Straykin is given a letter to deliver to Jack Reynolds.

The next day Rocky asks Straykin about the letter addressed to Reynolds, which he sees him read. He is advised to mind his own business. As Straykin talks with Taylor and Parradine, a shot is fired in his direction. Jack, the person who fired the shot, returns to the ranch to look around, believing everyone gone. Rocky catches him and gets him to confess to being Jack Reynolds. Jack reveals that his father was in perfect health when he died and that he has seen none of the money supposedly paid for the ranch. Rocky identifies himself and offers to help him get Straykin, the man Jack believes is behind his father's death.

Out on the trail, Rocky and Nugget spot a women in a buckboard who speeds off when seen. Her team gets away but Rocky rides to her rescue. The woman identifies herself as Carol Reynolds, Jack's wife. She is there to keep her hot-headed husband out of trouble but is informed by Rocky that all is well and that she should remain out of sight.

Rocky reports to Straykin that he has found no clues to the attempt on his life, so Murray accuses Nugget. Rocky takes exception to the accusation and is forced to defend himself against the burly badman. Rocky wins the tough battle as Parradine arrives and tells of Carol Reynolds arrival in town. Rocky pulls out a badge that he claims to have taken from the body of the marshal to whom he was cuffed and advocates that he pretended to be a lawman so that Carol can be done away with.

Murray sees Rocky head for town and informs Parradine that Rocky, the man they still believe to be Clune, lied about the badge. Fearful that Rocky is a lawman, Straykin tells Taylor that he must send his brother the necessary part to enable him to send money. Lawyer Jordon intervenes to help his client but is shot and killed. Taylor then reveals that he has given the proper part to Jack to send off for him.

Parradine and Straykin arrive in town with Taylor in tow and use him as a shield. Their hoodlums are ordered to shoot Rocky. Straykin engages Rocky in a bruising fist fight but goes down. Meanwhile, Nugget and the Reynolds escape and are chased by the gunmen. Rocky heads after them and single-handedly downs the gunmen with blasts from his guns.

Jack sells part of the ranch to Taylor as Rocky leaves to encounter adventure elsewhere

ROUGH RIDERS OF DURANGO

60 Mins .... Jan. 30, 1951

ALLAN LANE .... "Rocky" Lane
WALTER BALDWIN .... Cricket Adams
ALINE TOWNE. .... Janis
STEVE DARRELL .... .John Blake
ROSS FORD .... Sheriff Bill Walters
DENVER PYLE .... Lacey
STUART RANDALL .... Jed
HAL PRICE .... Johnson
TOM LONDON .... Evans
RUSS WHITEMAN .... Jim Carter
DALE VAN SICKEL .... Willis
and BLACK JACK

ASSOC. PRODUCER .... Gordon Kay
DIRECTED BY .... Fred C. Brannon
WRITTEN BY .... M. Coates Webster
PHOTOGRAPHED BY .... John MacBurnie
MUSIC .... Stanley Wilson

The town of Durango is experiencing trouble with the robbing of its grain shipments by a group of outlaws. The latest such attack is on the shipment of Cricket Adams, whose driver is killed in the attack. Desperate for help, Sheriff Bill Walters manages to get the grain buyers at the county seat to advance money for the next shipment to prevent the bank from calling in the notes on ranches in the area. The money is being sent by secret courier to hopefully allow the money to get through safely.

Rocky Lane, a special courier from the county seat, delivers the $40,000 in cash to Jim Carter, the courier set to take the money the last leg of the way. Outlaws attack and kill Carter before being chased by Rocky onto the property of Cricket. Awakened by the gunfire, Cricket drives Rocky off, believing him to be an outlaw.

The next morning Rocky informs Bill that the money was stolen and, he thinks, hidden in Cricket's barn. While Cricket and his niece Janis, Bill's girlfriend, are in town shopping, Rocky and Bill initiate a search of the barn to find the money.

John Blake, owner of the Durango Saddle and Harness Shop and brains behind the grain raids sends henchmen Lacey and Jed to Cricket's to recover the money upon learning that it was left there. Rocky and Bill encounter the gunmen and chase them off after an exchange of bullets. Cricket and Janis arrive to gunfire, causing Cricket's horse team to runaway with the feisty old-timer unconscious inside the buckboard. Rocky saves him and manages to hire on to continue his search for the money.

Blake learns from Cricket, who has returned to town on a trip to the bank, that Rocky has been hired to protect his ranch. Lacey, Jed, and Willis return to search the barn for the money after attempting to draw Rocky away. Rocky refuses to be drawn away by a claim that cattle are being rustled and swaps lead with the gunmen. Lacey is killed and Jed runs off, leaving Willis to defend himself against Rocky's wild two-fisted assault.

Cricket returns and follows Rocky's suggestion that they weigh the grain bags in the barn for uniformity. After weighing the grain sacks and finding the hidden money in the heaviest sack, Rocky admits to Cricket what is going on.

Blake sends Jed back to get the money and dispose of Rocky. Preparing to leave with the money, which he plans to take to Bill, Rocky is shot at by Jed and pretends to be hit. He trails the gunmen and runs him down on Black Jack. After a brief fight, Rocky advises Jed to tell his boss that he will split the money with him if he is cut in on the whole set up. He further instructs him to have his boss meet him after Cricket has joined the wagon train transporting the grain shipment.

Rocky hides the money in one of Cricket's grain sacks and asks that he leave the sack with Bill and instructs him to come to his ranch after safeguarding it. The load in Cricket's wagon shifts and the wrong bag is left with Bill. A jailed Willis, who has overheard Cricket convey the message to Bill, sees that the sheriff can't locate the money.

Blake enters the jail and asks to see if he can identify the prisoner as one of the men responsible for robbing his grain shipments. Willis is freed by his boss and is sent along with Jed to Cricket's to again try to eliminate Rocky. The roughnecks are overcome in a fierce gun battle with Rocky, who then leaves to warn Cricket.

Blake and his men attack the grain wagons with six guns blazing, but Rocky arrives and is joined shortly afterwards by Bill and a posse. The outlaws are captured but Blake manages to get away. Chased to his shop by Rocky, where he begins to empty his safe, Blake tries vainly to defend himself against Rocky's flying fists but fails and goes down to defeat at the hands of his brawling adversary.

With renewed confidence in Bill, whom he has always called "the pip squeak sheriff," Cricket offers no objection to the marriage plans of Bill and Janis. Rocky departs after having vanquished Blake and the rough riders of Durango.

NIGHT RIDERS OF MONTANA

60 Mins .... Feb. 28, 1951

ALLAN LANE .... "Rocky" Lane
CHUBBY JOHNSON .... Skeeter Davis
ROY BARCROFT .... Brink Stiles
CLAUDIA BARRETT .... Julie Bauer
ARTHUR SPACE .... Roger Brandon
MYRON HEALEY .... Steve Bauer
MARSHALL BRADFORD .... Sam Foster
MORT THOMPSON .... Jim Foster
LESTER DOBB .... Drummer
TED ADAMS .... Connors
GEORGE CHESEBRO .... .Hank Jamison
DON HARVEY .... Henchman
ZON MURRAY .... Joe
and BLACK JACK

ASSOC. PRODUCER .... Gordon Kay
DIRECTED BY .... Fred C. Brannon
WRITTEN BY .... M. Coates Webster
PHOTOGRAPHED BY. .... John MacBurnie
MUSIC .... Stanley Wilson

A meeting of the townsfolk of Westline reveals that Sam Foster has sought aid from the governor to hopefully alleviate constant horse rustling in the area. The authorization of the formation of state rangers has encouraged town representative Foster to offer the government the best mounts from the Westline herds. Having lost nothing to the rustlers, Steve Bauer refuses to give up his best mounts and join the other rancher gathering his horses in a secret place for the rangers. After the meeting, Roger Brandon, secret leader of the rustlers, suggests that Steve seek Foster and apologize, hoping this will enable him to learn the meeting place and attack the herd.

The next morning as Foster and his son Jim check the herds, Steve rides up. After encouraging his son to leave the brush, Foster is shot and killed. Steve chases the gunmen and exchanges gunfire with them, as Rocky Lane, the first of the state rangers, joins the fray. Rocky helps Steve drive the men off and heads for town with him.

Jim alerts Sheriff Skeeter Davis of his father's death and names Steve as the killer. Rocky and Steve arrive and are greeted by a mob intent on lynching the innocent man. Brink Stiles, Brandon's main henchman, has been ordered to escort Steve out of town. Brink and other masked men coerce Steve to leave with them at gunpoint, a fact only seen by Rocky. The ranger takes after the men but is stopped on the trail by Skeeter, who, aware that he is a ranger, causes him to lose sight of the masked men.

Brandon rides out to see Steve under the pretense that he hired the motley crew to prevent him from being hanged. Revealing that Foster was killed before he could learn where the herds would be assembled, Steve is encountered by Brandon to have his sister Julie join the ranchers so that she might learn of the gathering place.

As Rocky informs Skeeter that Steve was ushered from town at gunpoint, he spots Connors, another Brandon henchman, talking to Julie. Recognizing him as one of the masked men involved in Steve's departure, Rocky approaches the frightened man. Ducking into his boss's gunsmith shop, Connors panics and starts shooting at Rocky. Brandon shoots Connors to prevent him from being apprehended and questioned.

Rocky and Skeeter go to the Bauer ranch to question Julie about the dead gunman, believing that he might have given her some clue as to Steve's whereabouts. Hiding in an adjacent room is Steve, who is drawn out by a clever Rocky. Brink and two other men arrive to cloud the situation and Steve, still believing them to be employed by the concerned

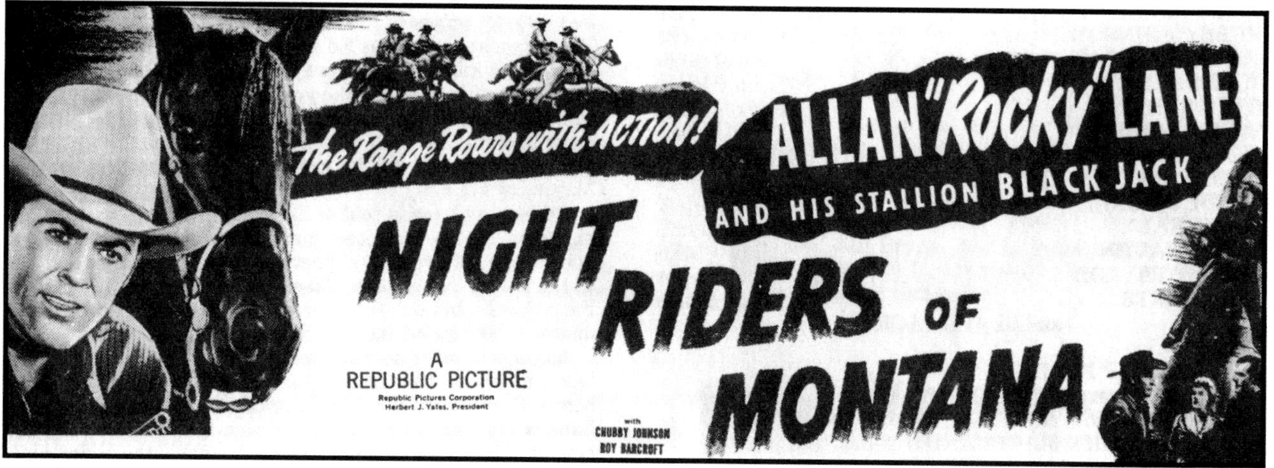

Brandon, leaves with Brink. Rocky disarms and thrashes the gunmen left behind to get rid of him. Seeing that her brother has fallen in with the wrong crowd, Julie offers to help.

Jim still believes that Steve killed his father, so he follows Julie hoping to find him. Rocky trails Julie as planned and is about to apprehend Steve when Jim shows up and attempts to shoot him. Jim chases Steve, but Rocky chases him. After roping Jim from his horse, Rocky takes up the chase but Steve gets away.

Jim goes to Brandon's shop to get a gun. He tells the gunsmith of his recent encounter with Rocky and Steve and indicates his belief that they are working together. Seeing this as a way to learn the secret gathering place of the herd, Brandon concurs with Jim and fuels his idea that the two men are working together. Jim departs after revealing that Rainbow Canyon is the meeting place. Brandon orders Brink to meet him there in the morning.

Jim and three of Brandon's henchmen are sent to take care of Steve, but Rocky learns of Steve's whereabouts too and engages them in a wild shooting match. One of the gunmen shoots a surprised Jim, but Rocky pulls him to safety and is informed by the wounded lad that Brandon dispatched the gunmen to dispose of him and Steve. Steve then reveals that Brandon is the man who has helped him remain hidden. Realizing now that the gunsmith is behind the rustlers, Rocky, after the defeat of the gunmen, sends Jim to town to get Skeeter and the rangers due to arrive that morning. Rocky and Steve depart for Rainbow Canyon. The attack on the herd has started, but Rocky and Steve hold off the rustlers until Skeeter and the rangers arrive. Rocky then takes off after Brandon and Brink who have rather hurriedly left for town. The badmen make it to Brandon's shop but no further. Rocky catches up and beats Brink in a brutal fist fight that wrecks the shop. He then outdraws and out guns Brandon.

With the attacks on the rancher's herds now ended, Rocky leaves Westline for his next assignment.

WELLS FARGO GUNMASTER

60 Mins .... May 15, 1951

ALLAN LANE .... "Rocky" Lane
CHUBBY JOHNSON .... Skeeter Davis
MARY ELLEN KAY .... Carol Hines
MICHAEL CHAPIN .... Tommy Hines
ROY BARCROFT .... Brick Manson
WALTER REED .... Ed Hines
STUART RANDALL .... John Thornton
WILLIAM BAKEWELL .... Charlie Lannon
GEORGE MEEKER .... Croupier
ANN O' NEAL .... Mrs. Feathergill
JAMES CRAVEN .... Henery Mills
FORREST TAYLOR .... Doctor
LEE ROBERTS .... Townsman
and BLACK JACK

ASSOC. PRODUCER .... Gordon Kay
DIRECTED BY .... Philip Ford
WRITTEN BY .... M. Coates Webster
PHOTOGRAPHED BY .... John MacBurnie
MUSIC .... Stanley Wilson

Rocky Lane, special Investigator for the Wells Fargo Company, happens upon a band of gunmen robbing Skeeter Davis of the Cedarville Wells Fargo Co. Rocky cuts down one of the gunmen with a well-placed bullet and chases off his companions before stopping to identify himself. Rocky finds a piece of paper on the dead robber containing what seems to be some type of code—Oasis 4-12-9-15, 4:30 p.m.. He has Skeeter agree to allow him to hold up his stage and steal his valuables before proceeding.

Sure, they say it's just a friendly game, but watch it, Rocky. The scene is from WELLS FARGO GUNMASTER.

Skeeter arrives and informs the townsfolk that he was robbed of $120,000 in bonds. Rocky, who is among the gathering, departs for the Oasis, the town's saloon, and arrives there at 4:30. After hearing a combination of four numbers bet on the roulette wheel, Rocky bets the combination on the piece of paper found on the dead robber. Seated nearby is Charlie Lannon, who remarks to Rocky that he played an interesting combination. Lannon takes Rocky to the back room where he meets Ed Hines, the saloon manager, and is told by him that his boss would probably pay $15,000 for the stolen bonds. After Rocky is told to meet him out front, Hines informs his boss John Thornton, the presumed respectable owner of a silver mine, about Rocky.

Under orders from Thornton, Hines escorts Rocky out of town where it has been decided that he will be killed and robbed of the bonds. On their way, the pair come across Hines' young crippled brother, Tommy, who is thrown and dragged by his horse. Rocky saves the lad and learns that he is badly in need of an operation on his leg. Grateful that Rocky has saved his brother, Hines can't go through with the plan to kill him and orders that he leave.

Skeeter Davis, who moments earlier attempted to secretly speak to Rocky at the ranch and in doing so unknowingly dropped the bonds, intercepts the departing Rocky. They watch as henchman Brick Manson tells Hines that the boss wants to see him. They follow at a distance and trail the men to the saloon where Thornton enters Hines' office from the back. A displeased Thornton exchanges words with Hines, who is then shot and killed by Manson. Rocky chases Hines' killer but loses him.

Rocky and Skeeter go to the Hines ranch the next morning to search for the bonds Skeeter has lost. While Rocky distracts Tommy and his older sister Carol, Skeeter finds the bonds. However, Tommy and Carol are alerted to his presence when the not-too-quiet man knocks over a chair. The ever-resourceful Rocky suggests that the bonds were probably hidden there by an outlaw and that Hines was probably killed because he knew of them. He further suggests that the bonds be left where they were found to help trap the culprit.

Rocky returns to the Oasis to rearrange a meeting with the boss but is told by Lannon to return at 1 A.M. Rocky sees a crew of motley characters arrive and suspects that an attempt will be made on his life. After meeting in the back room of the saloon, the ever polite Lannon opens the door to the street from which Rocky is to leave. Rocky refuses and is jumped from behind by a henchman, whom he beats in a fight and guns down. Forgetting what awaits the person exiting the saloon, Lannon runs out onto the street only to receive lead intended for Rocky. Rocky chases the gunman to the Blue Queen Silver Mine, where he finds Manson and his cohorts waiting for their boss. Thornton arrives and gets the drop on Rocky.

Rocky and Manson arrive at the Hines ranch to find no one there. Rocky tricks the burly henchman and soundly thrashes him in a fight which wrecks the room. Manson is tied up and hidden in a closet in the house.

As Thornton stirs the citizens into believing that Rocky killed Lannon and probably Hines too, Tommy and Carol inform the boss that Rocky and Skeeter are working together and that the bonds are at their ranch. Carol waits in Skeeter's office as Tommy accompanies Thornton to the ranch. Finding his house in a shambles from the fight between Rocky and Manson, Tommy turns over the bonds to Thornton, who learns of Manson's predicament and frees him from the closet. Tommy is taken hostage.

Rocky and Skeeter find out what has happened and quickly ride for the Hines ranch. Finding no one there, they ride for the mine. Greeted by flying bullets, the duo hold their own before Rocky chases Thornton and Manson who have escaped in an ore wagon in which Tommy is confined. After Manson is shot, Rocky manages to transfer to the speeding wagon. Thornton is bested in the fight which follows and is knocked from the still-moving wagon.

With problems now behind them, Tommy and Carol bid farewell to Rocky Lane.

Rocky's up to some typical rough-and-tumble action in the interior of the Duchess' ranch house. The scene is from WELLS FARGO GUNMASTER.

FORT DODGE STAMPEDE

60 Mins .... Aug. 24, 1951

ALLAN LANE .... "Rocky" Lane
CHUBBY JOHNSON .... Skeeter Davis
MARY ELLEN KAY .... Natalie Bryan
ROY BARCROFT .... Pike Hardin
TREVOR BARDETTE .... Sparkler McCann
BRUCE EDWARDS .... Jeff Bryan
WESLEY HUDMAN .... Butler
WILLIAM FORREST .... Hutchinson
CHUCK ROBERSON .... Ragon
RORY MALLISON .... Sheriff
JACK INGRAM .... Cox
KERMIT MAYNARD .... Settler
and BLACK JACK

ASSOC. PRODUCER .... Harry Keller
DIRECTED BY .... Harry Keller
WRITTEN BY .... Richard Wormser
PHOTOGRAPHED BY .... John MacBurnie
MUSIC .... Stanley Wilson

Deputy Marshal Rocky Lane helps to break up a gunfight in which a stranger is defending himself against three gunmen. Rocky swaps lead with the gunmen and succeeds in running them off, but the target of their gunfire has been severely wounded. Rocky learns that the dying man is Hutchinson, a participant in the recent Adams bank robbery in which he netted $30,000 after double-crossing his men. He tells Rocky that his companions will be found in Fort Dodge trying to use the key taken from him to find the loot.

Rocky leaves for Fort Dodge after turning in his badge, since the town is outside his jurisdiction. He arrives to find it a ghost town inhabited only by Skeeter Davis and a crew of men claiming to be surveyors for the railroad line. Pike Hardin and his men arrive and are questioned by Rocky about their railroad. Hardin is anything but cooperative and engages Rocky in a tough fistfight. Rocky wins and informs Skeeter that the men are not surveyors but outlaws in search of holdup money. Skeeter does not want to believe this since he has sold land to a group of settlers due to arrive soon.

The settlers arrive and are disappointed to find no railroad tracks and the town anything but prosperous. Sparkler McCann, spokesman for the settlers, is secretly the leader of the gang searching for the loot. McCann questions Hardin about the railroad but receives no answer. Hardin refuses to answer Skeeter when asked to admit being a railroad representative.

McCann meets with Hardin and chastises his head henchman for saying he worked for the railroad and threatens to dispose of him as he did Hutchinson. Hardin gives the key taken from Hutchinson to his boss, who suggests that the town be cleared so that a search can be started for the lockbox containing the $30,000. The cinch of settler Jeff Bryan's wagon team is cut, causing his wagon to run away and allowing the crooks a chance to begin their search. Rocky gives chase and saves Jeff.

Upon finding indications that the team was tampered with, Rocky returns to town and finds Skeeter being bullied by Butler and his place being searched. Rocky takes the badmen on and flails them in the room-destructing encounter.

Incited to riot by McCann, the settlers voice their displeasure of there being no railroad. They demand the return of their money but are informed by Skeeter that it has been spent. McCann allows Skeeter twenty-four hours to come up with the money.

Rocky and Skeeter search for the money so that Skeeter can use the reward to pay off the settlers. They abandon their search and pretend to leave town so that Hardin and his men can help find it. Trailed by one of the henchmen, Rocky subdues him, and he and Skeeter return to the junkyard prepared to confront Hardin and his men who have swallowed the bait. Jeff enters and questions the men, foiling Rocky's plan, but Rocky's bullets drive them off.

Chastised by Jeff for leaving the junkyard so wide open, Rocky learns that Jeff is in fact Jeff Adams, the son of the now-deceased banker accused of embezzling the money. Seeking to set the record straight, Bryan is informed by Rocky that he is a lawman. Together they are able to locate a set of lockboxes, one of which contains a coded map. Not knowing how to use the map, Rocky has Jeff leave town with the lockboxes on board a wagon, hoping to draw the outlaws out. The plan works as Rocky trails Hardin and orders him to tell his boss that they will split three ways with him if he divulges the way to decipher the code.

While working on a watch for Jeff's wife Natalie, McCann is informed of the predicament by Hardin. Natalie returns for the watch and is kidnapped by McCann and Hardin. They inform Rocky, Jeff, and Skeeter that they will take the map in exchange for Jeff's wife. Rocky and friends are tied up but escape and rescue Natalie from her captors.

Having located the bank money, McCann and Hardin abandon their partners and leave town in a speeding buckboard. Rocky, astride his stallion, runs the men down and battles them aboard the buckboard. McCann is shot while struggling with Rocky, after which Hardin bites the dust when pummelled by Rocky.

The future of Fort Dodge appears bright as Jeff is elected sheriff and news arrives that the railroad really is coming.

DESERT OF LOST MEN

54 Mins .... Nov. 19, 1951

ALLAN LANE ...."Rocky" Lane
IRVING BACON .... Sheriff Skeeter Davis
MARY ELLEN KAY .... Nan Webster
ROY BARCROFT .... Link Rinter
ROSS ELLIOTT .... Dr. Jim Haynes
CLIFF CLARK .... Carl Landers
BOYD "RED" MORGAN ....Frank
LEO CLEARY .... Dr. Roger Stephens
KENNETH MACDONALD .... Bill Hackett
STEVE PENDLETON .... Evans
and BLACK JACK

ASSOC. PRODUCER .... Harry Keller
DIRECTED BY .... Harry Keller
WRITTEN BY .... M. Coates Webster
PHOTOGRAPHED BY .... John MacBurnie
MUSIC .... Stanley Wilson

The Lost Men, a group of outlaws from all over the West, specialize in spreading death and wreaking havoc throughout Arizona. Deputy Marshal Rocky Lane is in the area of Bear Creek, Arizona, searching for the leader of the organization of killers when he comes upon Doctors Jim Haynes and Roger Stephens being fired upon by a host of masked gunmen. Rocky scatters the gunmen and saves Dr. Haynes whose buckboard has run away. Dr. Haynes heads for town with the wounded Dr. Stephens as Rocky tries to pick up the trail of the ruffians.

It looks as if Rocky has given Roy Barcroft the "old one-two" again in this scene from DESERT OF LOST MEN.

Rocky rides into town to check on Dr. Stephens and to report to Sheriff Skeeter Davis. Dr. Haynes informs Rocky of the death of his friend and further that he feels the gunmen were attempting to rob them of $40,000 they were expected to be bringing to town to build a new hospital. Fearing trouble, Dr. Haynes had ordered that the money be sent the next day by stage. Just then Rocky and Dr. Haynes discover the presence of Frank, one of the Lost Men, searching the office for the money. The bandit is sent packing after he loses a tough fistfight to Rocky.

Sheriff Davis informs the townsfolk that the money was stolen by masked bandits. Rocky has advised him to provide phony information and not reveal that he is a marshal, and, to further the plan, Rocky openly accuses Dr. Haynes of being a crook.

After hearing the sheriff's statement and witnessing the confrontation between Rocky and Dr. Haynes, Carl Landers, loyal cabinet maker and secret leader of the Lost Men, questions his head henchman, Link Rinter, only to be told that he didn't get the money because Rocky rode down and prevented him from doing so. Landers has Rocky followed by Link. Link is given the slip and then jumped by Rocky. Rocky tells Link to inform his boss that he is after the $40,000 hospital fund money and that he wants to join up with the Lost Men. Link departrs to tell his boss that Rocky desires a meeting with him later that night.

Rocky informs the sheriff and Dr. Haynes that he has made contact. He takes to the meeting a phony wanted poster accusing Dr. Haynes of murder. Rocky is told by Link that the boss is not interested. Landers' disinterest is because his suspicion of Rocky has been aroused when he questioned Dr. Haynes about him. Link and his men unholster their guns and prepare to make Rocky the target of their bullets, but Rocky outsmarts and outshoots his adversaries.

After Landers sees the wanted poster, he sends Link and Frank to get the doctor under the pretense of helping an injured comrade. His nurse, Nan Webster, informs them that he is at a nearby ranch seeing a patient. Nan rides to the sheriff's office but finds one of the wanted posters concerning her boss and fiance and refuses to reveal his whereabouts.

Rocky and Sheriff Davis follow Nan and save her

Rocky's on the lookout for the villains in this scene from DESERT OF LOST MEN.

from the gunfire of Link and friends who have intercepted Dr. Haynes and kidnapped him. Recovering from her rough encounter, Nan is informed by Rocky that the wanted poster is a phony and that her fiance is really in alliance with him. Relieved at the news, Nan helps to devise a plan to locate Dr. Haynes.

The next morning, Rocky is accused of attempting to break into the doctor's office. Link arrives and breaks into the office but is confronted by Rocky who offers to show him the location of the stolen money if he takes him to the doctor. Link swallows the bait and Rocky, following him to the hideout, drops bandages along the way to allow the sheriff to follow him.

Meanwhile, Landers learns that Rocky is really a marshal and that the money has not been stolen when Sheriff Davis announces this information to the posse formed under the pretense of capturing Rocky. He also learns that the hospital fund money is on the way and that Rocky is leaving a trail of bandages leading to the hideout, so he changes the trail. Rocky is apprehended and tied up.

With Rocky and Dr. Haynes in tow, Landers and the Lost Men prepare to intercept the stage carrying the money. Rocky manages to free himself and alert the stage driver to the trouble at hand. Dr. Haynes, who had been freed by Rocky, arrives with the posse and helps prevent the theft of the money. Rocky chases Landers and Link back to the cabinetmaker's shop, where the boss is felled by a shot from the marshal's gun and Link is pounded into submission.

The hospital fund money arrives safely to the joy of the citizens of Bear Creek as Rocky, having ended the existence of the Lost Men, leaves for his next adventure.

CAPTIVE OF BILLY THE KID

54 Mins .... Jan. 22, 1952

ALLAN LANE .... "Rocky" Lane
PENNY EDWARDS .... Nancy McCreary
GRANT WITHERS .... Van Stanley
CLEM BEVANS .... Skeeter Davis
ROY BARCROFT .... Piute
CLAYTON MOORE ....Paul Howarth
MAURITZ HUGO .... Randy Brown
GARRY GOODWIN .... Pete
FRANK McCARROLL .... Deputy Marshal
RICHARD EMORY .... Sam
and BLACK JACK

ASSOC. PRODUCER .... Gordon Kay
DIRECTED BY .... Fred C Brannon
WRITTEN BY . M. Coates Webster/Richard Wormser
PHOTOGRAPHED BY .... John MacBurnie
MUSIC .... Stanley Wilson

Marshal Rocky Lane, under the guise of a range detective, is dispatched to investigate the killing of a rancher near Amargo, whose death is believed to hold a key to the place where the loot of Billy the Kid is hidden. Stopped at his campsite for a moment, Rocky is called to duty by the eruption of gunfire and the sight of two masked men chasing a buckboard. He routs the bandits and is then called on to save the female passenger when her driver is shot. Rocky saves Nancy McCreary, daughter of the murdered rancher, and escorts her to town.

Once arriving in town, Rocky wires his agency in Santa Fe and the sheriff in the nearest town of the trouble he has encountered as an interested Van Stanley listens in. After Rocky departs, Piute, one of the gunmen who attacked Nancy's buckboard, reports to Stanley that Rocky prevented him from successfully stopping the buckboard and retrieving one-fifth of a map detailing the location of Billy the Kid's loot. Stanley orders Piute to stop an incoming stage on which passengers Randy Brown and a man named Gorman, each holders of part of the map, are riding.

Having escorted Nancy to the ranch of Skeeter Davis, Rocky learns from the ex-carnival barker that both he and Nancy own pieces to the map of Billy the Kid's treasure and that the soon-to-arrive stage has passengers with pieces also. Rocky rides to meet the stage and finds his anticipation of trouble to be correct as the stage is under siege by masked outlaws. Having killed the driver and a passenger, the outlaws scatter when Rocky tosses lead their way. The surviving passenger identifies himself as Paul Howarth and reveals that the dead passenger had told him that he was Randy Brown.

Rocky and Paul arrive at the junction safely but find a sweaty horse they believe to belong to one of the masked men. Rocky questions its owner, Piute, and finds him not too pleased by the insinuations. Rocky defends himself against a barrage of fists and comes out the clear-cut winner before his opponent takes flight.

Rocky and Paul go to Skeeter's ranch and inform him that Brown has been killed. A knock on the door reveals otherwise as Brown shows up and explains that he expected trouble and hired a man to take his place on the stage. It is further revealed that Paul won his piece of the map from Gorman in a poker game. The ranch is fired on by Piute and friends as they are about to follow Rocky's suggestion that he be given all five pieces. Rocky apprehends Piute and leaves him tied up in Skeeter's barn.

Rocky rides to town to wire for help from a neighboring town. His departure allows Stanley time to knock out Skeeter and free Piute. The burly gunman is told to learn Rocky's message from the telegrapher and then head for Amargo the next morning where all map pieces are to be assembled and the treasure located.

Rocky and his companions leave for Amargo and settle down for the night after traveling many miles. Brown is discovered knifed in the back later and his portion of the map stolen. About to search the others for the stolen piece, Rocky is shot at by the pesky Piute. He chases him off but abandons his search, feeling that the guilty party has had ample time to hide it.

The rest of the journey is safe as the group arrives in Amargo. Assembled in Nancy's room to put the pieces together, the group is startled as Rocky enters with guns drawn and steals the four map pieces. Party to a ruse to force the thief of the fifth piece to give himself away, Skeeter is given the four pieces by Rocky, who doubles back and turns them over for safe keeping.

Stanley dispatches Piute's accomplices to intercept the help Rocky awaits and to assume their identities. They succeed only briefly as Rocky, who is about to meet the deputies, becomes suspicious and overpowers them. Stanley observes the failure of his men and is about to shoot Rocky when Skeeter reveals that he has the map pieces and that Rocky is a lawman. Skeeter is relieved of the map pieces by Stanley, who is chased by Rocky after he latter shoots Piute. Rocky beats Stanley in a furious fight which sees the killer knocked from atop a mountain.

With the map assembled and the loot divided among the remaining parties, Skeeter makes plans to open a carnival with his share as Rocky rides on.

LEADVILLE GUNSLINGER

54 Mins .... March 22, 1952

ALLAN LANE .... "Rocky" Lane
EDDY WALLER .... Nugget Clark
GRANT WITHERS .... Jonathan Graves
ELAINE RILEY .... Carol Davis
ROY BARCROFT .... Chet & Pete Yonker
RICHARD CRANE .... Jim Blanchard
I. STANFORD JOLLEY .... Cliff Saunders
KENNETH MACDONALD .... Sheriff Nichols
MICKEY SIMPSON .... Monk
ED HINTON .... Deputy Ned Smith
ART DILLARD .... Sentry
WESLEY HUDMAN .... Driver
and BLACK JACK

ASSOC. PRODUCER .... Harry Keller
DIRECTED BY .... Harry Keller
WRITTEN BY .... M. Coates Webster
PHOTOGRAPHED BY .... Bud Thackery
MUSIC .... Stanley Wilson

U.S. Marshal Rocky Lane is on his way to the town of Leadville, Oklahoma, to pick up Chet Yonker, an outlaw who unsuccessfully attempted to rob the Leadville Security Bank. He stops off to see his friend Nugget Clark before arriving there. Rocky is introduced to Jim Blanchard, Nugget's neighbor and fiance of his niece Carol Davis, and is told by him that outlaws have made life so miserable for Nugget that the old-timer is having trouble making payments on his ranch. A meeting is to be held that evening at which time Nugget plans to offer to share with his fellow ranchers the oil thought to be on his land in exchange for them helping to pay his ranch note. Gunfire draws Rocky and Jim away from dinner, but they manage to drive off the bandits behind the trouble.

Rocky rides back to town with Sheriff Nichols, who happened to be in the area following the recent attack. They find Chet Yonker gone and Deputy Ned Smith tied up. Rocky feels that the jail break was probably tied in with the attack on the ranch. Rocky asks the sheriff to keep his identity a secret because he had hoped to break Yonker out himself and join the gang to gain information.

Rocky returns to Nugget's and informs his friend that the raids on his ranch are likely the result of someone hoping to gain his ranch because of the oil thought to be there. Rocky spots an outlaw looking into Nugget's window and chases the fleeing man. After being knocked from his horse, the man dies in a struggle with Rocky over a gun he had pulled to shoot the marshal. A watch on the dead man reveals him to be Pete Yonker, Chet's twin brother.

The next morning Nugget goes to see Jonathan Graves of the Leadville Bank to get an extension on his overdue note. Graves, the leader behind the plot to acquire Nugget's ranch, refuses him an extension even though told that a geologist is arriving on the afternoon stage to look over his land. Another meeting of the ranchers is to take place after the geologist gives his report, which, if favorable, will result in them helping to pay off Nugget's note.

Under orders from Graves, Chet and other outlaws attack the stage in which the geologist is a passenger. Chet guns him down in cold blood. The stage team is then run off, but Rocky, who is riding near by, stops the runaway and escorts the stage into town.

Rocky returns to Nugget's ranch to break the news but is informed that the geologist is on the premises. Cliff Saunders, pretending to be the geologist, informs Nugget that there is no oil there. After following Saunders across the Leadville county line into No Man's Land, a haven for outlaws, Rocky tells Nugget to inform his friends that there is oil, so that the person behind the scheme will hopefully give himself away.

Rocky and the sheriff devise a plan whereby Rocky crosses into No Man's Land under fire to convince the bandits that he is an outlaw. The plan works since Rocky is taken by the sentry to a cave where he finds Chet and Saunders. Rocky informs Chet of his brother's death and asks to join the gang. Before he is allowed to join, Rocky is told that he must fight burly gang member Monk to prove himself. Rocky takes the brute in a vicious fight, wins, and is allowed to join. Chet informs Rocky that he and his men are after oil on Nugget's land.

Nugget informs Graves that the geologist confirmed that there is oil on his land. After Nugget leaves, Saunders arrives to dispute Nugget's statement, whereupon Graves tells him to see to it that the old-timer is taken care of. After informing Chet of the orders, Rocky volunteers to do the job and is accompanied by Saunders and another man to Nugget's. Rocky tricks them and has Jim take Saunders to the sheriff.

Seeing Jim arrive with his henchman, Graves

asks about the prisoner and learns that Rocky is really a marshal. Graves goes to the cave to warn his men and finds Rocky informing Chet that Nugget has been taken care of. Learning that Rocky is a marshal and probably the killer of his brother, Chet assaults him as his men hold him down. Rocky pretends to be knocked out but escapes with Graves and Chet close behind. Seeing the posse headed their way, the men retreat to their hideout only to be chased by Rocky who out-shoots Graves and beats Chet in a brutal fight.

Rocky leaves Leadville after learning that oil is, in fact, on Nugget's land and that Carol and Jim will soon be wed.

BLACK HILLS AMBUSH

54 Mins .... May 20, 1952

ALLAN LANE .... "Rocky" Lane
EDDY WALLER .... .Nugget Clark
LESLYE BANNING .... Sally
ROY BARCROFT .... Bart
MICHAEL HALL .... .Larry Stewart
JOHN VOSPER .... Randall Gaines
EDWARD CASSIDY .... Sheriff
JOHN CASON .... Jake
WESLEY HUDMAN .... Buck
MICHAEL BARTON .... Clay Stewart
and BLACK JACK

ASSOC PRODUCER .... Harry Keller
DIRECTED BY .... Harry Keller
WRITTEN BY .... Ronald Davidson
& M.Coates Webster
PHOTOGRAPHED BY .... Bud Thackery
MUSIC .... Stanley Wilson

Rocky Lane is enroute to the Black Hills country to see his friend Nugget Clark, whose freight business is near bankruptcy due to bandit raids, when he rescues a youngster who experienced a bad fall from his horse. The sheriff rides up and identifies the youth as Larry Stewart, a member of the Black Hills outlaw gang. Larry has just prevented the sheriff from capturing the gang by supplying them with fresh horses after the holdup of a freight wagon. Larry is carried off to jail.

After confering with his friend Nugget, Rocky manages to have the sixteen-year-old released in the custody of Nugget and his niece, Sally. Larry is angered by the death of his brother Clay in the most recent display of outlawry by the gang and at first refuses to go but changes his mind. Rocky is in reality a deputy marshal, but he remains undercover to hopefully rehabilitate Larry and help capture his outlaw friends.

Attorney Randall Gaines, the brains behind the Black Hills outlaws, sees Rocky and Nugget leave town with Larry and dispatches Bart, his head henchman, to retrieve the youngster to prevent him from talking. Bart fails in his attempt to dry-gulch Rocky who chases him, knocks him from his horse, and downs him in a fight. Bart reveals to Rocky that he was trying to kill the youngster, a member of the dreaded Black Hills outlaw gang, before he manages to escape.

Larry is taken to Nugget's ranch where he is treated royally in the attempt to reform him. Since he fears Bart, Larry wants to return to the gang, but agrees to stay. Rocky prevents the youngster from going back on his word when he tries to escape, but Bart and fellow gang member Jack arrive to take him back as he and Rocky talk. The hoodlums pull guns but are tricked by Rocky, who bests them in a donnybrook before they manage to escape.

Realizing that his former friends wish to harm him, Larry tells Rocky where the hideout is. Rocky leaves in search of the hideout after telling Nugget to inform the sheriff. Larry leaves the ranch to help his new-found friend when he sees him leave for the hideout alone. Arriving to the sound of hot lead, Larry helps Rocky get away but returns with him to search for clues. Finding nothing, they return to town to see Nugget.

As he and Nugget try to determine a pattern to the attacks to Nugget's wagons, Rocky notices a freight wagon leaving town and follows it astride his faithful stallion, Black Jack. Rocky stops the wagon and finds gold bars in the crates marked tools. He hijacks the wagon from Buck, who informs the sheriff of what happened. Bart is ordered by Gaines to locate and retrieve the wagon.

Having hidden the wagon at Nugget's, Rocky locates Bart and offers to split the take if Bart takes him to his boss. Meanwhile, the sheriff arrives at Nugget's in search of Rocky and informs Larry and Sally of the theft of the wagon. Larry prepares to saddle his horse and leave when he discovers the wagon in Nugget's barn.

Unaware of Rocky's ruse, Larry then goes to town in search of Nugget, but unable to find him, makes the mistake of revealing to Gaines that the wagon is at Nugget's. Larry is taken to the gang's hideout where Rocky awaits the arrival of the boss. Gaines orders that Larry and Rocky be tied up as he departs.

The devious attorney arrives at Nugget's to

confiscate the wagon and decides to take Sally along as hostage. Meanwhile, Rocky manages to free himself and Larry after tricking their guard, Jake. Rocky sends Larry for a posse as he heads for Nugget's to encounter the crooks. Nugget informs him that they have gone and taken Sally with them.

Rocky takes off after the stolen wagon and succeeds in overtaking it. He gains possession but is chased by a host of lead-slinging bandits. The posse arrives to assist Rocky who then chases Gaines and Bart back to the hideout. Gaines goes down after a gunfight with Rocky, who now takes on Bart in a fistfight. Bart is mauled by Rocky and then turned over to the sheriff and held for trial.

With the end of the Black Hills outlaw gang now accomplished and the danger to his friend Nugget's freight business over, Rocky promises a reformed Larry that he can join him at the county seat and become a lawman after he has finished his schooling.

THUNDERING CARAVANS

54 Mins .... June 20, 1952

ALLAN LANE .... "Rocky" Lane
EDDY WALLER .... Nugget Clark
MONA KNOX .... Alice Scott
ROY BARCROFT .... Ed Brill
ISABEL RANDOLPH .... Deborah Crantston
RICHARD CRANE .... Dan Reed
BILL HENRY .... Bert Crantson
EDWARD CLARK .... Tom
PIERRE WATKIN .... Head Marshal
STANLEY ANDREWS .... Henry Scott
BOYD "RED" MORGAN. .... Joe
and BLACK JACK

ASSOC. PRODUCER .... Rudy Ralston
DIRECTED BY .... Harry Keller
WRITTEN BY .... M. Coates Webster
PHOTOGRAPHED BY .... John MacBurnie
MUSIC .... Stanley Wilson

Rocky and Nugget try to comfort Mona Knox after she reads the headline in the paper about her boyfriend, Deputy Richard Crane. He is accused of being an ex-convict. The scene is from THUNDERING CARAVANS.

Busy U.S. Marshal Rocky Lane, having just brought in the last of the notorious Crowder gang, is dispatched to the gold-mining town of Edgewater to help Sheriff Nugget Clark put an end to the constant attacks on the area wagons. The town's troubles become very evident to Rocky when he happens upon the attempted hijacking of an ore wagon. After the driver is shot, Rocky drops one of the bandits from his steed before routing the other and stopping the run-away wagon.

Rocky reports to Sheriff Clark upon reaching Edgewater to tell of the trouble he has encountered and finds the old-timer, who is up for re-election, having problems with mine owner Henry Scott. Scott assails Clark for the incompetency he feels has been shown by his inability to do anything about the repeated attacks on the ore wagons. Nugget also has problems with Deborah Cranston, owner-editor of the *Edgewater Bugle*, who just so happens to be the driving force behind the outlaws. Her attacks against the sheriff are supported by her brother Bert, the local express agent who is to oppose Nugget in the election.

Escaped convict Ed Brill arrives to fuel the fire when he informs Mrs. Cranston that Nugget's deputy, Dan Reed, is a former convict who served time with him in jail. With plans to print news of Dan's tainted past in the next edition, Mrs. Cranston advises Brill to confront the deputy and attempt to blackmail him to the tune of one thousand dollars.

Determined to up hold the law, Dan attempts to apprehend the prison escapee but fails. Rocky and Sheriff Clark arrive and chase Brill to Midas, a nearby ghost town, but lose him when the burly badman slips through a secret floor panel. Joe, an accomplice of Brill's, knocks the sheriff out, but is caught and pounded by Rocky, who then loses him while trying to aid Sheriff Clark. Brill mounts his horse and heads back to Edgewater, only to be chased and caught by Rocky who then manages to out draw and shoot his game.

Dan confesses to have served time and once being mixed up with outlaws. He informs Rocky that this girlfriend Alice Scott is the only one in town who knows of his former activities. Rocky asks Sheriff Clark

Rocky comes to the rescue of the sheriff's deputy (Richard Crane) in this scene in the famous Republic cave set.

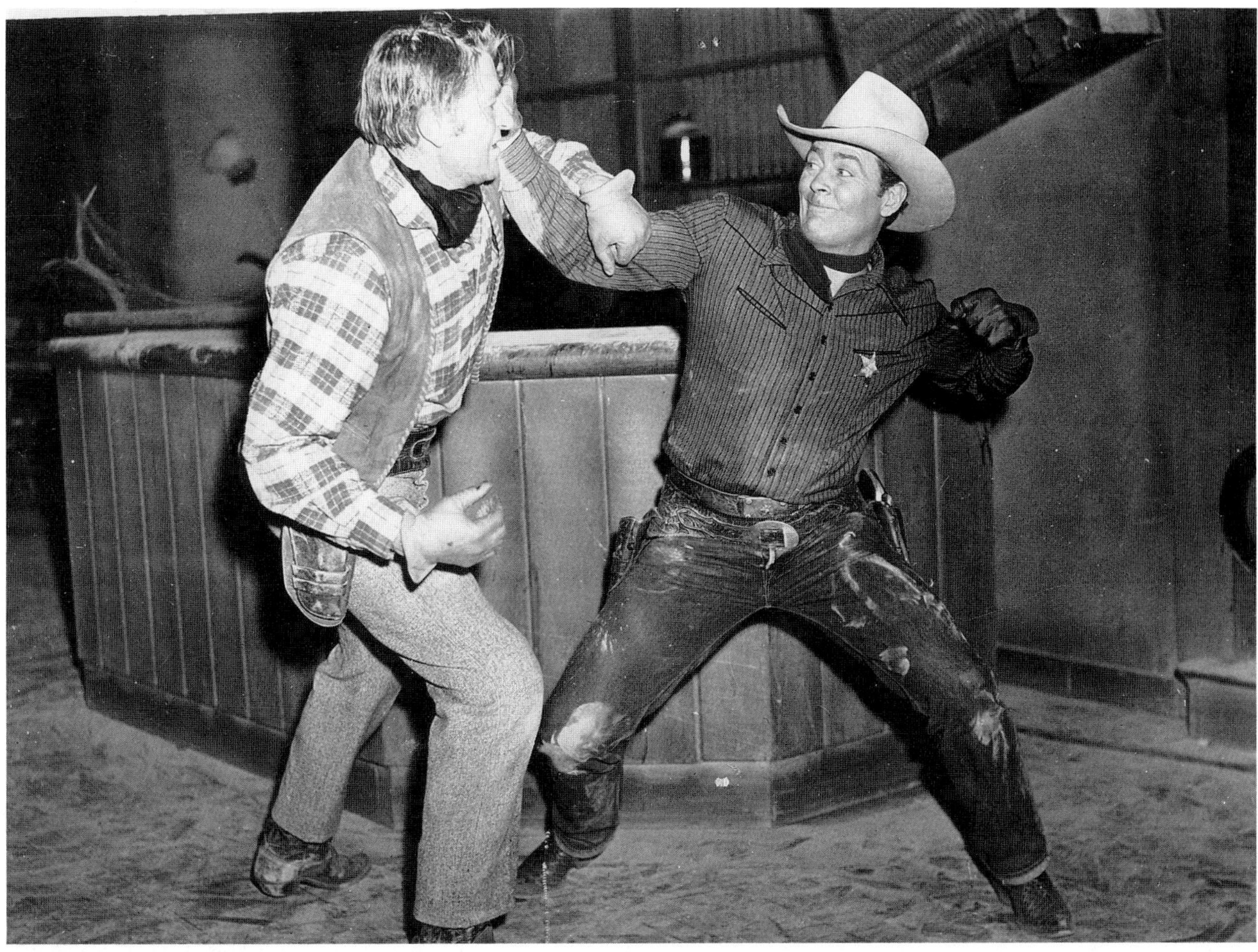

Rocky and Boyd "Red" Morgan have a scrap in the deserted bar of a ghost town. The scene is from THUNDERING CARAVANS.

to form a posse from the townsfolk who come to vote, and they will return to Midas to give the ghost town a thorough search.

After alerting his sister to the arrival of the miner's payroll, Bert joins her plan to take the money and frame Dan for stealing it. Bert gives the payroll to Dan who is joined by Rocky in his trip to deliver it. The Cranstons spot the departing duo and arrange for one of their hired guns to dispose of them. The attempt is foiled when Rocky chases the gunmen after ordering Dan to continue on his journey. Scott receives the payroll bag but opens it to find nothing but rocks after Dan departs. Heading back to town, Dan is captured by Bert and Joe when he spots the stolen ore wagons being moved.

As the townspeople read of Dan's past in the morning paper, Scott arrives to inform Sheriff Clark that the payroll money was missing from the bag. Refusing to believe that Dan is guilty of any wrongdoing, Rocky believes that the Cranstons are involved when he recollects that Bert gave the payroll pouch to Dan and further surmises that Brill informed Mrs. Cranston about Dan. Rocky devises a scheme to bring the Cranstons out in the open by having Nugget tell Mrs. Cranston that Rocky wounded one of the outlaws and is obtaining a confession.

Rocky watches the reaction of the Cranstons and follows Bert when he leaves town. The trail leads to Midas, where Rocky observes Bert entering the secret passageway through which Brill escaped earlier. Rocky locates Dan and frees him from his bonds as Bert and Joe continue to load the ore wagons. Rocky and Dan confront the men, who are joined by another of their number. A wild free-for-all takes place with Bert managing to escape in one of the ore wagons. Rocky gives chase in a second wagon, which wrecks during the chase causing him to continue by riding the wagon team. He jumps into Bert's wagon and takes him in the fight which follows.

With the Cranstons apprehended and incarcerated and Sheriff Clark's re-election a certainty, Rocky rides away to his next assignment.

Roy Barcroft has been thwarted again by Rocky in this scene from THUNDERING CARAVANS.

DESPERADOES' OUTPOST

54 Mins .... Oct. 8, 1952

ALLAN LANE .... "Rocky" Lane
EDDY WALLER .... Nugget Clark
ROY BARCROFT .... Jim Boylan
MYRON HEALEY .... Lieut. Dan Booker
LYLE TALBOT .... Walter Fleming
CLAUDIA BARRETT .... Kathy
LANE BRADFORD .... .Mike
LEE ROBERTS .... .Spec Matson
CHARLES EVANS .... .Major Seely
ZON MURRAY .... Tony
SLIM DUNCAN .... Army Sergeant
and BLACK JACK

ASSOC PRODUCER .... Rudy Ralston
DIRECTED BY .... Philip Ford
WRITTEN BY ....Arthur E. Orloff & Albert DeMond
PHOTOGRAPHED BY .... John MacBurnie
MUSIC .... Stanley Wilson

U.S. Investigator Rocky Lane is headed for El Mirado, California, to investigate the problems surrounding the mail shipments there when he encounters old-timer Nugget Clark in trouble. After having his last stage sent over a cliff by outlaws, Nugget and his niece Kathy decide to run for it when they spot Rocky and believe him to be an outlaw. Rocky stops the runaway buckboard and identifies himself. Desiring to remain incognito, Rocky hires on as Nugget's new driver.

Arriving in town, Nugget goes to the El Mirado Mortgage and Loan Company to get a loan. Walter Fleming, who is behind the attacks on the mail wagons, is not in favor of granting the loan but is talked into it by Rocky. Jim Boylan, foreman of the mine which supplies mercury to the U.S. Government and a Fleming accomplice, expresses displeasure at Fleming having granted a loan to the now-departed Nugget, especially since they were able to get $40,000 from the Mexican government for mercury which his men recently stole.

Rocky is introduced to Lieutenant Booker at Nugget's ranch and decides to inform him of his identity. A plan is implemented to allow Nugget's next stage to be attacked so one of the outlaws can hopefully be

captured. The plan works as Rocky guns down one of the lead-throwing bandits and captures another. The captive is loosely tied so that he can be trailed after escaping. Rocky's plan continues to work as Spec Matson escapes and is followed to the mines. He is seen reporting to Boylan by Rocky and Nugget. Rocky arrives and questions Boylan about the escapee and is told that he has not seen him.

ALLAN "ROCKY" LANE
and his stallion BLACK JACK
DESPERADOES' OUTPOST
with EDDY WALLER
ROY BARCROFT
MYRON HEALEY
LYLE TALBOT
CLAUDIA BARRETT
Written by Arthur Orloff and Albert DeMond
Associate Producer Rudy Ralston
Directed by Philip Ford
A REPUBLIC PICTURE

Lieutenant Booker wants to inspect the equipment in the mine because he has recently noticed a drop in mercury production. Boylan informs him that the trouble is in the smelting equipment and then decides to eliminate the curious man to prevent him from discovering that the mercury is being stolen. To attain his goal, Boylan arranges a fight between mine worker Mike and Lieutenant Booker. Accused of being involved in a drunken brawl, Lieutenant Booker is relieved of his duties of maintaining safe production of mercury at the mine by Major Sealey. Boylan then orders Mike to have Spec get rid of Rocky and Nugget's last stage.

Rocky returns to Nugget's after losing the trail and finds Lieutenant Booker wounded. When Rocky notices mercury in the water being used to treat his wounds, he inspects Nugget's faucet and finds that mercury comes out with the water. Rocky concludes that the raids on Nugget's stages are an attempt to force him into bankruptcy and enable the crooks to gain control of his ranch. Doing so would allow the crooks easier access to stealing the mercury.

Rocky, Lieutenant Booker, and Nugget go to the mine to verify that the pipeline runs to Nugget's but are confronted by henchmen Mike and Troy. The roughnecks fall to a brawling Rocky, who then discovers that the pipeline does not run to Nugget's ranch. In order to find out exactly who is behind the treachery, Rocky advises Nugget to put his ranch up for sale.

Nugget informs Fleming that he plans to sell his ranch, but the plan goes awry when Boylan is given a badge that Rocky dropped during the brawl with Mike and Tony. Suggesting that one last big haul be made before they depart, Boylan heads for the mine as Fleming waits at Nugget's for prospective buyers of the ranch. No buyers arrive and a nervous Fleming gives himself away. Rocky tricks Fleming who has pulled a gun on him, but Spec arrives to free him from his

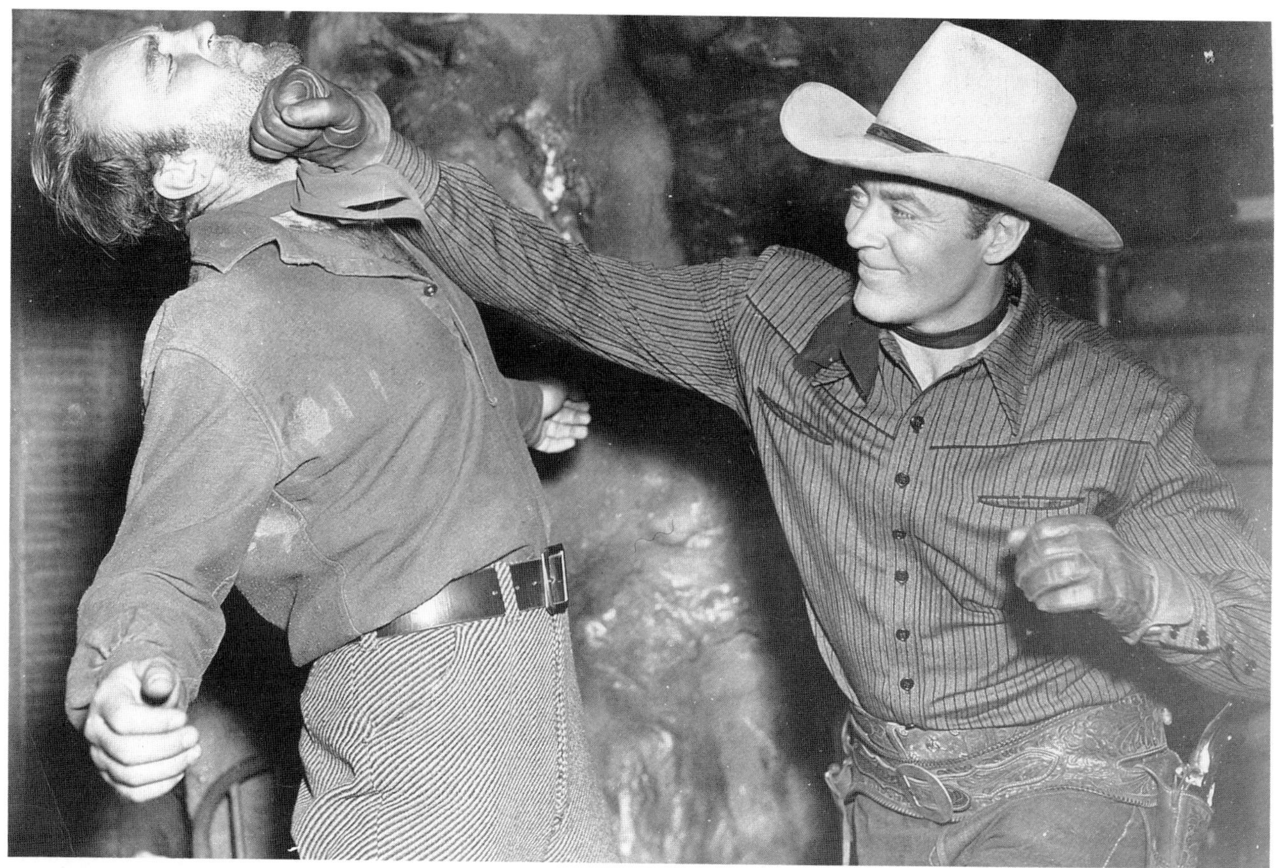

Lane Bradford takes a right to the chin from Rocky in this scene from DESPERADOES' OUTPOST.

That wound that Myron Healey has doesn't look too serious. Maybe leading lady Claudia Barret is just sweet on him.

Rocky and Nugget spy on the outlaws from some phony Republic Pictures' brush and rocks. The scene is from DESPERADOES' OUTPOST.

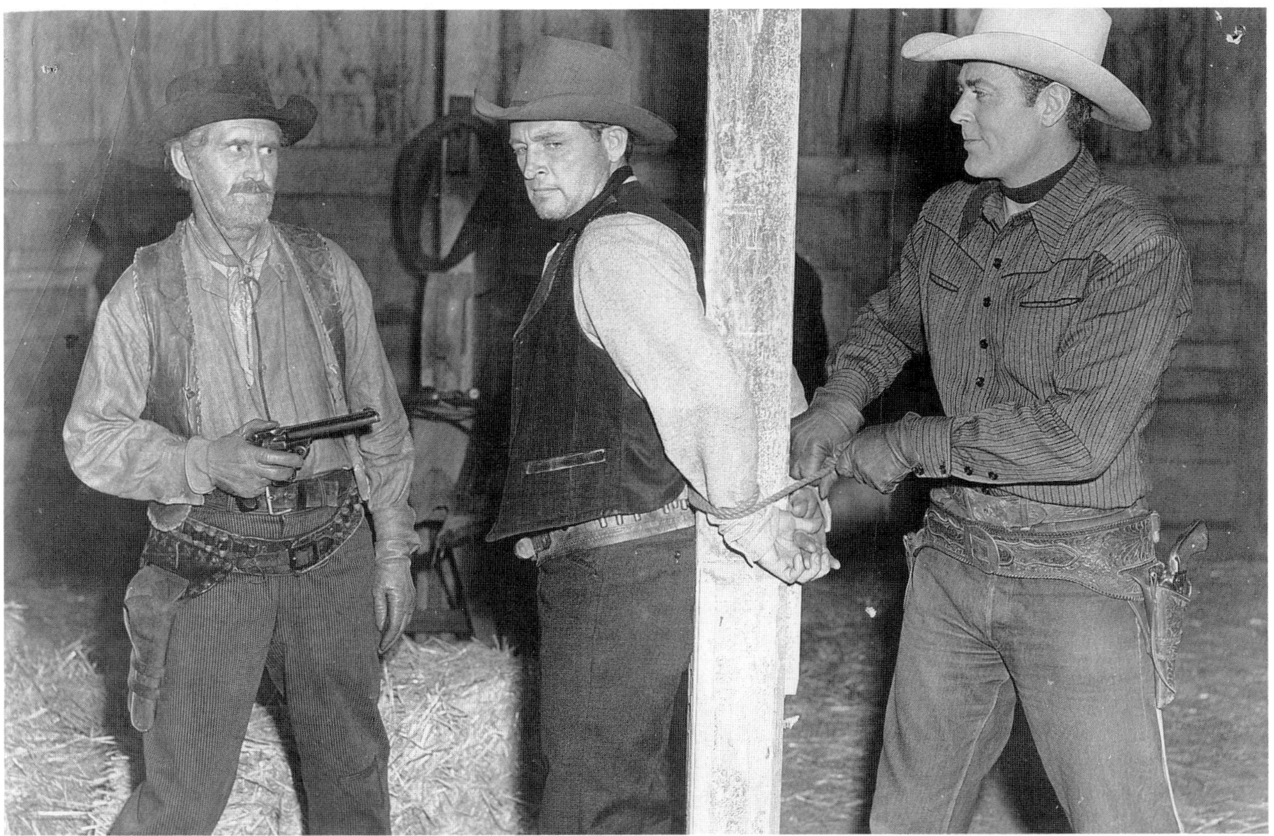

"You'll talk or else," Nugget informs Lee Roberts in this scene from DESPERADOES' OUTPOST.

Tracking the desperadoes requires stealth, as Rocky demonstrates in this scene from DESPERADOES' OUTPOST.

predicament.

Rocky and Nugget are taken to the mine where Boylan plans to hold them hostage. Rocky tricks Spec and metes out a dose of lead to the gunman. With Fleming and Boylan heading for town, Rocky manages to catch them. Fleming is shot in the gunfight and Boylan goes down to the hard-hitting Rocky.

Rocky bids farewell to his friends after telling Nugget that the government just might give him a stage for helping apprehend the crooks.

MARSHAL OF CEDAR ROCK

54 Mins .... Feb. 1, 1953

ALLAN LANE .... "Rocky" Lane
EDDY WALLER .... Nugget Clark
PHYLLIS COATES .... Martha Clark
ROY BARCROFT .... Henry Mason
BILL HENRY .... Bill Anderson
ROBERT SHAYNE .... Paul Jackson
JOHN CRAWFORD .... Chris Peters
JOHN HAMILTON .... Warden
KENNETH MACDONALD .... Sheriff Collins
HERBERT LYTTON .... John Harper
and BLACK JACK

ASSOC. PRODUCER .... Rudy Ralston
DIRECTED BY .... Harry Keller
SCREENPLAY BY .... Albert DeMond
PHOTOGRAPHED BY .... John MacBurnie
MUSIC .... Stanley Wilson

Bill Anderson, wrongfully imprisoned for the theft of $100,000 stolen from the Cedar Rock Bank and Trust Co., is allowed to escape from prison. The escape has been set up so that the stolen money can be recovered. Bill is forced to abandon his horse when it becomes lame, but he manages to get a ride with John Harper, a representative of the Western States Railroad, who is also on the way to Cedar Rock. Harper allows Bill to get out of the buckboard one mile from Cedar Rock as requested.

In town, Nugget Clark and his niece Martha attempt to get a loan from banker Henry Mason because the $100,000 theft has virtually cleaned out all the ranchers, Mason refuses the request and suggests that Nugget and his friends sell their ranches to the Consolidated Real Estate Co., which he is the head of, for two hundred dollars per acre. Knowing that the railroad is coming, an angry Nugget leaves.

Harper arrives at the bank and informs Mason that the railroad will be paying seven hundred dollars per acre for property in the area. Upon learning that his office was Harper's first stop, the crooked banker has henchman Chris Peters kidnap him.

The bank is the scene of much activity as Bill arrives shortly afterwards with gun drawn in an attempt to force Mason into confessing that he embezzled the stolen money. U.S. Marshal Rocky Lane, having been sent to watch Bill, shoots the gun from his hand. Mason rewards Rocky with an imported cigar, but Bill escapes

when outlaws ride in and shoot up the town. A busy Rocky is called on to save Martha after the gunfire causes her buckboard to run away. A grateful Nugget offers Rocky a job at his ranch.

Bill goes to Nugget's to see his girlfriend Martha, only to have the resentful old man pull a gun on him. After convincing her uncle that Bill can be trusted, Nugget puts away his gun. When Rocky arrives and questions Nugget about Bill, the secluded escapee takes flight. Rocky, on his stallion Black Jack, chases Bill and knocks him from his horse but two of Mason's henchmen, under orders to watch Nugget's ranch, have followed Rocky. Bill manages to get away while the marshal battles the men with guns and fists before dispatching them both.

Rocky returns to Nugget's and identifies himself as a marshal. Nugget and Martha are relieved to know that Rocky believes Bill to be innocent and that he thinks Mason has a hand in the skullduggery. Before the lawman leaves, Paul Jackson, hired by Mason to pose as a railroad representative, arrives and offers Nugget one hundred dollars per acre for his property. He suggests that Nugget and his rancher friends accept the generous offer made by Mason, whereupon Rocky, noting that the man is in possession of one of Mason's imported cigars, becomes suspicious.

Rocky and the Clarks head for Mason's office but are beaten there by Bill, who searches the office. He takes refuge in a closet upon hearing Mason, Rocky, Nugget, and Martha arrive but exits quickly when he hears them discuss the ridiculous offer made by the railroad. Prepared to make known what Harper told him, Bill is knocked out from behind by Mason in an attempt to hold the escapee for the sheriff.

Bill is lead away by Rocky, who confesses to the young man that he is a marshal. Jackson overhears as Bill reveals his knowledge of the railroad representative to the marshal. Rocky and Bill catch up to Jackson at his hotel room and force him to confess. Under intense questioning, Jackson reveals to them that Mason is about to kidnap Nugget, who has been granted power of attorney for all ranchers, in an attempt to force him to sign over their lands.

Rocky forces Jackson to accompany him and Bill to the place the Clarks are being held. The imposter dies in hail of gunfire as he enters the barn first. Rocky and Bill dispose of Mason's henchmen in the ensuing gunfight. Left to fend for himself, Mason is subdued by Rocky in a tough fistfight.

Rocky wires his superiors that Bill is innocent and that the guilty parties have been apprehended.

SAVAGE FRONTIER

54 Mins .... May 15, 1953

ALLAN LANE .... "Rocky" Lane
EDDY WALLER .... Nugget Clark
BOB STEELE .... Sam Webb
ROY BARCROFT. .... William Oakes
RICHARD AVONDE .... Cherokee Kid
BILL PHIPPS .... Johnny Webb
JIMMY HAWKINS .... Davie
LANE BRADFORD .... Tulsa Tom
JOHN CASON .... Buck Madsen
KENNETH MACDONALD .... Bradley
BILL HENRY .... Dan Longley
GERRY FLASH .... Pete
and Black Jack

ASSOC. PRODUCER .... Rudy Ralston
DIRECTED BY .... Harry Keller
WRITTEN BY .... Dwight Babcock & Gerald Geraghty
PHOTOGRAPHED BY .... Bud Thackery
MUSIC .... Stanley Wilson

The Cherokee Kid, Tulsa Tom, and Buck Madsen, three outlaws, head for Bitter Springs to report to William Oakes who has sent for them. A deputy trailing them is caught and riddled with bullets.

The gunmen arrive in town and Cherokee, who needs a dentist, goes to Bitter Springs Tonsorial Parlor run by Sheriff Nugget Clark. Cherokee is given gas by the rather dimwitted sheriff/dentist. Deputy U.S. Marshal Rocky Lane arrives in search of the outlaws and is fired upon by Tom and Buck, who escape after the gunbattle. A gassed Cherokee is easily caught. William Oakes, owner of the hotel and cafe, introduces himself to Rocky and informs him that the town has been peaceful for many years with little need for a lawman. Oakes intimates that the need for law will now be necessary since Cherokee, Tom, and Buck, members of the Sam Webb gang, are on the loose. Sheriff Clark informs Rocky that Webb is now reformed and is a respectable citizen.

Having been informed by his sister, Elizabeth, and brother Johnny of the presence of his former partners, Sam departs to confront them and make sure they realize that he is no longer interested in their line of work. He heads for the office of Oakes, a former gang member, who still, though deemed respectable, is as crooked as ever. Oakes tries to get Sam to rejoin the gang by threatening to inform his brother Johnny who helped in a bank holdup.

Sam returns to his ranch to find Rocky and Sheriff Clark questioning Elizabeth and Johnny. Rocky warns him that being involved with his former partners is a parole violation and suggests that he stay away from them. After the lawmen leave, Elizabeth suggests that Sam tell the whereabouts of the villains but he refuses, knowing that doing so would cause problems for Johnny.

Back in town, Oakes takes a meal to the jail for Cherokee in which a gun has been concealed. Cherokee forces Deputy Dan to free him. After shooting the deputy in the back, Cherokee pumps more lead into his fallen body before escaping in a wagon provided by Oakes. Rocky arrives and cuts cross-country on Black Jack to catch the fleeing criminal. After jumping into the wagon, he and Cherokee fight, but the wagon wrecks and Cherokee gets away.

Rocky and Sheriff Clark are confronted by Oakes, who informs them that a meeting of the townsfolk has resulted in the request that the sheriff resign. Sheriff Clark turns in his badge, but Rocky informs Oakes that Cherokee is wanted by the government for the senseless murder of a deputy and that he will bring him in.

As Rocky is being shaved by Nugget, he asks him about Oakes. He suggests that Oakes be watched since he feels that who ever delivered the meal to the jail from Oakes' cafe also smuggled the gun in. As they talk, they see Sam arrive at Oakes' place. For the first time in years, Sam is wearing a gun. Although realizing that confronting Oakes could mean trouble for Johnny, Sam is willing to take the risk if it will end the senseless killings. Rocky arrives and listens at the door as Sam chastises Oakes for causing Nugget's firing. Sam is taken to jail by Rocky who must arrest him for violating his parole.

Sam is questioned by Rocky at the jail but refuses to cooperate. He changes his mind and prepares to talk, but is shot from outside the jail by Cherokee. Johnny arrives to get Rocky for locking his brother up. He accuses him of shooting Sam and is himself jailed. A badly-wounded Sam is ordered left at the jail for treatment because moving him would pose a threat to his life. Elizabeth remains to look after him.

Buck arrives to inform his boss of the impending arrival of a gold shipment. Oakes is very interested but feels Rocky is watching him. He decides to leave town so that Rocky will trail him, allowing Buck an opportunity to gun him down. Nugget, ordered to remain at the jail, sees Buck following Rocky so he leaves to help his friend. With Nugget gone, Johnny tricks Elizabeth into freeing him. He departs bent on killing Rocky.

Rocky realizes that he is being trailed by Buck and fells the outlaw with a bullet from his six-gun. Rocky chases Oakes and catches him at the Golden Queen Mine. A gun-battle takes place in which Rocky, with the help of Nugget, manages to fend off the attack of Oakes and Cherokee, who are hiding in the mine. The trigger-happy Cherokee is wounded by Rocky and then killed by Johnny, who learns that Cherokee wounded Sam.

Rocky chases Oakes back to town and prevents him from killing Sam. A donnybrook takes place that spells doom for Oakes. Sam recovers from his wounds and Johnny is forgiven, since his help resulted in the end of the Cherokee Kid.

BANDITS OF THE WEST

54 Mins .... Aug. 8, 1953

ALLAN LANE .... "Rocky" Lane
EDDY WALLER .... NUGGET CLARK
CATHY DOWNS .... Joanne Collier
ROY BARCROFT .... Bud Galloway
TREVOR BARDETTE .... Jeff Chadwick
RAY MONTGOMERY .... Steve Edrington
BYRON FOULGER .... Eric Strickler
HARRY HARVEY .... Judge Wolters
ROBERT BICE .... Dutch Clyburn
and BLACK JACK

ASSOC. PRODUCER .... Rudy Ralston
DIRECTED BY .... Harry Keller
WRITTEN BY .... Gerald Geraghty
PHOTOGRAPHED BY .... Bud Thackery
MUSIC .... Stanley Wilson

The Landale Gas Company, operated by Joanne Collier, is about to bring natural gas to the citizens of Landale, Texas, the first such community to provide its wholesale use. To attain this goal, her head engineer, Steve Edrington, and a friend, Nugget Clark, prepare to cut down a fence on the property of Jeff Chadwick, erected to keep them out. As they do, burly foreman Bud Galloway stops them and unleashes a verbal assault which threatens to become physical as Marshal Rocky Lane rides up to cool things off. Rocky informs the parties that Judge Wolters will have to determine if the gas company is within its right.

In town, Steve and Joanne are admiring the new goods brought in for the general store when Dutch Clyburn and another of Chadwick's hands ride into town and almost run the duo down. Rocky observes their reckless behavior and follows them to the stage depot. After warning them that another such incident will result in their being jailed, Rocky is set upon by the roughnecks but bests them in a bruising fight.

Character actor Eddy Waller came to Hollywood in 1936 and worked regularly in movies and television until about 1960. He died at the age of eighty-eight in 1977. He is probably best remembered for his role as Nugget Clark in the Allan "Rocky" Lane film series.

Jeff Chadwick arrives on the incoming stage after serving a seven-year jail term for the murder of Joanne's father and posts bail for his men who Rocky is about to jail. Chadwick vows vengeance on those he finds guilty of causing him to spend time in jail for a crime he didn't commit. When the judge decrees that the gas company can put an underground line on his property, Chadwick sees this as more proof that the town is out to get him.

Galloway is worried that his boss will discover that much of his cattle has been sold but remarks to Dutch that Chadwick will merely have to be removed again as he was framed for the earlier murder which was actually committed by Galloway. The means to this end are implemented when Dutch is dispatched to sabotage the gas project. After turning a valve and releasing gas, Dutch is spotted and chased back to the Chadwick ranch by Rocky. Believing that Chadwick is responsible for the trouble, Rocky chastises and threatens to jail him.

During a routine check of the gas pressure, Steve learns that there is a leak somewhere. He and Rocky find the trouble spot on Chadwick's land although Nugget has found it first. After rescuing a passed-out Nugget, Rocky finds the judge's decree handed Chadwick upon his return to town. Rocky goes to the Chadwick ranch to jail the ex-convict who has discovered the rather sparse herd. Chadwick is told by Galloway that he sold the cattle and will pick up the money the next day.

Now in jail, Chadwick sees the beautiful view provided by the natural gas lamps, which are lit by Joanne and Steve for the first time that night. Chadwick is permitted by Rocky to light the lamps in the jail and marvels at the spectacle. Told by Rocky that this is what he is fighting, Chadwick is questioned about the murder he is thought to have committed. Galloway arrives with money from the cattle sale to bail his boss out.

The plot to eliminate the now-freed Chadwick continues as Dutch knocks out a storekeeper who happened to be the jury foreman when Chadwick was found guilty. Dutch douses the gas lamp in his store. The still-flowing gas results in an explosion and the storekeeper's death. Chadwick is again blamed for the trouble by an unruly mob bent lynching him. Judge Wolters and Eric Strikler, owner of the local coal and wood company, ask that Rocky arrest Chadwick, but the marshal refuses as he believes him innocent.

After resigning from office, Rocky goes to Boulder City to check on the cattle sale alleged by Galloway. Dutch overhears Rocky asking questions and heads for the Chadwick ranch to tell Galloway. Nugget spots him and decides to follow. The old-timer hears Dutch report to Galloway and informs Chadwick, but the twosome is caught and tied up.

Rocky and Steve go to Chadwick's to get Galloway but are fired on by Dutch and fellow henchmen. After eliminating the gunmen and learning that Nugget and Chadwick are captive at the warehouse, Rocky goes there and engages Galloway and a henchman in a fistfight. After besting the ruffians and pulling Nugget and Chadwick to safety from the building now filled with gas, Rocky is about to go back to pull Galloway out, but the foreman is blown to bits as he pulls his gun to shoot Rocky.

Though asked to stay on as marshal, Rocky leaves for California after Chadwick has been cleared and the bandits of the West have been eliminated.

EL PASO STAMPEDE

54 Mins .... Sept. 8, 1953

ALLAN LANE .... "Rocky" Lane
EDDY WALLER .... Nugget Clark
PHYLLIS COATES .... Alice Clark
STEPHEN CHASE .... Mason Ramsey
ROY BARCROFT. .... Floyd Garnett
EDWARD CLARK .... Josh Bailey
TOM MONROE .... Marty
STANLEY ANDREWS .... Marshal Zeke Banning
WILLIAM TANNEN .... Joe
and BLACK JACK

ASSOC. PRODUCER .... Rudy Ralston
DIRECTED BY .... Harry Keller
WRITTEN BY .... .Arthur Orloff
PHOTOGRAPHED BY .... John MacBurnie
MUSIC .... Stanley Wilson

Cattle herds for the soldiers fighting in the Spanish-American War are a constant target of raiders near the Mexican border. U.S. Marshal Zeke Banning is on the way to Clarksburg, a town near the boarder, when a group of raiders attack the stage and kill him. Special Investigator Rocky Lane is alerted to the trouble by the sound of gunfire and rides up to stop the runaway stage. Rocky helps the wounded driver who informs him that the cattle rustlers are responsible for Banning's death.

Arriving in Clarksburg to investigate the rustling problem, Rocky goes to see Nugget Clark at the local feed store. Rocky learns from the old-timer that the cattle rustlers and the herds seem to just vanish after each occurrence. Nugget also reveals that only he and his daughter Alice were aware of the impending arrival of Banning. Rocky hires on at Nugget's so he can operate undercover.

Town dentist Mason Ramsey, the picture of responsibility, is secretly behind the raids on the herds. Josh Baily, Nugget's hired hand and informer to Ramsey, lets his boss know that Banning is now dead. Ramsey orders Floyd Garnett, his head henchman, to steal some feed from Clark's store for the cattle they have rustled.

At dinner, Rocky and Nugget have their meal interrupted by a rancher who was wounded in the attempt to steal his cattle. They get help from other ranchers to fend off the attack on the rancher's herd. After blocking the pass with wagons, they trade gunfire with the rustlers and drive them off. Rocky suggests that the ranchers hold up their shipments for a while.

Rocky is introduced to Bailey the next morning and asks Nugget if he was present when it was learned that Banning would arrive. Alice intervenes and reports that a lot of feed is missing. Suspecting theft, the shop key is left in a conspicuous place so that the culprit can be caught.

That night Rocky sees Bailey and others stealing feed and he follows their wagon. Rocky is trailed by a rustler who spots him. The feed wagon comes loose from the team and plunges into the river. Rocky chases one of the rustlers and drops him from his horse with a well-placed bullet.

Bailey denies Rocky's accusations of any wrongdoing and is tied up and left with Nugget while Rocky looks for clues. Bailey cons Nugget into getting Ramsey to come and examine his persistant toothache and informs his boss that Rocky saw the feed wagon being stolen. Garnett knocks Nugget out and frees Bailey, only to have him recaptured by Rocky when he is unable to leave town with his cohorts.

Upon learning that Bailey was a frequent visitor to dentist Ramsey's office, even though he had false teeth, Rocky and Nugget search the office but find no file card on him. However, they do find a clipping in his office concerning a man across the border to whom stolen cattle have been sold.

When Nugget prepares to ship some feed back to his suppliers after ordering too much, Rocky suggests that Ramsey, whom he suspects of being the boss, be made aware of the shipment so they can trap him. Under the pretense of paying on a bill, Alice provides Ramsey with the information. However, when Ramsey gets fresh, she gets angry and reveals that he is suspected of being involved in the rustling. Alice is taken hostage as Ramsey orders Garnett to attack the feed wagons.

Nugget finds a note from Alice indicating that she went to Ramsey's. He and Rocky go in search of her and find only her purse. Feeling that Ramsey is aware of the trap laid for him, Rocky heads off to warn the wagon train.

The rustlers attack the wagons. Rocky helps to hold off the gunmen, who are apprehended when Nugget arrives with a posse. Ramsey manages to escape to a cave underneath a waterfall. It is here that Alice is held hostage but freed by Rocky, who bests the crooked dentist in a bruising fistfight.

After discovering the cave leads to a hidden valley through which the rustled herds had been driven, Rocky closes the books on the case and heads back to headquarters.

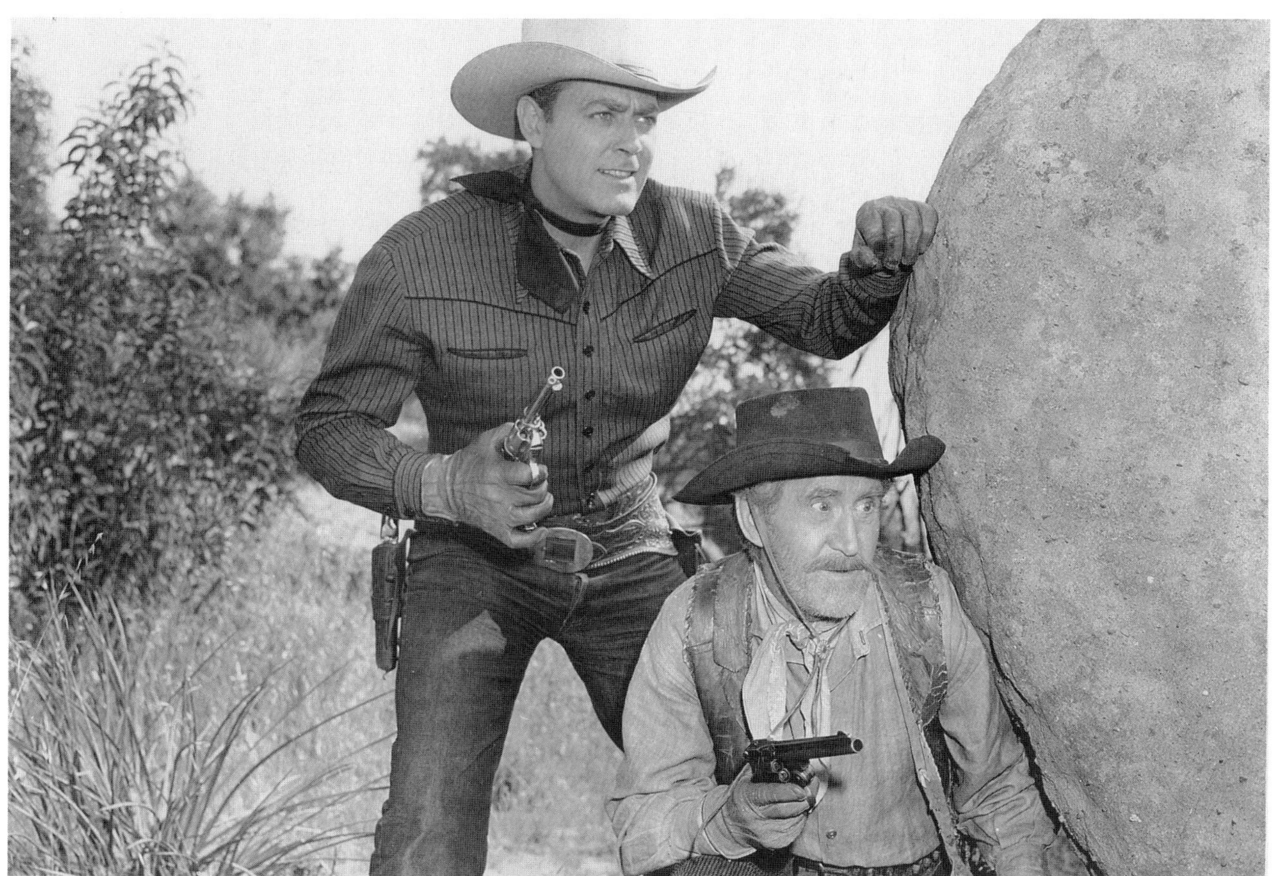

Rocky and Nugget seem to be looking to new adventures in this scene from EL PASO STAMPEDE. Unfortunately, this was to be their last shoot out.

CHAPTER 5

STRAIGHT FROM THE HORSE'S MOUTH; ALLAN LANE AND MR. ED—1961-1966

Three stars in a stall. Alan Young, Mr. Ed, and Connie Hines are all smiles as they pose for this publicity picture.

The concept of a talking animal movie star began in 1949 when Universal Pictures bought the rights to David Stern's novel about an English speaking army mule named Francis. The highly successful FRANCIS movie series starred Donald O' Connor as the discombobulated human companion of the loquacious quadruped. Popular character actor Chill Willis provided the gravelly voice of Francis. Six more popular features followed over the next seven years, but then Universal Pictures decided that they had gotten all the mileage they could out of the talking mule idea.

A fellow by the name of Arthur Lubin (who had directed all but the last FRANCIS feature film) felt that the "one joke idea" of a talking animal could still tickle a lot of funny bones and checked in to the possibility of purchasing the rights to the FRANCIS series. Universal informed him that it wasn't interested in selling the rights to its talking mule character even though no more feature films with the mule were planned.

Lubin didn't give up, however, and explored the possibility of a similar comic situation for an eventual television series. It took him until 1961, but finally his conception, MR. ED, made it to television on the CBS Television Network as a thirty-minute weekly situation comedy.

Mr. Ed, the title character, was a talking palomino horse. Alan Young starred as the horse's owner, a befuddled character named Wilbur Post, who was the only human with whom the horse would communicate. Connie Hines co-starred as Wilbur's sometimes perplexed and always scatterbrained wife. Allan Lane, of all people, provided the voice for Mr. Ed.

No one seems to know for sure how Allan Lane got the role. One story is that Lane (while at the studio for other purposes) was overheard by Arthur Lubin and Young, and from their eavesdropping they concluded that his voice would be right for the voice of the palomino horse. The story seems unlikely, but, then, there's no better one floating around.

MR. ED
THE TALKING HORSE and
HIS BARN FULL OF LAUGHS
starring:

ALAN YOUNG,
CONNIE HINES

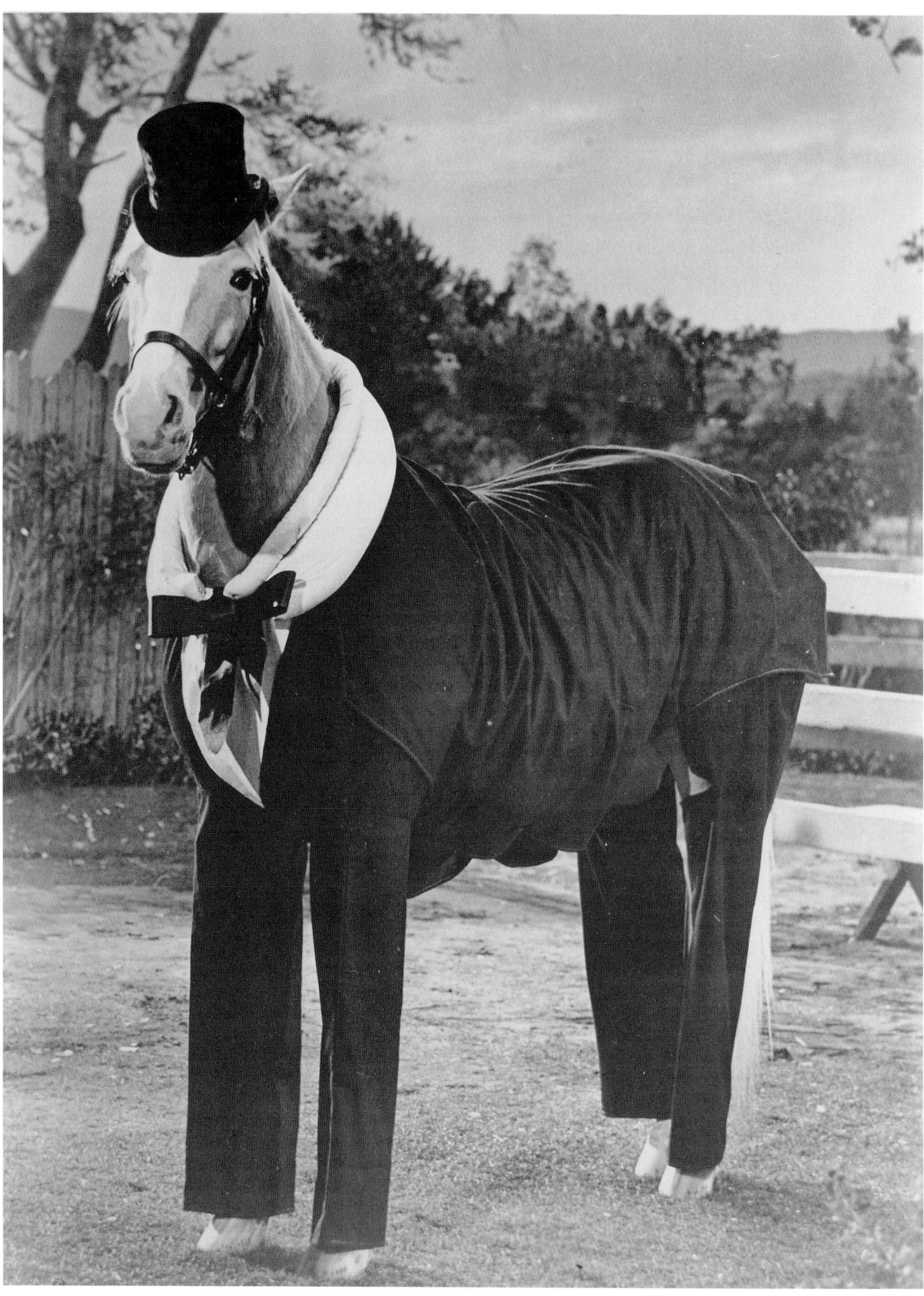

Mr. Ed is all dressed up with no place to go as he poses for this publicity picture for the series. Allan Lane never received any publicity for being the voice of the horse during the run of the show.

The one thing most likely is that he must have needed the work. After his Republic Pictures series concluded, Allan Lane batted around the movie and television studios finding a little work here and there but nothing that provided a steady income. There was a Red Ryder pilot in 1955 for a potential television series, but nothing ever came of it. He had supporting roles in television shows such as BONANZA, TEXAS JOHN SLAUGHTER, COLT 45, CHEYENNE, THE DAKOTAS, BRONCO, and GUNSMOKE, but, in most cases, the parts were small and in some you would have missed him if you had blinked. One of his better TV outings was an ALFRED HITCHCOCK PRESENTS episode entitled "Lamb to the Slaughter," which was actually directed by Hitchcock (Hitchcock only directed a very few TV episodes in the long-running series.)

Lane never received any billing on the MR. ED television series, and, again, there is some mystery as to why he never got on-screen credit. One story is that he was embarrassed by the downward turn in his career and that he considered the voice-over job as a talking horse the bottom of the acting barrel and didn't want credit—that is, until the show became a hit. When he then asked for on-screen credit, so the story goes, the producer decided that it would be a bad idea to publicize the voice of the horse because it might destroy the illusion which had been successfully attained of the horse *really* talking. At the very least, the series gave Allan Lane a good income for a period of five years and allowed him to retire comfortably.

Ron Honthaner was the sound effects editor on the MR. ED television series during the last year it was in production. Although he never had any contact with Allan Lane in person, he did, of course, have a close acquaintance with the workings of the show. I talked with Ron recently about the series.

RON HONTHANER: That was my first series job; in fact, my first job in the industry. When I was working on sound effects for the show, one of the things I had to do was split off Lane's sound tracks because we always did some fussing with the horse's dialogue to make it a little different. We would split the tracks onto separate units so that we could do that without effecting Alan Young's voice.

DAVID ROTHEL: Did you modify Lane's voice in some way?

RON HONTHANER: Yes. We modified it somewhat with filters. It made the voice a little deeper, as I recall.

DAVID ROTHEL: Did they do the voice live on the set as they were shooting the program?

RON HONTHANER: Yes, they did. The trainer handling the horse and Lane were so in sync on the dialogue that we didn't have to do much in that regard when we were doing the sound effects for the show. Lane's voice and the trainer's manipulation of the horse's mouth were right on target. They did the manipulation with wires attached to the horse's mouth.

DAVID ROTHEL: I was told that after the television series another Mr. Ed horse was trained by Glenn Randall to do the mouth movements by hand signals from the trainer. This was for some commercials that featured the horse.

RON HANTHANER: I think they used the wires on the TV show because they were actually playing scenes, which, of course, they wouldn't be doing in a commercial. It wasn't just Alan Young doing his dialogue and then cutting to the horse and making his mouth move. Allan Lane was giving a performance with Alan Young. They were doing scenes together with the horse. These were two performers going at it. The only difference was that Alan Young had to play his part to the horse while the horse's voice was coming from off camera.

It was an easy show in the sense that everybody was very relaxed about it, and they were all very nice people.

* * *

To expand on the techniques that Allan Lane and the Mr. Ed trainer had to develop for the MR. ED series, I would like to refer to an interview I did with horse trainer Glenn Randall when I wrote *THE GREAT SHOW BUSINESS ANIMALS*. Randall, a crusty old cowboy curmudgeon, trained some of the great movie horses such as Roy Rogers' Trigger, Dale Evans' horse Buttermilk, Rex Allen's Koko, and Gene Autry's last Champion.

GLENN RANDALL: The first Mr. Ed was trained by a dear friend of mine, Les Hilton, who was a very good horse trainer. He trained Mr. Ed to work (talk) on wire.

DAVID ROTHEL: Explain that to me.

GLENN RANDALL: You know how puppets work? Mr. Ed had a wire through his mouth, then up through his halter and down the side of his neck on the side away from the camera. When you pulled the wire, he opened his mouth.

DAVID ROTHEL: So the wire was the way they made Mr. Ed appear to talk.

This photo of horse trainer Glenn Randall and author David Rothel was taken in the spring of 1987.

GLENN RANDALL: If you remember the original Mr. Ed, you remember that you only saw him photographed from his shoulders to his head, unless it was some scene where he did mouth work—where he picked up a bowl or something. That was for the simple reason that a wire was on the off-camera side and the trainer was standing by his backside. When the trainer would pull the wire that ran through his mouth through the halter, the horse would open his mouth. When he released it, the horse would shut his mouth. That was the gimmick.

* * *

Allan Lane, to the best of my knowledge and research, never gave out an interview during the run of the MR. ED series. In fact, I have never been able to locate a printed full-fledged interview with the actor from *any* period of his career. He is known through his film roles and through the publicity that Republic Pictures (mostly) circulated while his films were being distributed.

Writer Jon Tuska (in his book *THE FILMING OF THE WEST*) quotes the retired Lane as saying, "I'm old, bald, and fat. I haven't done anything in years except the voice of the horse on TV in MISTER ED." And as far as this writer can determine, those were the last public words of Allan "Rocky" Lane.

This was a common two-shot camera position for Alan Young and Mr. Ed. It allowed the horse's trainer to stand behind the horse and manipulate the wires connected to its mouth, thus making it appear that the equine was talking.

CHAPTER 6

ALLAN "ROCKY" LANE— THE DISLIKED COWBOY

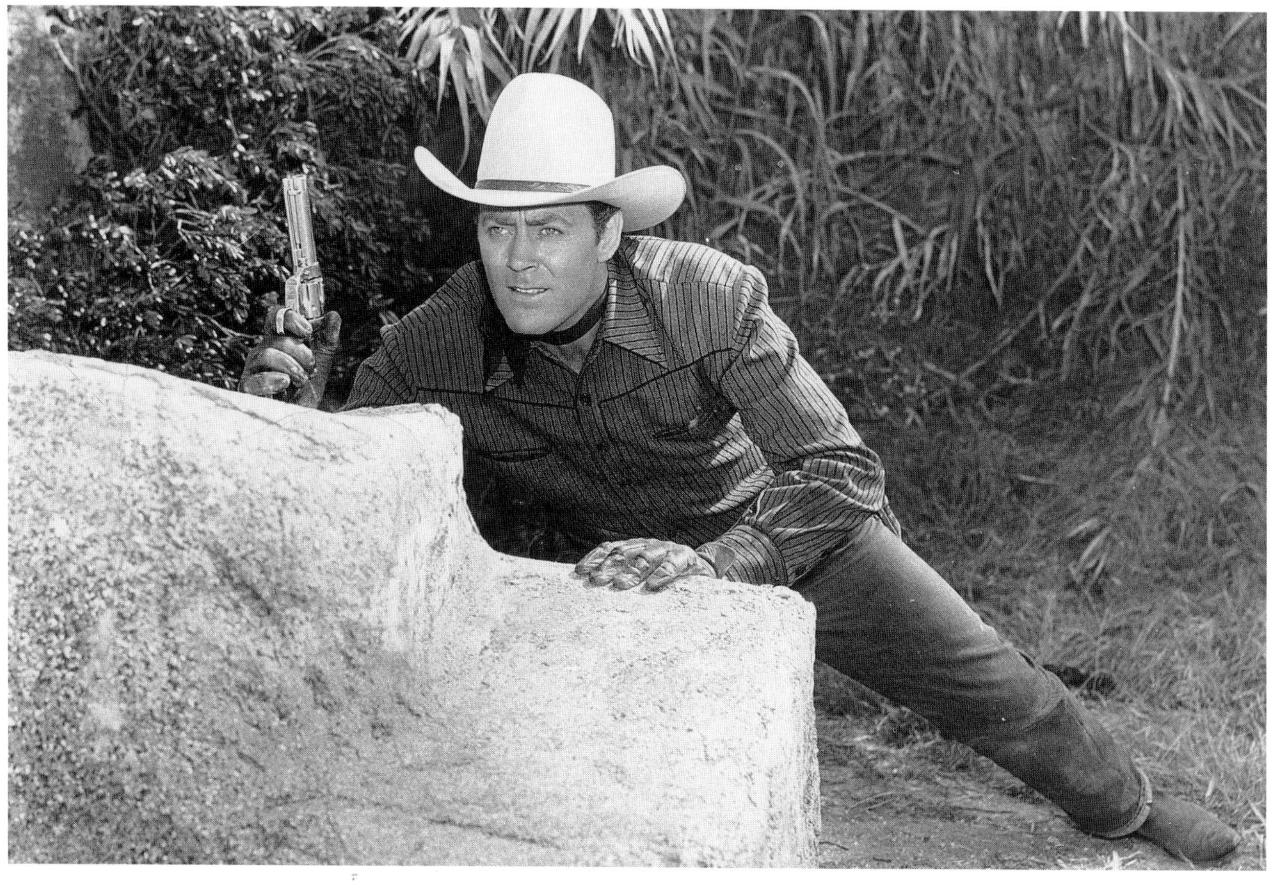

Allan "Rocky" Lane was a cowboy hero to all of us fans during the 1940s and early 1950s and very popular. We sat thrilled as he rode Thunder or, later, Black Jack to thwart the bad guy--more often than not Roy Barcroft. Because Lane was a hero on the silver screen and exuded all of the quantities of a cowboy hero through his characterization, we Saturday matinee fans assumed that most of these qualities were a part of the real man—that in real life Allan Lane was probably pretty much the same man we saw up there on the screen. We knew that he wasn't always rescuing damsels in distress, of course, or saving the nesters from the cattlemen, but we assumed that off screen and off Black Jack that he had lots of friends and that he was liked and respected by the people who worked with him on the production of his films.

It wasn't until many years later that word began to leak out that Allan Lane was not nearly as popular with the actors, directors, and production crew on the set at

Republic Pictures as he was to us fans in the motion picture theaters. As a writer who has interviewed many many Western actors and directors, I have found surprising the vehemence with which these people have spoken out about the negative qualities they saw and experienced working with the man. Some people would just not talk about him at all. Almost all of those who would talk about Lane had little good to say about him. Unhappily, it also became clear that those who had a few nice things to say about him didn't really know him well.

It is intriguing to me that of all the cowboy performers I have researched for my writing, Rocky Lane is the only one who was overtly disliked by many of his fellow workers. A performer such as Smiley Burnette had his detractors, I discovered, but he also had those who were close to him, thought the world of him, and would overlook annoying idiosyncrasies that may have been a part of the man. The same could be said about a few other performers I have checked on, but it was not so with those who knew Allan Lane. They carried their dislike for the man years after the last Allan Lane film had cranked through the camera, and they didn't mind telling a writer or the public about their feelings—on the record.

Back in the summer of 1979 at the St. Louis Western Film Fair, Yakima Canutt—actor, pioneer stunt man, and film director—was asked during a guest star panel session about working with Allan Lane. Yak, as gentle and kind a man as one is wont to find, reluctantly responded.

YAKIMA CANUTT: This is a person I hate to talk about.

Rocky Lane was a man who could have been one

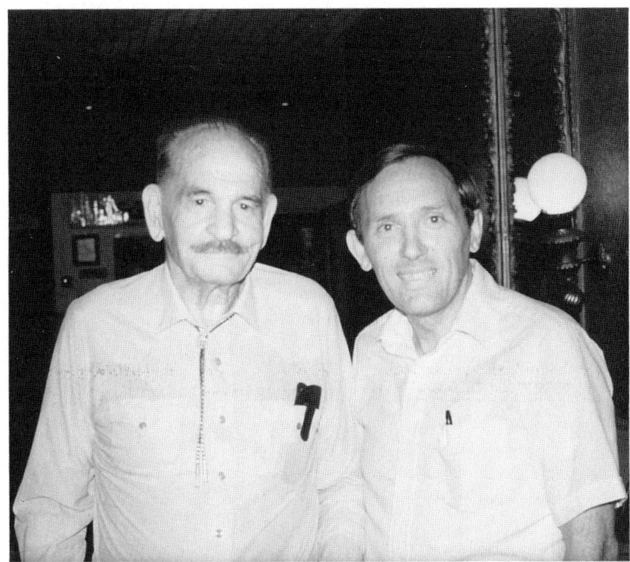

Director Yakima Canutt and author David Rothel at the 1979 St. Louis Western Film Fair.

Yakima Canutt pauses for photographer Howard Moore at the Raleigh Western Film Fair several years ago.

of the big stars if he had just behaved himself. He had a good personality on the screen; he was a good actor, but he wanted to run the whole show. I made a picture with him at Republic and it was nothing but fight and trouble all the way through, so I said that's the end of him. I'll do no more of that.

Well, he'd had the same trouble with all the other directors. So the next picture they started to do with him, no one [director] would take him. They called me and said, "You're going to have to do a picture with Rocky Lane." I said, "You can have him; I don't want him." They said, "Well, you're under contract, you know. That's your next job." I said, "I'll do it under one condition and one only. If he comes into your office screaming, run him out of there and tell him I'm running the show." They said, "Okay, we'll do that."

So I invited him over to my home for dinner the night before we started. I walked through the script with him and went over all the different points he was interested in. We talked it over. Then I said, "Allan, we've got to understand one another. You're going to act; I'm going to direct." He said that was fine.

The first day if was good; the second day he began to move in. The third day he was right back at his old self. I had a scene where I had two or three horses on wires crossing in the background, and he was walking across the foreground with

Kay Aldridge listens intently as Yakima Canutt completes his comments regarding Allan Lane at the 1979 St. Louis Western Film Fair.

the girl. The scene didn't amount to anything. If there was something wrong with it, I could cut in, but I wanted to get the long shot. Right in the middle of it he stopped and hollered, "Cut." I said, "What are you hollering cut for?" He said, "Look, I've got an investment in this business that I've got to protect. There's something wrong." I said, "Listen, I'll tell you when to cut, and from here on, no more out of you." He headed for the front office to get me fired right quick.

He came back in about thirty minutes with his head hanging down, and from then on, he was pretty good. They ran him out and told him to go down and do his job the way he [Yak] wants it or "we'll cut you loose, break your contract." That was the last time I worked with him.

Kay Aldridge, Allan Lane's leading lady in the serial DAREDEVILS OF THE WEST, was sitting on the same guest star panel as Yakima Canutt discoursed on Rocky. When he was through, she reminisced about working with her leading men in serials.

KAY ALDRIDGE: I get very wistful about Kane Richmond and Clayton Moore, and I enjoyed working with them very much. I liked Allan Lane, but I don't ever get wistful about him. . .I first met Allan Lane in New York when I was a model and he was a boy model, so it was hard for me to take him all that seriously as the great lover or great star. We worked together without, let's say, falling in love. He was, I think, a very handsome fellow, and I think he was his own worst enemy because he could have been the biggest star there was [at the studio.] He had it all going for him, especially when I first met him in New York. He just seemed like a horse with a burr in his tail—isn't that what you all say?

In the 1989 publication of Richard Lamparski's book WHATEVER BECAME OF. . .?, Eleventh Series, the author's profile on Kay Aldridge includes this comment: "She recently described him [Allan Lane] as 'the most conceited human being I have ever met.'"

In THE FILMING OF THE WEST by Jon Tuska, the author quotes another Allan Lane leading lady.

PEGGY STEWART: I don't mean to sound unkind, but he was the *dullest* man I ever met. Truly, I think the main problem with Allan was that he had absolutely no sense of humor—none at all. I was known to be kind of round in the derriere and so was Allan, so I nicknamed him Bubblebutt and he didn't think that was a bit funny. Why, anything like that you said in jest, it didn't get through to him at all. So, you just took Allan for what he was. As an actor doing his business or trade, he was one hundred per cent professional.

Peggy Stewart was asked about her Bubblebutt reference to Lane when she was on a guest star panel at a film festival in July of 1981.

PEGGY STEWART: It had nothing to do with him being hard to get along with. Allan was pleasant enough to get along with. You'd "Hi there" in the morning

Kay Aldridge was Allan Lane's leading lady in the 1943 serial DAREDEVILS OF THE WEST. This publicity still is from the film.

Peggy Stewart was Allan Lane's leading lady in five features. She is seen here with Lane in a scene from STAGECOACH TO MONTEREY.

Peggy Stewart is still a beautiful heroine. This photo was taken by the author at the 1982 Memphis Film Festival.

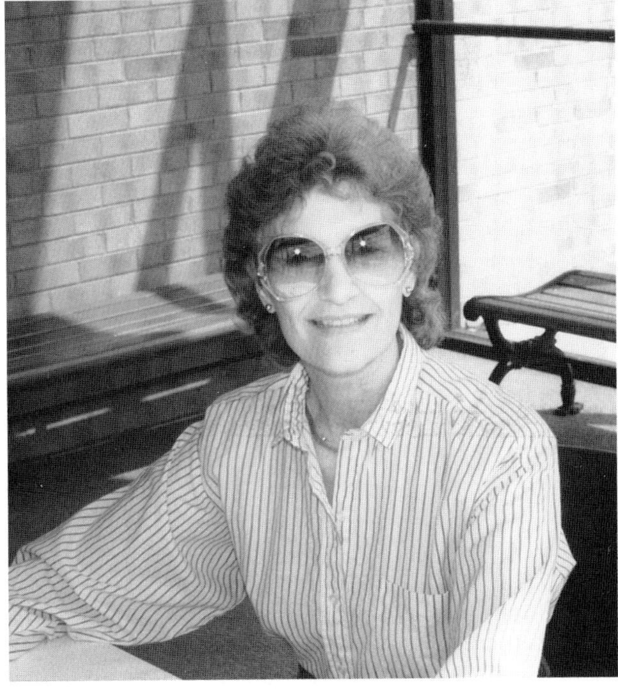

Peggy Stewart looks up from signing an autograph for a fan at the 1986 Riders of the Silver Screen Caravan at Knoxville, Tennessee.

and do your scenes, and you didn't really see each other between scenes. Republic was so darned much fun, and it was such a little family. All of the crew and all of the actors were always kidding each other. It was a playground. We really had fun over there. Allan didn't have a good sense of humor on the set. Maybe it was fine in his personal life; he was a very giving person; he was a very charitable person and all those wonderful things. We were only talking about his sense of humor. He was just a dead duck as far as that was concerned. He was a very conscientious person. He wanted that series to go; he wanted to be good in it; he had a tremendous ego like a lot of us have.

He was very conscious of his build, and he would worry you to death. The last thing you wanted to do on the set during the day when maybe you were having fun or maybe having some problems of your own was to worry about Allan's darned wardrobe. He would be figuring out whether he should wear a dark shirt and light pants or vice-versa, dark pants and a light shirt, and which one would make him look thinner. It caused us to say he had a bubblebutt. The highway to the Western street was very long and had quite an echo chamber. So I yelled down the street one day; I yelled, "Hi ya, Bubblebutt." I only called him that because it takes one to know one!

Former juvenile performer Twinkle Watts was a guest at the Knoxville, Tennessee, Riders of the Silver Screen Film Festival in the spring of 1988. She commented that Rocky Lane was very aloof on the set and treated her like a very little girl—which she was at the time, of course. She said that he was not the type to bounce her on his knee or anything of that sort. He didn't kid around while they were working. He treated her the way a serious adult would treat a little girl who was working on the set.

TWINKLE WATTS: He was a serious man, maybe too serious. I wasn't as serious as he was. Maybe that is why actors don't like children too much; they take it too seriously. I didn't. I think he had

Twinkle Watts appeared with Allan Lane and Linda Stirling in this scene from SHERIFF OF SUNDOWN.

a sense of humor when it came to something like, you know, when I made a mistake or something, and then it was like. . .I think he had a little sense of humor. People like that always took things seriously. After all, they were paid to take it seriously. I was paid to be a child, and that's what I was.

I only met him one time after we made pictures. I was riding some years later when I met him. He said, "Hi, Twinkle. How are you?" I was always surprised when anyone recognized me as an adult. But he recognized me and said, "Hello." That was it.

* * *

According to writer/stunt man Neil Summers, Rocky's sidekick Eddy Waller acknowledged a few years before his death that Rocky was hard to get to know, but that their working relationship was amicable.

* * *

Frequent heavy Marshall Reed, who was up for the Red Ryder role but lost out to Lane, told SERIAL WORLD writer Gregory R. Jackson that "Lane was a hard man to work with. In my way of thinking he was not one of the nice guys, because he had an ego that did not allow him to be.

Tris Coffin, who could be heavy or hero in films, told writer Jackson: "He was a practically impossible

Popular Western character actor Marshall Reed is seen here at the 1978 St. Louis Western Film Fair.

Western villains and character actors Terry Frost and Tris Coffin had a ball together at the 1976 Nashville Western Film Festival.

kind of a guy. He was so egotistic, so impressed with himself, and he gave the impression that nobody else had any ability or any talent."

* * *

Duncan Renaldo told SERIAL WORLD writer Gregory R. Jackson: "Allan wasn't too sweet, but I got along with him fine. He used to be damned temperamental at times and he was stubborn."

* * *

Supporting actor House Peters, Jr. commented to this writer at a recent film festival, "He [Lane] didn't impress me from the standpoint of being a very friendly person, but then again, I might not have spent enough time with him. I'm not one for knocking a fellow performer."

* * *

When I asked character actor/villain Terry Frost about Allan Lane, he tried to avoid commenting by changing the subject. Finally, he reluctantly answered my query with "I only worked a couple of pictures with him. I used to call him Mother Lane. He was one of these guys who had to have his makeup just right. He was always fussing about one thing or another. If it wasn't his makeup, it was his costume. I worked enough that I wanted to work with the good guys like Bill Elliott or Johnny Mack Brown, Gene Autry, or Roy Rogers. They were the good guys."

* * *

R. G. Springsteen directed a great many of the Allan Lane films over the years. In 1989 Springsteen was a guest at the Knoxville Riders of the Silver Screen Film Festival. He was asked to comment on directing Wild Bill Elliott and Allan Lane in the Red Ryder films.

R. G. SPRINGSTEEN: Allan Lane was a little tough in comparison with Bill Elliott. The only thing I can remember about him [Lane] is that he once went to Mr. Yates and told him he didn't think that I was directing the picture [Lane's starring feature] very well. Yates took us into a viewing room to look at the picture up to that point. Afterwards, we came out and Lane said, "Well, I guess it's all right." And that was the end of it. I had no trouble [with him] after that.

* * *

Outstanding action director William Witney was on the same guest star panel with R. G. Springsteen in Knoxville. Bill Witney was on his best public behavior that evening and had nothing to say about Lane. The next day he talked with me privately and told me "on the record" what his feelings were about Rocky Lane.

Director William Witney posed for this picture with author David Rothel right after the director's panel session at the 1989 Knoxville Riders of the Silver Screen Film Festival.

WILLIAM WITNEY: He would have made a goddamned good Buick salesman, which is what he started out doing before he came to Hollywood. He just couldn't do anything well. I thought he was a terrible rider. He aggravated everyone. Jack English, a director who worked with me a lot, could not stand him. One time they got into a fist fight.

I remember when we were shooting a serial one time, Lane indicated that he wanted to do a Crupper mount for one of the scenes coming up. I told him I didn't think he could do it. "Oh, Yes," he said. "I can do it!" Davey Sharpe, one of the best stunt men in the business, was standing back of Allan and said, "Go ahead; go ahead, let him try it."

So when they were ready, Lane came running up behind the horse and put his hands on the horse's rump to do the leap, went up about six inches, and hit his chest on the horse's behind. The horse didn't kick him, thank God, or I could have lost my job.

* * *

And, finally, character actor and one-time serial star Walter Reed tried to defend Allan Lane but in the process revealed just how little he really knew the man.

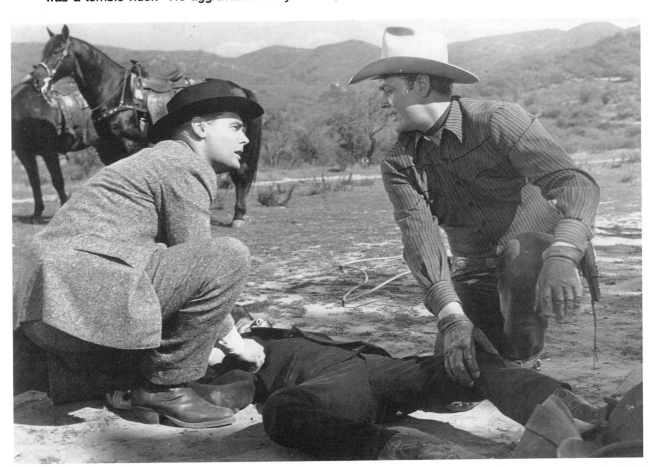

Character actor Walter Reed helps Rocky check out a wounded hombre in this scene from WELLS FARGO GUNMASTER (1951).

WALTER REED: Listen, he had a reputation for being very hard to work with. Let me tell you, he was a perfectionist. I never had any trouble with Allan. I couldn't understand why everybody thought he was hard to work with. After we'd get through work for the day, we'd go around the corner and have a drink, and he was the nicest guy you ever met in your life. He liked [working] with experienced people. It was his series, and he wanted it to be good.

I knew him when he was a juvenile in films wearing a tuxedo. He *became* a cowboy. I don't think he was ever a cowboy [in real life]. He became a cowboy [for films]. He got that horse Black Jack and learned to be a good rider. He was very good on a horse, but I don't think that he was a born cowboy who lived on a ranch or anything like that. He was the first guy to wear Levis in films.

When I went on the MR. ED set, I saw Allan and I said, "What are you doing here?" He responded with, "I'm the voice of Mr. Ed, the horse." Somebody said to me later, "God, he's slipped." I said, "No, that's an important job." I hear Sterling Holloway doing voices all the time, and nobody says that about him. There is nothing wrong doing voice-overs for a show like that. There's a lot of money to be made in that if you have a distinctive voice.

I wasn't socially with Allan except after a day's shooting when we would have a drink together. I found him a delightful guy. I liked him very much. I don't understand why others didn't like him.

DAVID ROTHEL: Some have said he didn't have a sense of humor.

WALTER REED: You're right. He didn't have a sense of humor on the set. Oh, no, he didn't smile very much. But when we'd go for a drink after the show, he'd be delightful. He'd talk to the crew and all of that stuff, but it was like he was a different person. But he didn't have much of a sense of humor. But I like him very much. I haven't seen him in years. In fact, if you ever see him, tell him Walter Reed said hello.

DAVID ROTHEL: Rocky died fifteen years ago in 1973.

WALTER REED: He did? Oh, my God. I didn't know that.

*   *   *

CHAPTER 7

AN ALLAN "ROCKY" LANE SCRAPBOOK

Allan Lane appeared in many films beyond those Westerns which are featured in this book. The following is a filmogaphy of other films that he made.

ADDITIONAL FILMOGRAPHY

FILM	*YEAR*	*PRODUCTION COMPANY*
NOT QUITE DECENT	1929	Fox
FORWARD PASS	1929	First National
DETECTIVES WANTED	1929	Fox

Many fans preferred Allan Lane's characterization of Red Ryder to those of Bill Elliott and Don Barry, who preceded him in the role. This comic scene is from STAGECOACH TO DENVER (1946). Red Ryder (Lane) and Little Beaver (Bobby Blake) try to suppress their laughter as the Duchess (Martha Wentworth) is none too happy to have her unmentionables dumped onto the sidewalk by Coonskin (Emmett Lynn) for all to see.

Notice the A L initials on Black Jack's bit. The publicity still is from DESPERADOES' OUTPOST (1952).

FILM	*YEAR*	*PRODUCTION COMPANY*
KNIGHTS OUT	1929	Fox
LOVE IN THE ROUGH	1930	MGM
MADAM SATAN	1930	MGM
WAR MAMAS	1931	MGM-Hal Roach
SMART MONEY	1931	Warner Brothers
NIGHT NURSE	1931	Warner Brothers
STAR WITNESS	1931	Warner Brothers
HONOR OF THE FAMILY	1931	First National
LOCAL BOY MAKES GOOD	1931	First National
IT'S TOUGH TO BE FAMOUS	1932	First National
FAMOUS FERGUSON CASE	1932	First National
THE TENDERFOOT	1932	Warner Brothers
MISS PINKERTON	1932	First National
CROONER	1932	First National
ONE WAY PASSAGE	1932	Warner Brothers
THE CRASH	1932	First National
STOWAWAY	1936	20th
LAUGHING AT TROUBLE	1937	20th
FIFTY ROADS TO TOWN	1937	20th
BIG BUSINESS	1937	20th
CHARLIE CHAN AT THE OLYMPICS	1937	20th

FILM	*YEAR*	*PRODUCTION COMPANY*
SING AND BE HAPPY	1937	20th
THE DUKE COMES BACK	1937	Republic
NIGHT SPOT	1938	RKO
THE MARRIAGE BUSINESS	1938	RKO
HAVING A WONDERFUL TIME	1938	RKO
MAID'S NIGHT OUT	1938	RKO
CRIME RING	1938	RKO
FUGITIVES FOR A NIGHT	1938	RKO
THE LAW WEST OF TOMBSTONE	1938	RKO
PACIFIC LINER	1938	RKO
TWELVE CROOKED HOURS	1939	RKO
THEY MADE HER A SPY	1939	RKO
PANAMA LADY	1939	RKO
CONSPIRACY	1939	RKO
THE SPELLBINDER	1939	RKO
GRAND OLE OPRY	1940	Republic
KING OF THE ROYAL MOUNTED	1940	Republic
ALL-AMERICAN CO-ED	1940	UA
KING OF THE MOUNTIES	1942	Republic
DAREDEVILS OF THE WEST	1943	Republic
THE DANCING MASTERS	1943	20th
THE TIGER WOMAN	1944	Republic
CALL OF THE SOUTH SEAS	1944	Republic

Leading man Allan Lane takes a phone call as Heather Angel and an unidentified actor look on anxiously in this scene from THE DUKE COMES BACK (1937).

FILM	*YEAR*	*PRODUCTION COMPANY*
BELLS OF ROSARITA (guest star)	1945	Republic
GAY BLADES	1946	Republic
A GUY COULD CHANGE	1946	Republic
NIGHT TRAIN TO MEMPHIS	1946	Republic
OUT CALIFORIA WAY (guest star)	1946	Republic
TRAIL OF ROBIN HOOD (guest star)	1950	Republic
THE SAGA OF HEMP BROWN	1958	Universal
HELL BENT FOR LEATHER	1960	Universal
POSSE FROM HELL	1961	Universal

* * *

ROCKY LANE COMIC BOOKS

The ROCKY LANE WESTERN comic book started in May 1949 and ran until November of 1959. There were eighty-seven issues in all. The comic was first published by Fawcett (issues 1-55) and later by Charlton (issues 56-87). The comic had a photo cover of Rocky for the first fifty-seven issues. After that, artist's renderings of Rocky were used.

A popular feature in the early issues was a page entitled ROPING "N" RIDING WITH ALLAN "ROCKY" LANE AND BLACK JACK. The page consisted of a letter from Rocky to his fans. Rocky would thank the

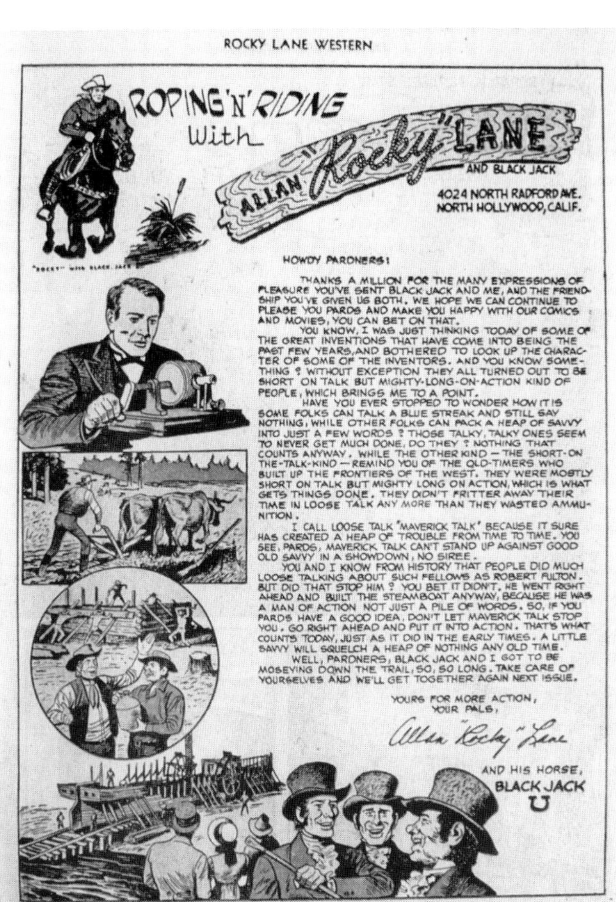

ROCKY LANE WESTERN

ROPING 'N' RIDING With ALLAN "Rocky" LANE AND BLACK JACK

4024 NORTH RADFORD AVE.
NORTH HOLLYWOOD, CALIF.

HOWDY PARDNERS!

THANKS A MILLION FOR THE MANY EXPRESSIONS OF PLEASURE YOU'VE SENT BLACK JACK AND ME, AND THE FRIENDSHIP YOU'VE GIVEN US BOTH. WE HOPE WE CAN CONTINUE TO PLEASE YOU PARDS AND MAKE YOU HAPPY WITH OUR COMICS AND MOVIES, YOU CAN BET ON THAT.

YOU KNOW, I WAS JUST THINKING TODAY OF SOME OF THE GREAT INVENTIONS THAT HAVE COME INTO BEING THE PAST FEW YEARS, AND BOTHERED TO LOOK UP THE CHARACTER OF SOME OF THE INVENTORS. AND YOU KNOW SOMETHING ? WITHOUT EXCEPTION THEY ALL TURNED OUT TO BE SHORT ON TALK BUT MIGHTY-LONG-ON-ACTION KIND OF PEOPLE, WHICH BRINGS ME TO A POINT.

HAVE YOU EVER STOPPED TO WONDER HOW IT IS SOME FOLKS CAN TALK A BLUE STREAK AND STILL SAY NOTHING, WHILE OTHER FOLKS CAN PACK A HEAP OF SAVVY INTO JUST A FEW WORDS ? THOSE TALKY, TALKY ONES SEEM TO NEVER GET MUCH DONE, DO THEY ? NOTHING THAT COUNTS ANYWAY. WHILE THE OTHER KIND — THE SHORT-ON THE-TALK-KIND — REMIND YOU OF THE OLD-TIMERS WHO BUILT UP THE FRONTIERS OF THE WEST. THEY WERE MOSTLY SHORT ON TALK BUT MIGHTY LONG ON ACTION, WHICH IS WHAT GETS THINGS DONE. THEY DIDN'T FRITTER AWAY THEIR TIME IN LOOSE TALK ANY MORE THAN THEY WASTED AMMUNITION.

I CALL LOOSE TALK "MAVERICK TALK" BECAUSE IT SURE HAS CREATED A HEAP OF TROUBLE FROM TIME TO TIME. YOU SEE, PARDS, MAVERICK TALK CAN'T STAND UP AGAINST GOOD OLD SAVVY IN A SHOWDOWN, NO SIREE.

YOU AND I KNOW FROM HISTORY THAT PEOPLE DID MUCH LOOSE TALKING ABOUT SUCH FELLOWS AS ROBERT FULTON. BUT DID THAT STOP HIM ? YOU BET IT DIDN'T. HE WENT RIGHT AHEAD AND BUILT THE STEAMBOAT ANYWAY, BECAUSE HE WAS A MAN OF ACTION NOT JUST A PILE OF WORDS. SO, IF YOU PARDS HAVE A GOOD IDEA, DON'T LET MAVERICK TALK STOP YOU. GO RIGHT AHEAD AND PUT IT INTO ACTION. THAT'S WHAT COUNTS TODAY, JUST AS IT DID IN THE EARLY TIMES. A LITTLE SAVVY WILL SQUELCH A HEAP OF NOTHING ANY OLD TIME.

WELL, PARDNERS, BLACK JACK AND I GOT TO BE MOSEYING DOWN THE TRAIL, SO, SO LONG. TAKE CARE OF YOURSELVES AND WE'LL GET TOGETHER AGAIN NEXT ISSUE.

YOURS FOR MORE ACTION,
YOUR PALS,

Allan "Rocky" Lane

AND HIS HORSE,
BLACK JACK

kids for being loyal patrons of his comics and movies and then move on to a specific topic for that particular letter. In the September 1950 issue, for instance, he wrote about people of action and people who only do a lot of talking. He reminded us that the pioneers who settled the frontier were "short on talk but mighty long on action, which is what gets things done." The return address on Rock's letter was 4024 North Radford Avenue, North Hollywood, California—the address of Republic Pictures.

Another feature of the comic book in the early years was a "special offer" for a "large" photo of Rocky and Black Jack autographed personally to you. You were instructed to send your name, address, and twenty-five cents to the Republic Pictures address. If you wanted five photos

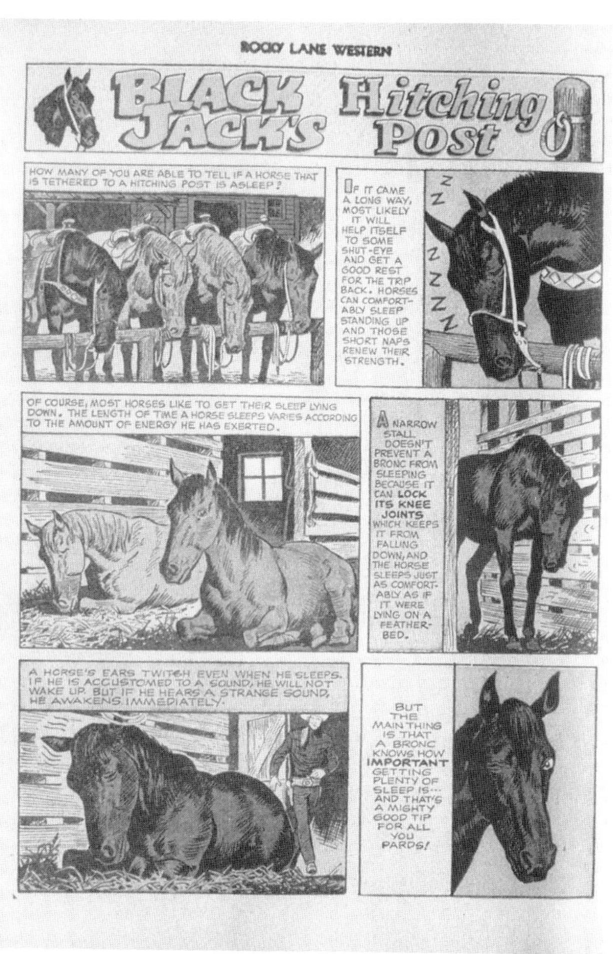

autographed to you, you were to send a dollar. What bargains life held for kids in those days! You don't get offers like that from Hollywood today.

A back-of-the-comics segment called BLACK JACK'S HITCHING POST began with issue fifteen and ran through twenty-five. Information about horses was presented on the HITCHING POST page. You could find out, for example, the standing and lying down sleeping habits of a horse in issue number seventeen.

Issues one through twenty had a short, humorous segment (usually consisting of four pages) entitled SLIM PICKENS. The cartoon character was a typical bumbling Western sidekick type, but the drawing bore no resemblance to the real-life Slim Pickens (who was a sidekick for Rex Allen, of course) and apparently had no connection with him.

The ROCKY LANE WESTERN is a sought-after Western comic book and has increased in value with the passing of each year. The first issue in near-mint condition is worth $280. In fine condition you could expect to pay around $120. In only good condition it would be worth $40. Succeeding issues, of course, diminish in value. When you get to the final issue (number eighty-seven), a near-mint copy would cost $24; in good-to-fine condition the copy would range in value from $3.50 to $10.50.

Mary Ellen Kay doesn't seem too cooperative as Irving Bacon and Rocky try to talk to her.

Rocky has the upper hand on Clayton Moore.

Here is Rocky Lane and Nugget Clark in a serious scene from CARSON CITY RAIDERS.

REPUBLIC PICTURES' FAN MAGAZINE PUBLICITY RELEASES

Kindness, patience, repetition and reward are the keys to successful training of trick horses.

training black jack

1. ROCKY tells Black Jack to get the paper.

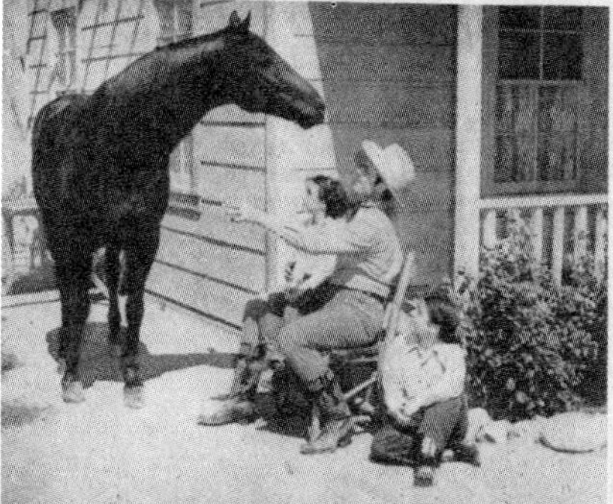

2. THE children beam as the horse turns to obey.

3. BLACK JACK's on his way to the mailbox.

7. NO TRICK. *And* no trick to get the paper!

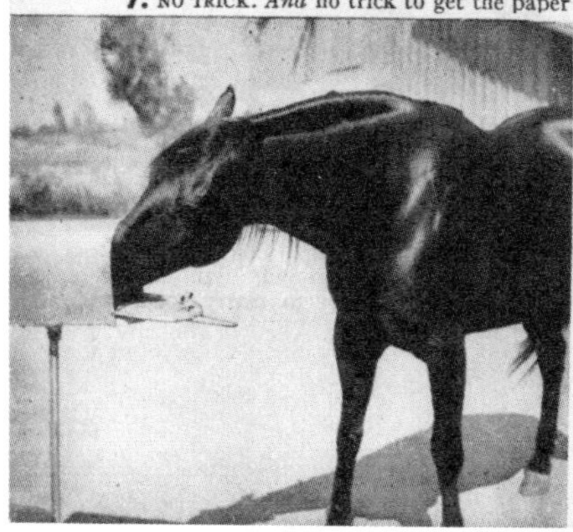

8. FIRMLY but lightly does it—no teethmarks on it.

9. SPEEDING up now on his way to Rocky.

A couple of youngsters were sitting with me one day, and Black Jack, my horse, was nuzzling around and begging for attention. Casually, as though it was the most routine request in the world, I turned to the horse and said, "Black Jack, go bring in the paper."

Like a friendly dog, the big, powerful animal trotted off, opened the mail box and returned with the paper in his mouth. The kids were delighted but they probably never realized the hours of careful training required for this trick. Or, for that matter, for his many other tricks—drinking water out of a pop bottle, kneeling to say his prayers, dancing the fox trot, and the hundred and one things Black Jack is called upon to do in the course of making a movie.

All methods of training are based on one system of *repetition, patience, kindness,* and *reward.* And the training requires many long hours of work, preferably very early in the morning.

He gets his lesson in various gradual degrees, starting with the most important of all—his confidence or foundation lesson, which is to develop the understanding so necessary between horse and master. The sooner the horse learns to trust his master, the sooner he gets going on the second step. Remember, all this takes time and patience. The exact amount depends on how willing a student the horse is, then on the number of hours each day they can work together.

After the trainer has gained the horse's confidence, he starts asking him to obey some of the more simple commands, such as to come to him, to stop, to back up, etc. All the while, the horse is learning to be on the alert for any command that might be given. These things perfected, he is ready to move along to the more advanced stages of his schooling. This phase includes such things as nodding "yes" and "no"; kneeling and bowing; counting; sitting on his hind quarters; mouth-work tricks like untying knots; picking up articles in his teeth; opening and closing doors; dancing.

All trained horses are "cued" into their various tricks. The most common method is touching the horse on various parts of his body, the shifting of his master's weight from one side to the other, and the different positions his master might take in relation to the horse's position.

Gradually, the horse can be brought to understand spoken commands as well as cues of touch or sight. Black Jack now understands such cues.

Such control takes patience; the commands must be repeated over and over in the training stages. It takes understanding, and the horse will reward *you* with almost-human understanding.

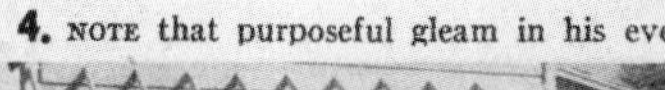

4. NOTE that purposeful gleam in his eye.

5. A CLOSED box poses no problem to Black Jack.

6. WHAT, no paper? Rocky playing tricks?

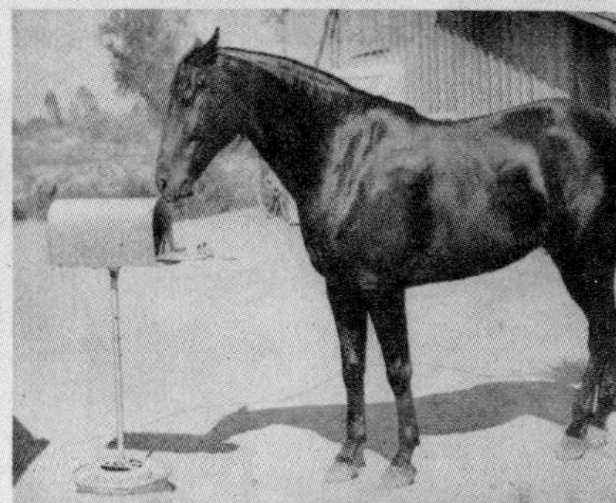

10. PROUD of himself as he has a right to be.

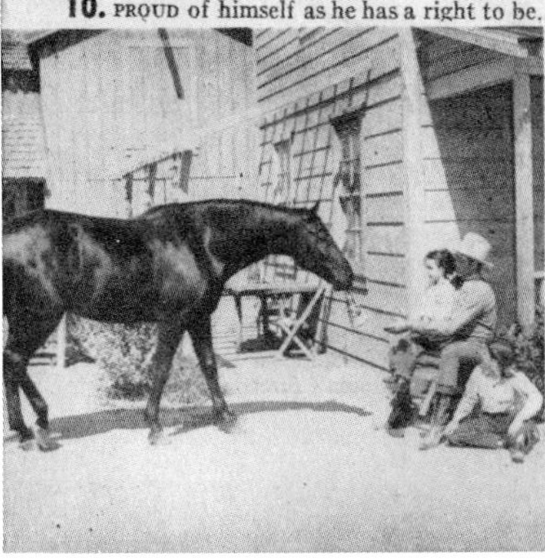

11. A NOSE for news? Shucks, yes. The comics, too!

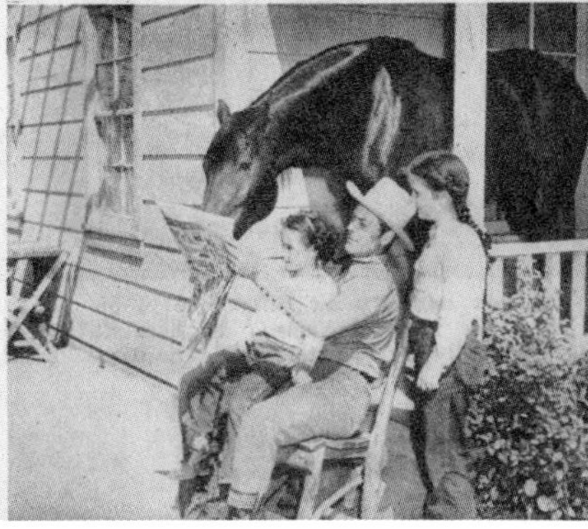

12. FUN finished, it's time for real action.

(The preceding publicity release originally appeared in *Western Stars,* Vol. 1, No. 2, March-June 1949.)

One of the most popular among action heroes is the gentleman known as "Rocky"—otherwise, Republic star Allan Lane. Allan's pictures are always full of fast action and have good stories to back up the fisticuffs and hard riding in which Rocky engages. Like other big Western stars, Allan has his own special horse in all his movies—Allan's steed is Black Jack, almost as famous as his master.

When movie scripts call for location scenes some distance away from the studio, transporting the horses is a major concern. Allan has his special trailer for the convenience of Black Jack when it comes to traveling. As matters sometimes work out, Black Jack may travel more comfortably than Allan does himself.

A WESTERN star who features fast action in all his movies is Allan "Rocky" Lane. Action is the keynote in the Rocky pictures, just as in pictures of other Western stars, music or comedy may be the element stressed. It's no chance thing, either, that Allan's physical prowess has become one of his most popular characteristics. He was formerly a champion athlete and his ability made him a natural for outdoor pix.

The road to outdoor pictures wasn't a simple one or an easy one for Allan, however. In his first years in the movies he played leading man in drawing-room dramas and light comedies, for his good looks typed him as a likable foil to the charms of feminine screen stars. But it was Allan's hope throughout this time that he could eventually turn to Western movies, and a few years ago his wish came true when Republic assigned him to Western pictures exclusively. Fans agreed with Allan, too, that action pix were his best, and he's continually rising in popularity with movie-goers who like pictures with hard riding and quick shooting.

Tall—he's six feet one—Allan Lane was born in Indiana and studied at Notre Dame (it was there he first made his reputation as a star athlete). Besides acting in the movies his experience includes acting on the stage and working for a time as an actors' agent. During his time as a motion picture actor Allan's been one of the busiest, for he's made more than 75 movies, which include dramas, comedies, Westerns and serials. He is unmarried and like most Western stars leads a quiet private life far from the glamorous night spots of movietown. Allan's real name is Harry Albershart,

(Continued on the following page)

Western heroes rarely use doubles for their action scenes. Above you see Allan completing a slide for a scene in Republic's "Sheriff of Wichita." Below, in a quieter moment on the set, are Allan and another of Republic's Western stars, Monte Hale, who is currently in "Law of the Golden West."

"ROCKY" (CONT'D)

When Allan Lane isn't busy before cameras he keeps himself occupied with other duties around Republic Studios. Above left you see him cleaning some of the guns from his own large collection, and above right he's checking the "cutting" of one of his films with film editor Robert Leeds in the studio cutting room.

(Continued from the preceding page)

but his movie success as "Rocky" has completely identified him with that well-known nickname.

FEW fans realize the amount of work, other than that done before the movie cameras, which a Western star must do. Typical of so many Western stars, Allan Lane takes an active interest in all the matters connected with turning out his movies. He personally cleans his guns and checks with the gunsmith on their firing. He checks with the property men and his director on the props which are used in his pictures as authentic details of the Old West which is pictured. And after scenes have been rehearsed and shot by the cameras, Allan—or "Rocky"—is on hand at the cutting room to see how the scenes have come through and to learn how action sequences may be improved for future pix. All this detail work pays off invaluably, too, for with each of Allan's movies there is improvement in the picture.

"There is a lot of work to be done between pictures," says Allan. "There are guns to clean, horses to train, and lots of equipment to repair." Below left you see him in the studio gun room with his gunsmith, and below right, as you see, he's in the prop department checking personally on his movie props for a scene.

(The preceding publicity release originally appeared in *Movie Spotlight*, October 1949.)

Future Annie Oakley on TV, actress Gail Davis was Rocky's co-star in two films/

Black Jack gives Rocky the horselaugh in this publicity photo for the Western series. Notice the A L on Black Jack's bit.

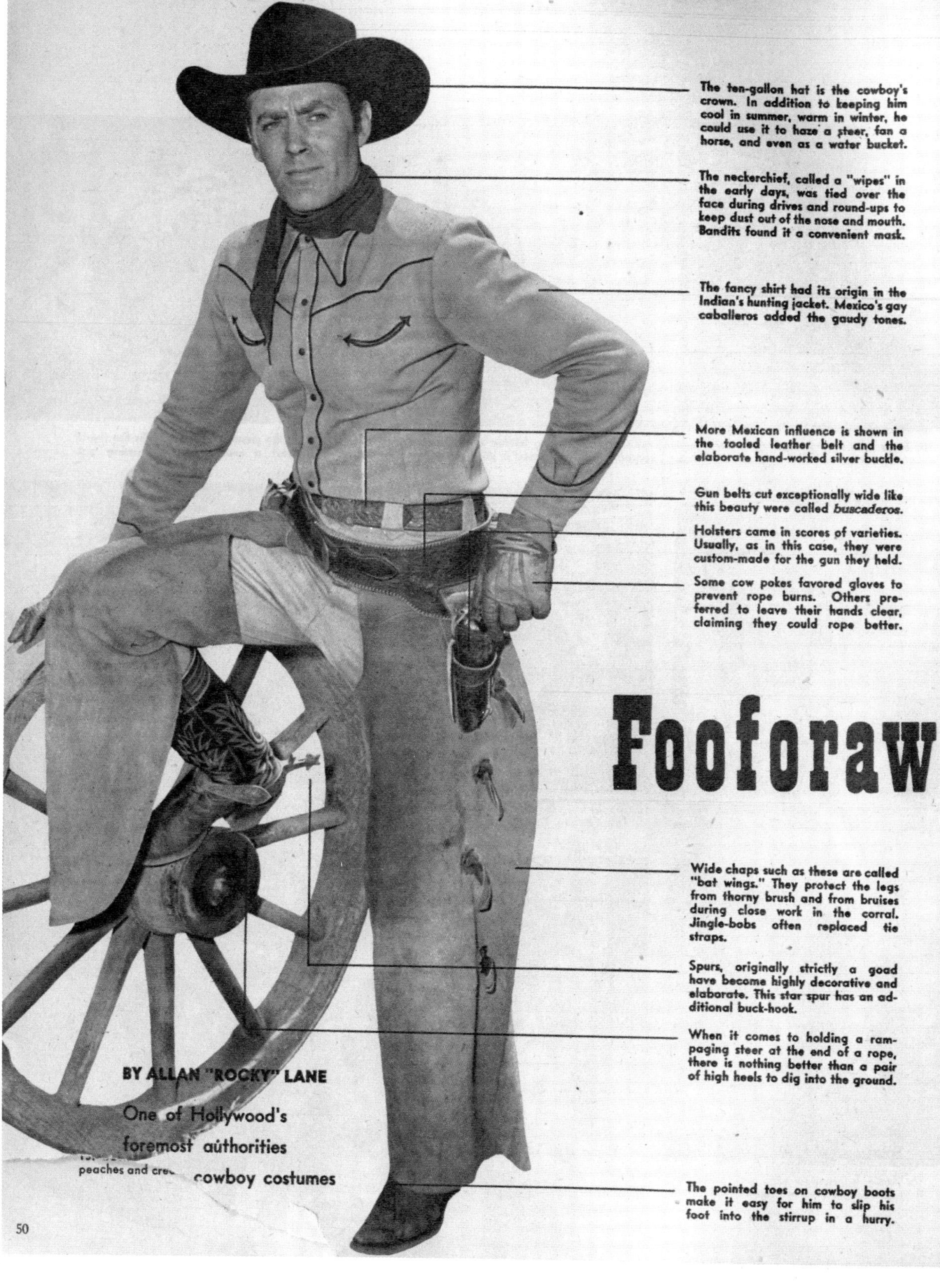

Fooforaw

BY ALLAN "ROCKY" LANE

One of Hollywood's foremost authorities ... cowboy costumes

peaches and cre...

The ten-gallon hat is the cowboy's crown. In addition to keeping him cool in summer, warm in winter, he could use it to haze a steer, fan a horse, and even as a water bucket.

The neckerchief, called a "wipes" in the early days, was tied over the face during drives and round-ups to keep dust out of the nose and mouth. Bandits found it a convenient mask.

The fancy shirt had its origin in the Indian's hunting jacket. Mexico's gay caballeros added the gaudy tones.

More Mexican influence is shown in the tooled leather belt and the elaborate hand-worked silver buckle.

Gun belts cut exceptionally wide like this beauty were called *buscaderos*.

Holsters came in scores of varieties. Usually, as in this case, they were custom-made for the gun they held.

Some cow pokes favored gloves to prevent rope burns. Others preferred to leave their hands clear, claiming they could rope better.

Wide chaps such as these are called "bat wings." They protect the legs from thorny brush and from bruises during close work in the corral. Jingle-bobs often replaced tie straps.

Spurs, originally strictly a goad have become highly decorative and elaborate. This star spur has an additional buck-hook.

When it comes to holding a rampaging steer at the end of a rope, there is nothing better than a pair of high heels to dig into the ground.

The pointed toes on cowboy boots make it easy for him to slip his foot into the stirrup in a hurry.

50

■ No fancy city tailor ever had a hand in designing the distinctive garb of our Western cowboys. No fashion plates ever served as models. The master designers were the blazing sun, the bucking horse, the dusty trail and the tearing claws of mesquite and cactus. Hard necessity was the dictator of style, and every article, from ten-gallon hat to pointed boot, was designed to do a special job.

Take the hat, the first garment the cow poke puts on when he gets up in the morning. Originally it was the straw sombrero of the Mexicans, ideal for protecting the face from the blistering sun, while the high crown provided cooling ventilation for the top of the head. But straw couldn't stand the abuse of the cowboy's hard life, nor was it good in winter. Hatmaker Stetson made his famous ten gallon hat of felt and the problem was solved.

The next most distinctive item is a pair of chaps, the name coming from the Spanish *chaparejos*. They are designed to protect the rider's legs while racing after cows through thorny underbrush. In their original version they were just a stiff leather apron split up the center to fit over the saddle, but this didn't satisfy the punchers. They began tying the split apron around their legs to prevent flapping, and the present style was born. Wide chaps are called bat wings, tight, round ones are called shotguns, and northern versions with the hair on are called woolies. These latter also serve to keep the legs warm and dry in winter.

The most popular item of cowboy garb is his boots which are now beginning to appear even in the eastern cities. The pointed toes are not designed to satisfy the cowboy's vanity. They permit him to jab his foot swiftly and surely into the stirrup. The high heel serves to keep his foot from going through the stirrup while riding a mean bronco, and is designed also for ground work in the corral. With his high heels, he can anchor himself firmly in the ground after getting his rope over "a hot one," rank steer or calf.

Leather working reaches a high art in cowboy boots. Tall ones with projecting lifts are called mule ears.

Like gloves, gauntlets are worn to avoid rope burns; to fend off branches when riding in thorny brush.

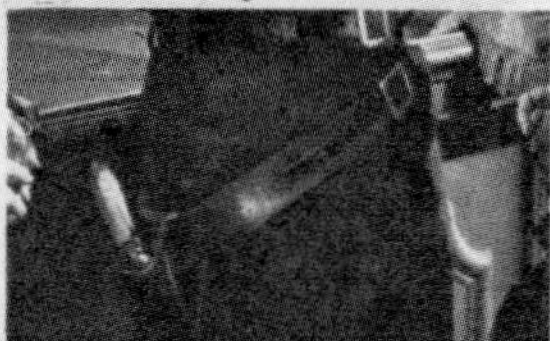

When cowboys took to wearing their guns in low-slung holsters, trouble was seldom very far in the distance.

in the Wild West

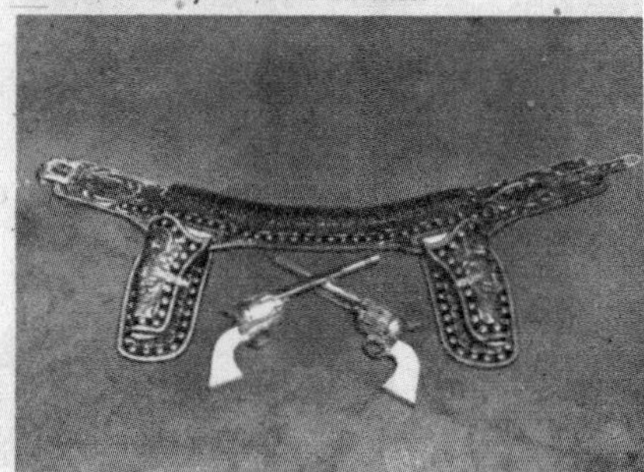

Roy Roger's gold-plated "Forty-niners" and *buscadero* belt, which holds holsters firmly in place.

The gloves and gauntlets are likewise designed to protect the hands and arms against rope burns, though many an old time puncher claimed it was cheaper to grow new skin than buy gloves.

Their Levis (jeans) got their name from Levi Straus of San Francisco, the first man to make those popular, durable pants. The shirt was first just a plain old work shirt, but some of the "Fancy Dans" began to combine certain features of the Indian's fringed hunting jacket with fancier touches from the California Spanish dons and the Mexican caballeros. The fancy vests came directly from the beaded and quill-worked vests of the Indians. Even the neckerchief, now worn in many brilliant colors, was originally a plain bandanna used to keep dust out of the lungs while on the trail.

Because some cowboys liked noise and glitter, they wore danglers or jingle-bobs on their spurs, and *conchas,* little silver bells, on their chaps. Spurs came in all shapes and sizes, as did the belts on which they hung their artillery. Decked out in all his fooforaw, the cowboy became the most colorful figure in our history.

Above, a Mexican "Chihuahua" spur. Below, a spur with "buck hook" which hooks cinch for rough ride.

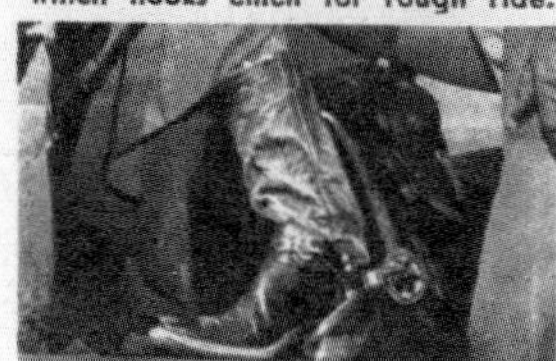

(The preceding publicity release originally appeared in *Western Stars*, Vol. 1, No. 3, October-December 1949.)

A cowboy star and his sidekick: Rocky Lane and Eddy Waller.

A cowboy hero gets to spend a lot of time crouching behind rocks shooting at bad guys.

rocky lane:

taming a tough bronc is fun!

■ For a long time, Rocky appeared in movies as Alan Lane, a well-muscled hero of polite dramas opposite actresses such as Joan Fontaine and Ginger Rogers. He wasn't too happy with his lot. The son of an Indiana farmer, he had visited the New Mexico ranch of relatives when seven years old, and been captivated by the West. Back in Indiana, he dreamed of being a cowboy until finishing his schooling, then once more made tracks for the West. While attending a rodeo he was spotted and hauled into Hollywood drawing room scenes. About to leave town in disgust, he was offered a cowboy role and has stayed on ever since, starring in Westerns as Rocky Lane. He has never married, is in his mid-thirties, well over six feet and husky in build. Since his first chance at Western roles, he has worked overtime to make himself a worthy cowboy, and today is proud of his talents in riding, roping and bulldogging. He lives in the San Fernando Valley in a house decorated mannishly in leather and wood, and filled with Western gimcracks. Shelves in his bedroom are stacked with scores of ten-gallon hats and the floor of his closet is littered with boots. He makes up for lost time by wearing nothing but cowboy clothes and riding his stallion, Blackjack. Rocky is one of the few cowboys who never sings or plays a guitar even though he has a very fine voice. He goes in completely for rough, tough, rugged, action-packed films with lots of shootin' and fightin'—the real he-man stuff. His films always show a hard-riding cowboy who sees that right always prevails. Rocky feels if you're right and fight hard, you win through. Being an action cowboy, Rocky chafes under the restriction imposed by his studio that he cannot compete in rodeos because of the physical danger.

draws like greased lightning!

Rocky likes the rough and tumble of Western life, the guns and the shooting in particular. He owns dozens of firearms, many of them relics from pioneer days, and keeps them scattered around his bachelor home, in corners and in most of the drawers. At the drop of a hint he will drag a guest out the back door and start potting away at a target set in the trees.

(The preceding publicity release originally appeared in *Who's Who in Western Stars*, Vol. 1, No. 1, 1952.)

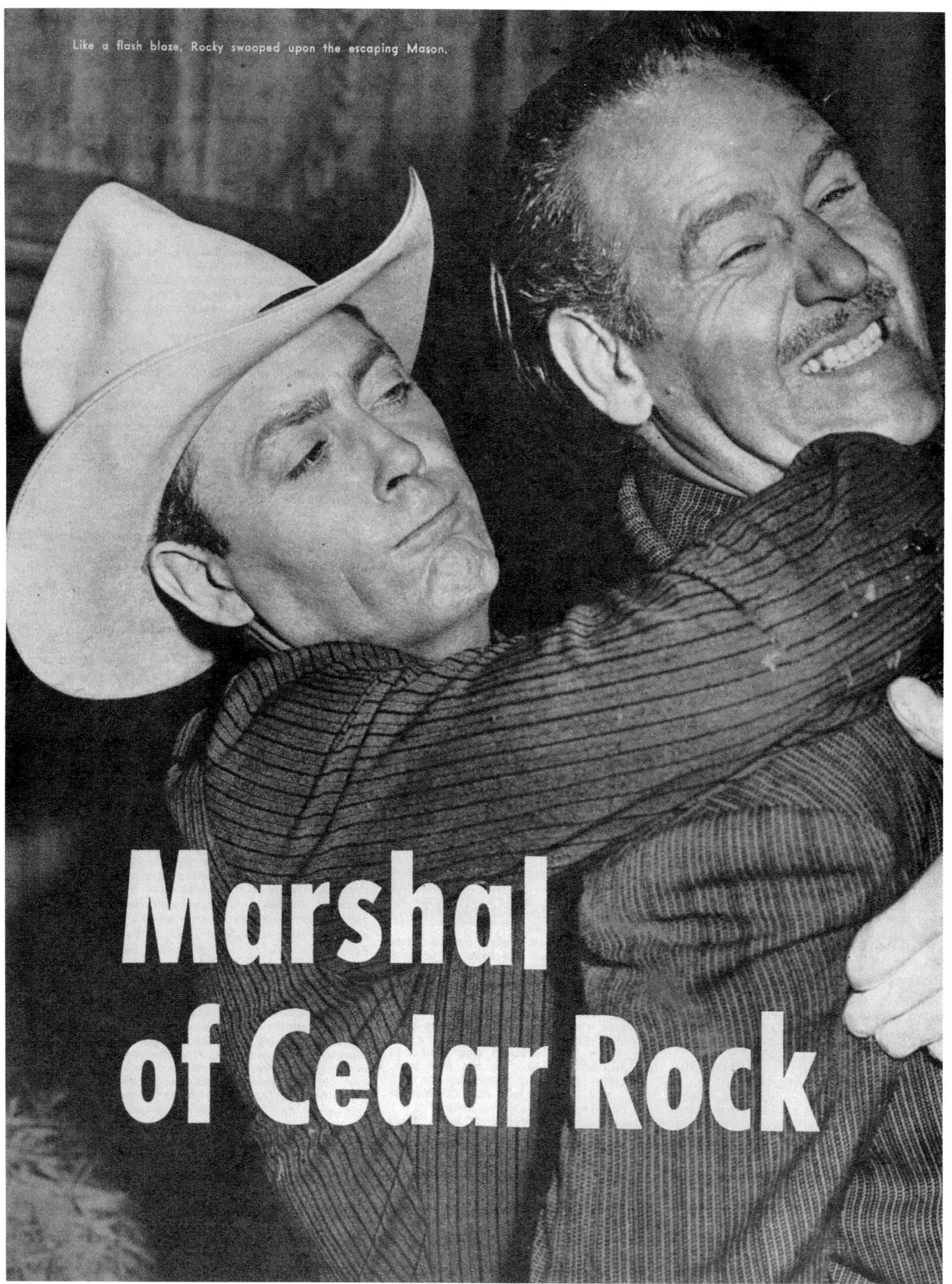

Like a flash blaze, Rocky swooped upon the escaping Mason.

With a jailbreak as bait, Rocky Lane tends the gun trap he aims to spring on a crook

■ United States Marshal Rocky Lane had followed the nice-looking, young escaped convict clean across the state and into the ranch-country town.

It hadn't been a tough tailing job. Bill Anderson headed back to Cedar Rock like a homing pigeon. East of town, when his horse went lame, he'd accepted a lift from a stranger in a buggy. But just short of his destination, he'd taken to bootleather. Hat down to cover his face, he'd lined up the street straight for the Cedar Rock Bank & Trust.

Obviously, the fugitive hadn't a suspicion that his successful jailbreak had been carried out with the help of the warden. Help provided because of Rocky's hunch that Anderson might lead them to the other bandits.

Every cowman nearby had lost his shirt in that bank holdup. Rocky aimed to recoup the loss. Hard times gripped this rangeland. Unless a projected rail spur came through, buying up land, the ranchers would be ruined.

Having tailed Bill Anderson into town, Rocky now saw him slip into the bank via a small door opening off the rear alley. Flat to the wall under a half-open window, silent as a shadow, the Marshal crouched to listen.

"Anderson!" gasped a voice inside. "I thought you were in prison!"

"I broke out—to settle with the man who put me there. You're going to Sheriff Blake, Mason, and tell him what happened here the night of the robbery. You're goin' to tell him I was here because you sent for me—so you could frame me, 'cause I was cuttin' you out with Martha!"

The man called Mason—and Rocky recollected that the bank's sign was lettered *Henry Mason, President*—blustered. "Now, look, Bill—"

"You'll tell Blake I didn't keep you covered while bandits were in the bank. And when I went after 'em, I was chasin' 'em—not escapin'!"

"You said all that at the trial, and they didn't believe you," Mason murmured. "Why should I conspire to rob my own bank? Put that gun up and—"

"Get your hand outa that drawer, Mason, or I'll shoot it out!"

Anderson's sudden sharp warning explained itself. Rocky straightened at the window, whipping his own gun into action. One deft shot spun away the weapon with which Bill was dominating a nervous Mason.

Through that rear door to the bank office Rocky launched himself. At the same moment, a startled employee burst in from out front. Mason sent him to fetch the Sheriff. Then he turned to Rocky, smiling a thin smile.

"Much obliged, stranger. You got me out of a mighty tough spot."

Rocky shrugged. "I don't like to see people get hurt. If it'd been the other way, and you had a gun on him, I'd have done the same thing. I'm Rocky Lane, mister. I just drifted into town, lookin' for work."

"Did you—happen to hear what this fellow was saying?"

Rocky thought Mason sounded worried. He shook his head. "Didn't hear anything. Happened to glance in the window as I was passin' by."

The Sheriff elbowed in, just then, to take Anderson into custody. Despite Bill's denials, Mason charged him with attempted murder.

"Well," smiled the banker, as Bill was led away, "that's that!" He produced a box of costly cigars. "Have a smoke? They're quite good."

Rocky just was tucking two unwanted cigars into a pocket when the din erupted outside. Hoofs pounded the street; men screeched; guns blasted.

Just as a buckboard went careening by, a girl fighting its gun-shy team, Rocky reached the front of the bank.

THE CAST

Allan "Rocky" Lane . . . . himself
His Stallion . . . . Black Jack
Nugget Clark . . . . Eddy Waller
Martha Clark . . . . Phyllis Coates
Henry Mason . . . . Roy Barcroft
Bill Anderson . . . . Bill Henry
Paul Jackson . . . . Robert Shayne
Chris Peters . . . . John Crawford
Prison Warden . . . . John Hamilton
Sheriff . . . . Kenneth MacDonald
John Harper . . . . Herbert Lytton

Adapted from the Republic Picture

Rocky and Bill paid a surprise visit to the bogus John Harper.

Rocky ducked into a stall for cover from those guns above, reloaded and fired again, taking dead aim at the figure in the hayloft.

Forced into the open, the real despoiler of Cedar Rock took

He heard more shots, and the Sheriff's voice bawling: *"Hey, Anderson!"* Bill must be loose again, while masked riders churned the street into a dust storm, firing and howling.

A bullet caught the Sheriff in the arm, and he doubled over.

Through the turmoil, Rocky spun to the spot where Black Jack waited—forking his saddle in a catlike leap. Out for open country raced the runaways, hoofs battering hard earth. Up a stony, shrub-covered hill streaked the vehicle, its slim driver fighting gamely as she jounced about.

A good mile out of Cedar Rock, he finally cut off the horses and hauled them to a standstill. Once sure they would behave, he turned to the girl.

She smiled at him shakily. "I—I don't know how to thank you."

"I was standin' just outside the bank when your horses broke loose." Rocky doffed his hat respectfully. "My name's Rocky Lane."

"I'm Martha Clark." The girl smiled again. "I guess I better be getting back into town. My Uncle Nugget'll be worried sick."

They found weathered old Nugget Clark near the bank and surrounded by jabbering townsfolk. Rocky picked up plenty of random information. Anderson, so folks said, had been engaged to Martha Clark. Martha still didn't believe him a bank robber, despite Henry Mason and the courts. Rumor had it Bill was headed for the south hills—now he was loose again.

Old Nugget shrewdly studied the stranger who had rescued his niece.

"Wish we had some protection here against Anderson and gunmen! A few young fellows like Lane— Say, Lane, you wouldn't be needin' a job?"

Rocky grinned modestly. "Well—yes, I could use one."

"Our ranch is straight out the town road, just beyond the fork."

Rocky spent the day getting a picture of the local situation. Nugget was leader of all the ranchers and so sincerely respected that he held a legal power of attorney to act for them. They all were praying—hard—for the railroad to come in and buy them out at a good price. Else they'd all have to sell for peanuts to a land outfit represented by Henry Mason . . .

Rocky's hunch rewarded

He had a hunch Bill Anderson would head, sooner or later, to see Martha. A few hours after dark had fallen, Rocky's vigilance was rewarded. A horse came spurring head on for Nugget's place—and Anderson rode it. Following cautiously, Rocky saw the fugitive slip in by the kitchen way.

It wasn't hard to fill in their reunion scene. Bill would be holding Martha close. She'd be clinging to him, probably begging him to go back to jail before the law killed him. And Anderson would be vowing never to return to a cell until he'd made Henry Mason clear his name.

After he'd allowed them time together, Rocky rode Black Jack up to the front of the ranch house. Old Nugget answered his knock—but tardily.

"Good evening," nodded Rocky. "That job you offered me—"

Nugget gulped. "Well—yuh see—I'm fresh out o' cows!"

"You change your mind in a hurry." Rocky was circling carefully, working toward the kitchen door. "Have you seen Anderson?"

"Bill Anderson?" Nugget looked very vague. "Why should *he* come here?"

"He might show up anywhere. Mind if I get a drink of water?"

Before Nugget could move to check him, Rocky had ducked out into the kitchen. He found Martha standing there, quite alone. But she was near a window. And the rear door stood ajar. Rocky sprinted through it.

As Bill galloped off into the night, Rocky rounded the house at a full run and leaped for Black Jack's saddle. As he took off across country in the fugitive's wake, two other horses crashed from cover nearby. Somehow, he doubted the Sheriff's men were watching Nugget's ranch. Among the potentially interested parties, then, that left—only Henry Mason.

The other riders came on him hell-for-leather as Rocky urged Black Jack on. In Bill's desperate wake, they crossed open country. Bill hit a road, followed it for a swift mile, then veered again across a clearing. Rocky sprang from his saddle to drag the runaway to earth.

Writhing beneath him, Martha Clark's recent caller fought gamely. But Rocky was heavier. "Hold it, Anderson! If you'll listen to me—"

A shot's sharp crack interrupted. That pair who had ridden out on Rocky's trail now were loitering behind boulders, off to the clearing's left. A bullet bit up dust at Rocky's boot tip. He and Bill flung apart—Bill to plunge for the brush, Rocky to dive for the nearest big stone formation.

Rocky was firing back as he made cover. Bill spurred away. But Rocky had more pressing work at hand. Past his rock, he lined quick gunfire.

Up in the hayloft, one sniper was knocked sprawling by a bullet from Rocky's sixgun.

even more desperate chances

One of the pair was circling in the brush, seeking to flank him. Rocky took careful aim and dropped the other man. Already reloading, he heard his target go sprawling. Then came another sound, as the one in the brush snagged a spur on rock and came plunging down the hillside.

Rocky jumped the man as he fell. They rolled together, slugging.

It was a long time before the other man went down again—and even then, he was not out. Snarling, he went for the gun dropped in his fall. Rocky jumped him just in time, twisting the black muzzle of the weapon aside. The trigger kicked and the gun exploded. The man shuddered and went limp. Panting, Rocky crouched above the body to search it swiftly.

In one of the corpse's pockets he found a costly cigar. Whistling, Rocky drew its mashed twin from his own pocket. Henry Mason, indeed! And—had Mason backed that flash raid in the town, too; maybe to scare down local land values?

He headed straight for Nugget's ranch. And this time he showed a Marshal's badge. "Has Bill been back here? I want the truth this time!"

Martha shook her head. "We haven't seen Bill since you left."

"You after him 'cause he escaped prison?" Nugget probed curiously.

"The Warden and I let him escape. I'm comin' to feel he wasn't involved. I overheard Bill talk to Mason at the bank. And tonight a couple of gunmen tried to kill us both. Bill got away. I found an imported cigar on one of 'em—just like a couple Mason gave to me."

"Maybe there's a reason for Mason to want Bill dead. But why *you?*"

Rocky looked back at Nugget. "He probably figures I heard him and Bill talkin'. I wanted to see what I could uncover."

"Why don't you camp here, like you planned to?" Nugget offered.

So Rocky Lane became a hand at the Clark ranch. And that was how he was introduced to the respectable-looking gentleman who presently drove up and presented himself as the railroad's purchasing agent, John Harper.

While Harper talked with Nugget, Rocky took a look at the waiting buggy outside. It was identical with the one Bill had thumbed a ride in, headed for Cedar Rock. Harper's clothes were the same. Only the man wasn't.

"Mr. Clark," Harper was saying meanwhile, "I saw some of the other ranchers. You may have heard our railroad would like to run a spur here. We're willing to go to one hundred dollars per acre for property."

Nugget gaped at his caller. "A *hundred* an acre? That's what you're offerin'? Why, we can git *two* from that outfit Mason represents!"

"If you can do that, Clark," said Harper, "I'd say—take it!"

"So this is the end of my dream." Nugget looked sick. "A hundred—? Maybe we should see Mason quick, before he changes his mind!"

Listening, Rocky was worried. Mason could make a fortune, buying up acreage cheap and reselling it later—*if he somehow knew the railroad was set to pay a higher price.* But he doubted Nugget would listen to any warning to go slow now. The poor old man was getting too desperate.

Henry Mason was all cordiality when the little ranch party walked into his bank, an hour later. He offered Nugget glib sympathies, while Harper expressed regrets that Mason's land price was twice what he could offer.

"Hate to do it," Nugget sighed, "but you better start gettin' the papers ready, Henry. Feel like I'm sellin' Marthy outa house 'n—"

From the coat-closet, Bill Anderson stepped suddenly. He held a drawn gun, and he had been hidden—listening—all along. "This is another Mason fraud! That man there—" he indicated Harper "—he's a phony! I—"

Cursing, Mason hurled an inkwell off his desk. As Bill doubled in pain, Martha and Nugget both rushed to him. But Rocky got there before them.

"I'll take him over to jail," he said, catching Bill's arm firmly.

Mason's eyes glittered. "See that he gets there, this time!"

After he had guided his prisoner from the office, so Rocky heard later, Nugget had come mighty close to signing Mason's sale agreement. But Martha's pleas finally prevailed. He agreed to wait—until tomorrow.

At the moment, Rocky had concerns of his own. Instead of escorting Anderson into the Sheriff's office, opposite the bank, he pulled the younger man around the corner. There in the alley, he faced a startled Bill.

"You're *sure* this isn't the Harper who picked you up on the road?"

"Positive!" Bill nodded.

"Anderson—you hide where you can watch the hotel entrance." Rocky handed his companion back his gun. "I got something to do."

a sinister eavesdropper

But for once, Rocky had missed a trick. He hadn't seen a Mason hireling who followed them to the alley's mouth; who listened to their talk.

A brief spell later, Rocky and Bill Anderson paid a joint call upon the man registered at the local hotel as the railroad's John Harper.

Their unwilling host put up a game pretense of not comprehending their charge that he was an imposter; that he had attempted to swindle the ranchers by making them believe Mason's offer was better than the railroad's.

"Suppose I told you I'd telegraphed the railroad?" Rocky rapped. "To find what they *are* offering, and any details on John Harper?"

"It'll take a little time for the wire to get back."

"We'll just sit here and wait until the answer comes."

The clock ticked slowly, while they waited. Its hands inched on. At long last, their man sat upright on the bed where he'd been lounging.

"All right. So I'm Jackson, not Harper. You'll find out anyway."

"What happened to Harper?" rapped Rocky, his jaw set square.

"I don't know anything about him. Or about Clark and his niece."

Bill Anderson spun, aghast. "*Martha and Nugget?* Why—?"

"He's going to force Nugget to sell the ranchers out. After that—I don't know."

Rocky stood rigid. "Mason knows he can't get away with this!"

"Mason's ruthless. If you'd help me in court—?" Jackson paused, awaiting Rocky's nod. "I know where Clark and his niece are being held."

A boom for Cedar Rock only means new woe for Nugget

They took along the phony Harper's buggy, for the run to the abandoned barn the man had named. Rocky and a grim Bill Anderson rode after him on horseback. Rocky felt grave doubts Jackson was playing straight.

But nothing had gone amiss when their guide slowed before the weathered old structure. Jackson climbed down from his seat. Herding him ahead at gun's point, Rocky still smelled trouble. Before entering the barn, he detoured to peer in a dusty window. Trussed, gagged, Nugget and Martha sat in there on a broken bedstead! So much of the story, at least, was truth!

"They're not even guarded," Jackson said. "I'll wait here until—"

"You'll come along! Bill, stay outside in case somebody shows up."

Mouthing, Jackson tried to pull his gun. But Rocky twisted his arm, sent the weapon flying, and then forced his gasping guide through the door ahead of him. Over on the bedstead, the two Clarks regarded him with eyes bulging in terror—as if they were trying to warn him of some danger.

Rocky's keen glance swept the edge of the hayloft overhead. Suddenly, he caught Jackson and whirled him around as a cover. In the same instant, a gun spat from above. Jackson screamed and went down kicking.

Anderson dashed past the door. Rocky yelped, *"Get down, Bill!"*

A gun in the loft probed at Bill, but he sprang for a pile of crates. Whenever a shadow moved in the loft, Rocky fired—until his gun clicked empty. He paused to reload just as a bullet from Bill spilled one sniper across a mound of sacks. Then Bill himself went down; hurt, but not dead.

Rocky ducked another bullet to fire back again. Nugget and Martha were writhing to loosen their bonds, muttering wildly behind their gags.

Swinging from the ladder to the loft, Rocky clambered swiftly up it. Mason hurled an emptied gun full at him—and dove for a window. Like a flash fire, Rocky was after him . . . slugging, punching, wrestling. . . .

It was much later that day before Rocky Lane made ready to ride away from Nugget Clark's cozy ranch. Anderson's wounded arm had been dressed. Now Martha stood close beside him on the porch. But Nugget was scowling.

"Not worried about your money?" Rocky pressed. "Remember, you're going to get it all back, now that Henry Mason's confessed everything. When I get back and tell what happened, they'll release Bill right off. And it can't be about the railroad. You know they'll buy—and for big money."

"That's just it!" Nugget blurted. "Why *should* I sell? If the railroad comes, there'll be a big boom on here. I'm gonna keep my ranch."

"But the railroad can't come through here if you *don't* sell."

"That's right!" The old man glared back at Rocky balefully, deep in his worries, while Bill and Martha laughed. *"And it's all your fault, Lane!"*

THE END

Bill, Martha and Nugget all grouped together on the porch to bid Rocky goodbye.

* The set was crawling with marshals

Marshal Of Cedar Rock *was photographed at Burro Flat, country over which California's vaqueros used to ride roundup. When anyone asks how the place picked up its label, the answer is that the weather is trickier than a flat-headed burro.*

The picture was laid in the summer, supposedly. When Rocky Lane & Company started to work, the weather was perfect. On the third day of production, a typical Texas norther got lost in California, started as a sand storm, ended by leaving two inches of snow on the ground. Production had to be halted for a week while Burro Flats gradually returned to the season with which it had started the month.

Whenever Rocky Lane works at The Flats, a rooting section of kids gathers after school. Usually they have the good manners of junior cowboys. However, sometimes there's a slipup.

In one of the key scenes in Marshal, *Rocky passes himself off as a cowhand in search of work, leaving his U.S. Marshal's badge on his regulation clothes in his trailer.*

Once that scene was completed, Rocky went back to the trailer to change, noted that his badge was missing. He stepped out to the young wranglers, explained how important the badge was to the picture, said he thought he must have "lost" it among the rocks and bushes, and asked the posse to help him search. Sure enough, in a few minutes one of the boys "found" the badge. At the end of the day's shooting, Rocky gave the boy the gadget. (Rocky has them made up by the dozen because they tarnish quickly.)

The next day the rocks and rills surrounding the picture site were crawling with bright-eyed junior marshals, all in need of a badge. Rocky exhausted his stock, concluded that there is no need to worry about the enterprise of the younger generation.

The cast is still grinning about an off-camera incident that brightened one morning. Phyllis Coates, the love interest in the picture, confessed laughingly that the name on her baptismal certificate is Gypsie Ann Stell. The next day Rocky Lane presented her with a gift-wrapped parcel: a huge black chiffon square, suitable for the exit run of a burlesque queen. That gag was not her only present: the villain of the piece, Roy Barcroft (who has spent his cinema life in deviltry of all types) also brought an offering: a huge bouquet of peach blossoms, picked from his own trees. Roy operates a fruit ranch in the San Fernando Valley, insists that his peaches, plus walnuts, and citrus crops beat his movie pay checks all hollow. He says that he was born in Weeping Water, Nebraska, probably the true reason he has brought little but tears to most of his leading ladies.

(The preceding publicity release originally appeared in *Western Movie Hits*, Vol. 1, No. 2, 1953.)

The trademark of the Rocky Lane Western series was ACTION. . .

ACTION. . .

ACTION!

rocky lane:
he got those muscles the hard way

■ Known as "America's fightin'est cowboy," Rocky Lane has grown used to the fact that all the movies written for him are chock full of slugfests. The two he has just finished, *Savage Frontier* and *Marshal of Cedar Rock*, are no exception. They include some of the best knock-down-drag-outs ever filmed, and Rocky's fans won't be disappointed.

In order to blast their way through these fights, screen cowboys have to be in tip-top physical condition. They never know when some opponent is going to smash a piece of furniture over their noggins and, while many people think screen fights are faked, the brawls shown in Westerns are actually so tough that the actors go home at night as battered and bruised as a coon in a bear trap. It's as rough as a professional boxing match, if not more so, and it takes clean living to keep in condition.

Rocky stays with it religiously. He neither drinks nor smokes and hits the sack early, trying for ten hours sleep each night. He never goes to night clubs, preferring to spend quiet evenings with his friends and going to bed early enough for an alarm set at 5 a.m. When not working in a movie, he spends all day out-of-doors and many hours are devoted to his stallion, Black Jack. There isn't a day goes by that Rocky can't be seen loping around the ranch on Black Jack, and sometimes he puts the horse in a van and takes him out to wider country where they can have a longer ride. Black Jack has his own stable, a clean, strong building that makes the best quarters a horse could want. Not only that, he has his own radio, and Rocky insists that Black Jack enjoys the music.

Rocky is 6′ 2″ and 190 pounds of muscle. He has never believed in body building, preferring to keep in trim through natural activity. There's plenty of it around the ranch, and although Rock has help, he always pitches in and never asks anyone to do any work he wouldn't do himself.

The fondness for outdoors comes naturally, as he grew up on an Indiana farm and cut his teeth on a cinch buckle. There was a lot of work in those days, breaking the beans, feeding the hogs and weeding peppermint, and although he tried to get out of as much labor as any boy does, the work gave his body a hardness it still retains. When he was nine, he went to Clovis, New Mexico, to visit the ranch owned by an uncle, and it was there he got his first whiff of real Western life. He had already learned to worship the old-time movie cowboys like Tom Mix and Ken Maynard, and now on the ranch he spent hours goggling at the real-life cowhands. He admits he probably got in their way, but nevertheless he set about learning all he could. He spent every summer thereafter in New Mexico, and by the time he made his high school basketball, baseball and football teams back in Indiana, he was a real cowboy at heart.

His years as a fighting cowboy have kept him solid as his own name, and it's a rare extra who doesn't feel qualms before a movie fight with Rocky Lane. On the subject of fighting, Rocky has some good advice. "I've never gotten into a fight," he says, "without being on the right side. And I think that's a message for every kid. Don't be afraid to fight, but before you fight, make doggoned sure you're right."

Rocky Lane, "America's fightin-est cowboy," demonstrates his technique with a right cross to his opponent's chin. It looks mighty lethal.

he likes gals, all right, just doesn't have time

Rocky is the only leading movie cowboy who remains a bachelor. He lives in a rambling ranch-type home in the valley, surrounded by a good piece of land and stables that house the horses he raises. It's the kind of life for which a good many girls would give up their city homes. Some have the impression that Rocky likes it this way but he himself says, "I'm not enthusiastic about being a bachelor. I think women are the most wonderful and necessary creations the heavens ever produced, but although I see a lot of pretty creatures, I never have time to get acquainted with them." He may marry some day, but in the interim, his horse Black Jack is his best pal, sharing everything with Rocky except the morning paper.

Savage Frontier

Rocky's smashing fists deal swift punishment to the crime czar of Bitter Springs, each blow sending him reeling backwards.

1. As Deputy Marshal Rocky Lane knelt by his chief at the side of the young lawman bushwacked on the trail, he silently vowed retribution for the four fugitives Donovan had been following.

2. Having rendered the gun-happy Cherokee unconscious with his dentist's gas, grizzled Nugget Clark used the senseless killer as a shield and tried to take the other two into custody also.

The trail of the dead law man's killers took Deputy Rocky Lane to a cancer of old crimes long buried in the past of a bad man gone legitimate

THE CAST

Allan "Rocky" Lane	himself
Nugget Clark	Eddy Waller
Sam Webb	Bob Steele
Elizabeth Webb	Dorothy Patrick
William Oakes	Roy Barcroft
Cherokee Kid	Richard Avonde
Johnny Webb	Bill Phipps
Davie	Jimmy Hawkins
Tulsa Tom	Lane Bradford
Buck Madsen	John Cason
Bradley	Kenneth MacDonald
Dan Longley	Bill Henry
Pete	Gerry Flash

Adapted from the Republic Picture.

■ When the Cherokee Kid's boys kill a Deputy Marshal who is tailing them, fellow Deputy Rocky Lane vows to get the quartet. He kills one; then traces the others to Bitter Springs, home of ex-gunman Sam Webb, his sister Elizabeth and his kid brother, Johnny. The fugitives once rode with the old Webb gang. But now Sam is farming, honest since leaving jail. City Marshal of Bitter Springs, also its dentist, is Nugget Clark. He gasses Cherokee when the killer comes in with a toothache. The other gunmen, Tulsa and Buck, alarmed at Rocky's arrival, trade shots first with Nugget and then with Rocky—but escape. Cherokee is locked up. It is not long, however, before the respectable hotel owner, Oakes—the man Cherokee really came to Bitter Springs to see— slips in a gun. Oakes has plans regarding some up-coming gold shipments. Sam Webb does not dare betray these to the law, because Oakes also possesses evidence that young Johnny took part in one of the gang's old-time robberies. When Rocky visits the Webb farm, Johnny gets a notion the law is out to herd Sam back behind bars. Rocky and Nugget get back to town just after Cherokee shoots down a guard and breaks jail; and Rocky pursues and overtakes the wagon in which the killer is escaping. The wagon is wrecked. Tulsa and Buck spirit Cherokee away while Rocky is still groggy. But as they flee, Rocky shoots Tulsa from his saddle. Town talk blames Sam for smuggling Cherokee the gun. Oakes gets the Selectmen to ask for Nugget's badge, leaving Bitter Springs without law. But Rocky, a Federal man, keeps Nugget on as his helper. Together, they figure Oakes smuggled the gun on Cherokee's lunch tray; but they lack any proof. Watching Oakes' place, they see Sam Webb arrive—armed! Sam figures even Johnny is no fair swap for a killer's liberty. He aims to bring in Cherokee. Instead, Rocky takes Sam into custody. At the jail, he is quizzing Sam about the brain back of Cherokee—when Cherokee and Buck fire through a window and badly wound Sam. Rocky is at the door, in hot pursuit, when hot-headed Johnny halts him. Johnny has come to free Sam. Now he thinks Rocky has shot his brother. Rocky disarms the kid and locks him up. But the trail is cold. Doc Pearson says Sam cannot be moved from the room, so Elizabeth arrives to nurse him there. Oakes heads for the mine, leaving Buck to cover his trail. Nugget reports

To hold his power, a secret crime czar plotted murder

savage frontier, continued

the departure to Rocky, who follows at once—tailed by Buck. Left in charge, Nugget sees Buck quit town and dashes to warn Rocky. Elizabeth grabs the forgotten jail keys and frees angry Johnny, who also follows. On the trail, Rocky is ambushed and kills Buck; but Oakes escapes to the mine where Cherokee and the others are hiding out. Nugget catches up with Rocky, and together they close in on the mine. A fast gun fight follows. A wounded Cherokee and his last man are being put in irons when Johnny appears, to draw on Rocky. But Cherokee betrays his guilt of the assault on Sam by making a reckless grab for the spare gun he has previously concealed upon him. Only now are Johnny's youthful eyes open to the truth of who are the real friends of his reformed elder brother, and who are Sam's foes. In the light of this grim revelation, Johnny finds courage to make a fast draw and shoot Cherokee. Rocky now spurs back for town, aware Oakes will get to the wounded Sam ahead of him. He reaches the jail just in time to forestall Oakes' new murder attempt on Sam before Elizabeth's shocked eyes. In a savage battle, Rocky masters the gang's evil secret leader. Sam seems to recover; and Johnny will be forgiven his youthful mistake because of his bravery in gunning Cherokee. As Deputy Marshal Lane lopes out of town, Bitter Springs has back its law and order.

3. Darting to cover behind a cart in the Bitter Springs street, Rocky pumped lead fast and furiously toward the pair of outlaws who fled in sudden panic from the City Marshal's dental office.

4. With a smuggled gun gripped firm, the Cherokee Kid leeringly forced his jailer to open up the cell—and then pumped bullets into the man's back before fleeing to the wagon Oakes provided.

5. Rocky already had reached the door, in pursuit of the gunmen who had shot Sam from his seat, when Johnny burst in with drawn weapon to tax the stranger lawman with persecuting his brother.

6. Safe at the Golden Queen, the slippery Oakes warned Cherokee that law trouble was coming—and then doubled back into Bitter Springs with a deadly purpose in mind for defenseless Sam Webb.

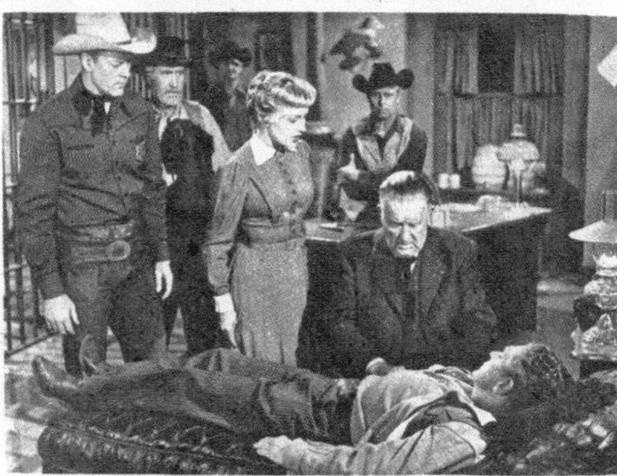

7. Examining the wound Oakes had sought to tear open again, the doctor was able to assure his tense listeners that the reformed badman stood a good chance of surviving Cherokee's wild bullet.

who's who in "savage frontier"

EDDY WALLER (Nugget Clark) first entered show business at the age of 14, much against the wishes of his preacher-father. He was living in New York City at the time, and had been offered a juvenile role with a touring stock company. After two years on the stage his parents bribed him into quitting, by offering to send him through college. But the longing for grease paint brought him back to Broadway after graduation. He's been working in pictures since 1927, and made 13 Westerns in a row with the late Wallace Beery. He's married to the former Doris Brownlae, stage actress. They live in the San Fernando Valley.

BOB STEELE (Sam Webb) knows just about everything there is to know about motion pictures, having started in the business when he was only 13 years old. Even before that, he had gotten a taste of cowboy life when he rode in the grand entry at the famed Pendleton, Oregon, rodeo, at the age of six. His first movie experience came pretty much by chance, when his father made some home movies of Bob and his brother. He has a horse, named Apache, which has appeared with him in nearly 50 movies and television films.

RICHARD AVONDE, (Cherokee Kid), hails from Ontario, Canada, where he was a championship fencer and tennis player, as well as a top-flight musician. Before the war, he directed his own orchestra, and was known as Canada's "King of Rhythm." In 1940, he became a member of the Black Watch regiment, rising to the rank of captain. He came to Hollywood on a furlough, was spotted by a motion picture executive, and offered a career in films. He's still active in sports, frequently is called upon to instruct other actors in the arts of foil and saber fencing.

KENNETH MacDONALD (Bradley) dates his acting career clear back to 1909, when he was a child actor on the legitimate stage. From that time until he entered movies in 1930, MacDonald appeared with stock companies all over the eastern United States and Canada. It was while appearing on the stage that he was picked up for motion pictures and placed under contract at Columbia studios. In addition to making movies he has been appearing on television with Gene Autry, Bill Williams and Jack Mahoney. Kenneth is the father of two boys and a girl.

DOROTHY PATRICK (Elizabeth Webb) has been a career girl ever since she was twelve years old. She started by modeling children's dresses in Winnipeg, Canada, where she spent the early years of her life. When she was seventeen, she took a modeling job with the famed John Powers' agency in New York City, and, the following year, beat out 2,000 other entrants in a film talent contest. Since coming to Hollywood, she has played several important roles in M-G-M pictures. Dorothy plays a good game of golf. Swims, too.

BILL PHIPPS (Johnny Webb) owes his big break in pictures to Charles Laughton, who saw him appearing in a little theater production in Hollywood, and was so impressed with his ability that he wangled a screen test for him. Producer Dore Schary, immediately put him in pictures. Phipps was born in Vincennes, Indiana, and received his first dramatic training while attending Eastern Illinois State College. During the war, he served as a radio operator with the Navy, saw considerable combat duty in the Pacific. He's single.

(The preceding publicity release originally appeared in *Who's Who in Western Stars*, Vol. 1, No. 3, 1953.)

Publicity shots for the Red Ryder film series.

Allan Lane, Bobbie Blake, and Martha Wentworth are seen here posing for publicity pictures for the Red Ryder series of Westerns.

Okay, Allan, let's get a shot of you on the back of the covered wagon.

Lean back, relax, and I'll get another one.

Allan Lane is seen here during a personal appearance to promote the Red Ryder movie series.

Allan Lane protects Linda Stirling, THE TIGER WOMAN, in the 1944 Republic serial.

Allan Lane helped the inexperienced Roy Acuff act his way through NIGHT TRAIN TO MEMPHIS.

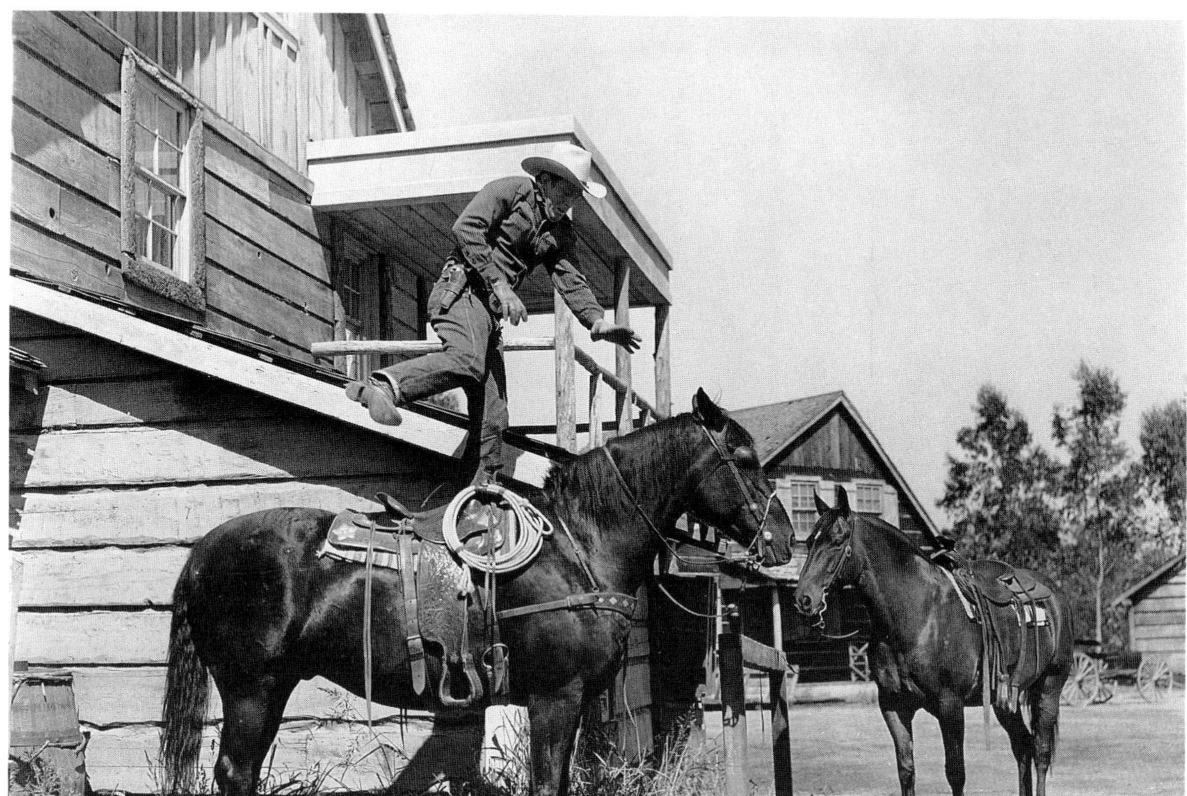

A close examination of the photo reveals that it is, indeed, Rocky taking the jump. Notice the blinders on the horse to keep him from seeing the impending mount. Unfortunately, Rocky lands directly on the saddle horn! The scene from RUSTLERS ON HORSEBACK always elicits a loud groan from audiences when the film is shown at Western film festivals.

Allan "Rocky" Lane, the balletic cowboy, leaps from rock to rock on the Iverson Movie Ranch location.

Rocky warns Myron Healey not to rush in where angels fear to tread.

Villainous actor Roy Barcroft was Rocky Lane's most frequent nemesis in the film series.

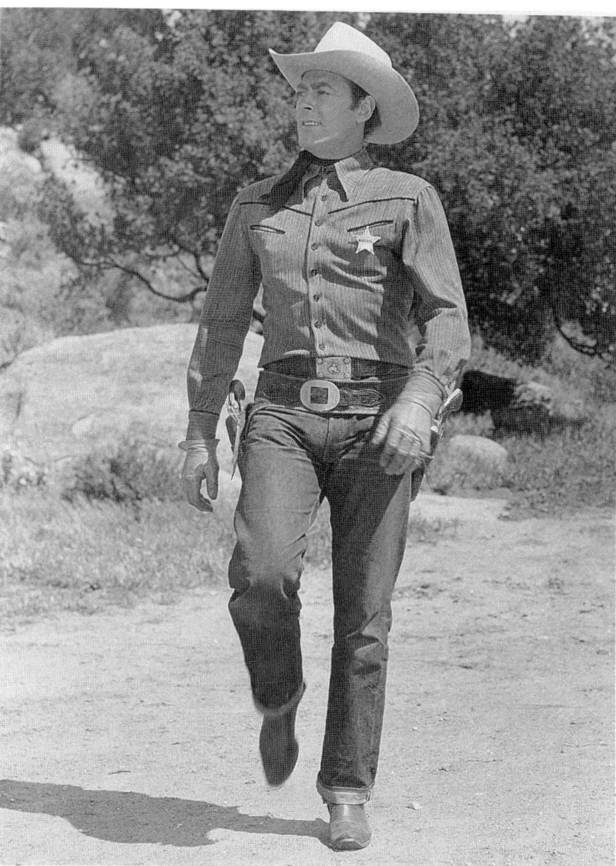

It's break time on the Rocky Lane set and time for some relaxed publicity photos.

This gallery of photos from the 1960's was undoubtedly taken to promote Lane as a middle-aged character actor. The photos reveal a still ruggedly handsome man—even with his receding hairline.

A rather pensive looking Allan Lane poses here in costume for a role in an unidentified Walt Disney television production.

Allan Lane is seen here in costume for his small role in the 1960 Audie Murphy movie HELL BENT FOR LEATHER.

SELECTED BIBLIOGRAPHY

Barbour, Alan G. *The Thrill of it all*, New York: Collier Books, 1971.

Jones, Ronnie. *Saturday's Heroes*, privately published.

Lahue, Kalton C. *Riders of the Range*, New York: Castle Books, 1973.

Lamparski, Richard. *Whatever Became of ?* (Eleventh Series), New York: Crown Publishers, 1989.

Miller, Don. *Hollywood Corral*, New York: Popular Library, 1976

Pitts, Michael R. *Western Movies*, North Carolina and London: McFarland & Company, 1986.

Pontes, Bob. "Who Was Allan 'Rocky' Lane?" *Favorite Westerns #28*, (1989).

Rothel, David. *The Great Show Business Animals*, San Diego and New York: A.S. Barnes & Company, 1980.

______. *Those Great Cowboy Sidekicks*, New Jersey and North Carolina: Scarecrow Press and World of Yesterday, 1984.

Tuska, Jon. *The Filming of the West*, New York: Doubleday, 1976.

ABOUT THE AUTHORS

Chuck Thornton

Hershel Edward "Chuck" Thornton was born at the end of the B-Western film craze, and, therefore, his primary exposure to these films came through television and through later theatre reissues to which his mother took him. After attending many B-Western festivals over the years, and being greatly impressed by the work of his friend Bob Carman on several Western books, Mr. Thornton compiled his first book, *The Western Adventures of Allan Lane*. Later efforts yielded *The Western Adventures of Lash LaRue* and *The Western Adventures of Tim Holt.* Mr. Thornton received a degree in Business Administration from Georgia State University and afterwards graduated from Gypton Jones College of Mortuary Science in order to work in the family funeral home in Atlanta, established by his father over 40 years ago. In 1975, he married his high school sweetheart, the former Marcia Lanette Edwards. The couple has two children—an eight-year-old daughter, Gloria Lorraine, and a five-year-old son, Brandon Elliott. Mr. Thornton is very grateful for the support and encouragement given to him by fans of the most enduring of all film genres, the B-Western.

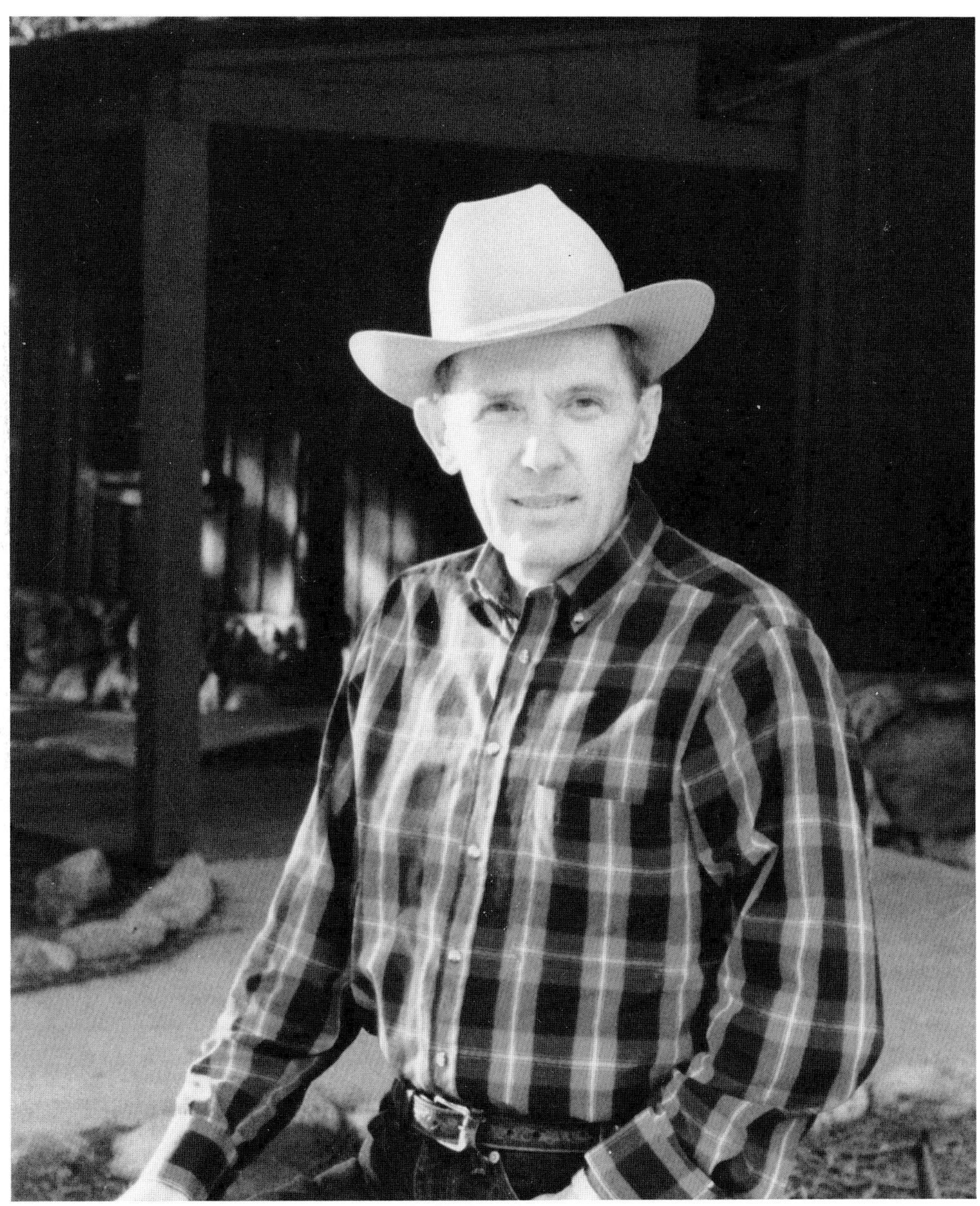

David Rothel

David Rothel's lifelong fascination with show business began with frequent visits to his local movie theater, where he followed the adventures of his favorite Western heroes. He has since gone from youthful observer to performer, producer, director, teacher, and published authoriity on various aspects of popular entertainment. His first book, *Who Was That Masked Man?: The Story of The Lone Ranger*, received enthusiastic reviews, was a main selection of the Nostalgia Book Club, and has been expanded and revised. Mr. Rothel's second book was *The Singing Cowboys*, an informative, back-in-the-saddle examinatiion of the B musical Western films. Next came *The Great Show Business Animals*, a charming work that reflects Mr. Rothel's ability to capture the spirit and analyze the impact of show business phenomena. *Those Great Cowboy Sidekicks* is an in-depth examination of such fondly remembered comic character actors as George "Gabby" Hayes, Smiley Burnette, and Andy Devine. *The Gene Autry Book* and *The Roy Rogers Book*, both reference-trivia-scrapbooks, have been popular with Mr. Rothel's readers. Most recently, he co-wrote the revised edition of *Lash LaRue, The King of the Bullwhip* with Chuck Thornton. Mr. Rothel's writing is characterized by thoroughness of research, warmth, wit, and understanding.

The authors wish to thank Ronnie Jones for allowing his article, "Allan 'Rocky' Lane, The Fightin'est Cowboy on the Range," to be reprinted in this book.

Ronnie Jones was born and raised near Hollis, Oklahoma, and became fascinated by movies at an early age. The B Western and its heroes topped his list of favorites during those early years. He says he was fortunate to grow up in a town that harbored two movie palaces that catered to his interest in Western films—the LaVista and the Watt. The LaVista entertained with the likes of Randolph Scott and Audie Murphy-type Westerns. The Watt was, according to Jones, "a Crackerjack box paradise (that had to have been designed especially in heaven) that housed Rocky Lane, Lash LaRue, Charles Starrett, etc. flicks." Jones feels that his movie fascination has remained with him because of those two theatres ahd the times that produced such movies as those shown at the theatres. Mr. Jones has B.A., M.A., and administration degrees and has worked as a teacher, coach, and administrator in the Muleshoe, Texas, school system for the past several years. In addition to his work in education and his hobby of Western film and memorabiilia collecting, Mr. Jones is currently studying and collecting materials connected with Billy the Kid and the Lincoln County War.

Other fine books from EMPIRE PUBLISHING COMPANY, INC.

THE GENE AUTRY BOOK, a reference, trivia, scrapbook by David Rothel, is the definitive source of information on "America's favorite singing cowboy." Containing a life profile, filmography, discography, TV log, personal interviews, memorabilia, rare fan magazine and news stories, over 200 photos, and much more, you'll want to have this exceptional publication in your personal library. Mr. Autry, himself, has praised the book and purchases it for re-sale in his Western Heritage Museum in Los Angeles, California. Available in hardcover ($30) and softcover ($25), the book is a giant 293 pages in length and is printed on heavy glossy stock. Please add $2.00 for shipping.

THE ROY ROGERS BOOK, a reference, trivia, scrapbook by David Rothel, is a companion volume to *THE GENE AUTRY BOOK*. A best seller at the Roy Rogers-Dale Evans Museum and with Western film fans, the book presents everything you ever wanted to know about "The King of the Cowboys." You'll find a personal interview by the author, a filmography, discography, TV log, memorabilia, fan magazine and news clippings, around 200 photos, and much more. Available in both hardcover ($25) and softcover ($20), this huge 233 page volume is printed on heavy glossy stock. Please add $2.00 for shipping.

IRON EYES CODY, THE PROUD AMERICAN, by Iron Eyes Cody and Marietta Thompson, is the life story of the Keep America Beautiful, tear-in-the-eye proud American, Iron Eyes Cody. Told in words and beautiiful pictures, Iron Eyes' story includes his long Hollywood career (with such personalities as Cecil B. DeMille, Gene Autry, Roy Rogers, and Ben Johnson), his world-wide personal appearances, his dedication to civic and community work, and his concern for the environment through his association with the Keep America Beautiful organization. A truly great American, Iron Eyes Cody has lived a fascinating life, and now you can read about it in this beautiful book. The 142 page hardcover volume is printed on heavy glossy stock and is available for only $18.00 plus $2.00 shipping.

COWBOY SHOOTING STARS, by John A. Rutherford and Richard B. Smith, III, is the ideal booklet for the Western film fan. This softcover, 100 page volume contains a check list of all the tiitles of those thrilling, never-to-be-forgotten B-Western films and their cowboy stars. In addition, you'll find the year each film was released, the production company, and the running time. Here is the perfect way to keep track of the films you have seen and those that you want to see. Profusely illustrated with photos from many of the films, this popular book costs only $7.50 plus $1.00 shipping fee.

LASH LaRUE, THE KING OF THE BULLWHIP, written by Chuck Thornton and David Rothel, includes almost everything you ever wanted to know about the man in black who rode fast and lashed his way across the silver screen. Over 150 photographs, complete filmography, personal comments and interviews highlight this book which is available in softcover for only $15.00 plus $2.00 shipping.

TOM MIX HIGHLIGHTS, by Andy Woytowich, is a 52-page book with 40 illustrations. Tom'Mix's life story is told in brief storybook form. The characters are drawn to a perfect likeness by a lifelong fan of Tom Mix. The cover is in beautiful color. This book is available for only $5.00 plus $1.00 shipping fee.

DON'T LOOK UP—THE REAL STORY BEHIND THE VIRGINIA UFO SIGHTINGS is a day-by-day account of the strange "goings on" in the western Virginia skies where more than 1,000 Unidentified Flying Object sightings were recorded in less than a 12-month time period. This book can be yours to examine for $12.00 plus $1.00 shipping fee.

Coming soon from Empire Publishing: *AN AMBUSH OF GHOSTS: A GUIDE TO FAVORITE WESTERN FILM LOCATIONS* by David Rothel.

Empire Publishing, Inc. has been in business for 16 years and is ready to serve **you**. Orders my be placed by phoning 1-919-427-5850, or you may write to: Empire Publishing, Inc., Route 3, Box 83, Madison, NC 27025. Book dealer inquiries are welcomed.